# Per~~~~ Practice

## THIRD EDITION

D1335169

THE LEARNING CENTRE
HAMMERSMITH AND WEST
LONDON COLLEGE
GLIDDON ROAD
LONDON W14 9BL

**Malcolm Martin** BSc, MCMI, FCIPD has been involved in the design and delivery of Certificate in Personnel Practice programmes for eight years primarily at the training provider, MOL. As a young graduate he joined British Steel and subsequently moved to Dunlop, Guthrie, and the BBA Group, where he held managerial positions in industrial relations, project management and personnel. Since then he has directed numerous CPP courses for corporate clients and for public programmes.

His own business, Malcolm Martin Associates, provides training and consultancy advice in the application of personnel practices with particular emphasis on industrial relations aspects. Malcolm lives in Lancaster.

**Tricia Jackson** BA, MSc, MInstAM, FCIPD is a freelance training and personnel consultant, an accredited mediator and a tutor in personnel and development on open learning and college-based CIPD programmes. Tricia has many years' experience as a generalist practitioner in both the private (engineering and metallurgy) and public (local authority) sectors and as a senior lecturer. She has been involved in the design and delivery of CPP programmes for a number of public open and corporate programmes.  ~~~~ law and has written five books in the CIPD Good Practice se~~~~ ~~~~ ~~~~nd Alcohol Policies_, _Career Development_, _Handling Grievance~~~~ ~~~~ ~~~~ s in Weybridge.

Hammersmith and West London College

302514

# • Other titles in the series

The Chartered Institute of Personnel and Development is the leading publisher of books and reports for personnel and training professionals, students, and all those concerned with the effective management and development of people at work. For details of all our titles, please contact the Publishing Department:

*tel* 020 8263 3387
*fax* 020 8263 3850
*e-mail* publish@cipd.co.uk

The catalogue of all CIPD titles can be viewed on the CIPD website:
www.cipd.co.uk/bookstore

# Personnel Practice

### THIRD EDITION

## Malcolm Martin
## and
## Tricia Jackson

Chartered Institute of Personnel and Development

© Malcolm Martin and Tricia Jackson
1997, 2000, 2002

First published in 1997
Reprinted 1998, 1999
Second edition 2000
Reprinted 2000
Third edition 2002
Reprinted 2002, 2003

All rights reserved. No part of this publication may be reproduced, stored in an information storage and retrieval system, or transmitted in any form or by any means, electronic, mechanical, photocopying, recording or otherwise, without written permission of the Chartered Institute of Personnel and Development, CIPD House, Camp Road, London SW19 4UX.

Design by Pumpkin House

Typeset by Fakenham Photosetting Ltd, Fakenham, Norfolk

Printed in Great Britain by
the Cromwell Press, Trowbridge, Wiltshire

British Library Cataloguing in Publication Data
A catalogue record of this book is available from
the British Library

ISBN 0 85292 941 2

The views expressed in this book are the authors' own and may not necessarily reflect those of the CIPD.

CIPD Enterprises Ltd has made every effort to trace and acknowledge copyright holders. If any source has been overlooked, CIPD Enterprises would be happy to redress this for future versions.

HAMMERSMITH AND WEST
LONDON COLLEGE
LEARNING CENTRE

17 JUN 2004

DAW
L9115100 E 29-49
302 514
658.3124 MAR
Business

cipd

Chartered Institute of Personnel and Development, CIPD House,
Camp Road, London SW19 4UX
Tel: 020 8971 9000   Fax: 020 8263 3333
E-mail: cipd@cipd.co.uk  Website: www.cipd.co.uk
Incorporated by Royal Charter. Registered Charity No. 1079797.

302 574

# • Contents

# • Abbreviations

| | |
|---|---|
| ACAS | Advisory, Conciliation and Arbitration Service |
| CIPD | Chartered Institute of Personnel and Development |
| COSHH | Control of Substances Hazardous to Health Regulations 1999 |
| CPD | Continuing Professional Development |
| CPP | Certificate in Personnel Practice |
| CRE | Commission for Racial Equality |
| DPA | Data Protection Act |
| DRC | Disability Rights Commission |
| ECJ | European Court of Justice |
| EOC | Equal Opportunities Commission |
| ERA96 | Employment Rights Act 1996 |
| ERA99 | Employment Relations Act 1999 |
| EU | European Union |
| GOQ | Genuine Occupational Qualification |
| HASWA | Health and Safety at Work Act 1974 |
| HR | Human Resources |
| HRM | Human Resource Management |
| HSC | Health and Safety Commission |
| HSE | Health and Safety Executive |
| IAM | Institute of Administrative Management |
| IiP | Investors in People |
| IMS | Institute of Manpower Studies |
| IPD | Institute of Personnel and Development |
| IPM | Institute of Personnel Management |
| IT | Information Technology |
| ITD | Institute of Training and Development |
| LEC | Local Enterprise Company |
| LSC | Learning and Skills Council |
| MbO | Management by Objectives |
| MCIPD | Member of the Chartered Institute of Personnel and Development |
| NACEPD | National Advisory Council on Employment of People with Disabilities |
| NVQ | National Vocational Qualification |
| NTA | National Training Award |
| PC | Personal Computer |
| PDP | Personal Development Plan |
| PMS | Performance Management System |
| PRP | Performance-Related Pay |
| RIDDOR | Reporting of Injuries, Diseases and Dangerous Occurrences Regulations 1995 |
| SBS | Small Business Service |
| SVQ | Scottish Vocational Qualification |
| TEC | Training and Enterprise Council |
| TUC | Trades Union Congress |

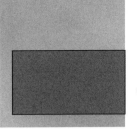

# • Acknowledgements

We recognise that directly or indirectly those with whom we work, and have worked, help create such practical knowledge and skill as we have. We would like to acknowledge their contribution to the content you see here. This new edition has primarily been driven by the changes to the CIPD standards but contributions from students, delegates and business clients, often in responding to specific enquiries, have again been invaluable in providing insights into current trends and organisational procedures and practices.

Preparation of the material itself has been greatly helped by comments, informed suggestions and contributions from our fellow tutors, associates and publisher. We would like to thank them all for their assistance.

Finally, Malcolm and Tricia would like to thank their respective partners, Christina and David, for their continuing understanding and support during the second revision of this book.

## Our purpose

The contents of this book follow the rationale set down in the Chartered Institute of Personnel and Development (CIPD) Professional Standards for the Certificate in Personnel Practice (CPP). This programme is self-standing but also provides an access route to the professional scheme. CPP students, enrolled at a CIPD-approved centre, will find that this book provides essential background reading to reinforce their learning.

The central purpose of the CPP is to develop competence in a range of core personnel and development skills together with the acquisition of underpinning knowledge and understanding. This book has been written to provide you, the reader, with a grounding in the basics of personnel activities. Thus it considers the breadth of knowledge and range of skills necessary for the effective performance of personnel work, while taking into account the organisational culture and environment.

A summary of the book's structure and an overview of its contents follow. But first we consider the type of reader most likely to benefit from the book and the learning sources you should use.

### You, the reader

This book's focus on the core skills required in managing and working effectively with people makes it suitable for a large range of potential readers. The CPP programme is widely regarded as an ideal course for all newcomers to the profession, but we expect that readers will belong to one or more of the following groups:

- personnel officers and managers who are newly appointed to the role but who lack previous generalist experience (you may be the sole personnel practitioner within your organisation, or your post may be a newly established one)

- personnel assistants, administrators and secretaries who support more senior personnel staff

- employees working for new but rapidly expanding organisations who acquire the responsibility for establishing and formalising personnel policies, procedures and practices

- staff who work in personnel-related areas, for example a personal assistant to a managing director or a payroll supervisor

- staff who work in specialist areas of personnel practice, such as training, employee relations or job evaluation, who wish to progress into or have more knowledge of generalist roles

- line managers or supervisors who have responsibility for personnel activities

- owners or managers of small businesses who have overall responsibility for the 'people element' within them.

NB: We use the title 'personnel practitioners' throughout this book as a generic term to cover all the above types of job and all levels of personnel work.

### Learning sources

This book has been written by two authors, both experienced in the field of personnel but with very different experiences, styles and, sometimes, perspectives. In order to understand each of the issues tackled within your own organisational circumstances, you will need to draw upon your own experience and perspective. To gain the maximum benefit from the book you will find it valuable to discuss the issues raised with appropriate people, particularly if you are relatively inexperienced in the areas under consideration. These people or 'learning sources' may include:

- senior colleagues, such as personnel specialists and line managers, peers and subordinates who have knowledge and experience of the organisation and how it operates

- personnel managers and officers from sister, parent and outside organisations

- specialists within your organisation such as company solicitors, health and safety officers, computer programmers/analysts, medical personnel and occupational health advisers

- members of your local CIPD branch and other networking bodies

- college tutors and fellow students

- other contacts that you have made through networking activities

- employees of advisory bodies such as the Advisory, Conciliation and Arbitration Service (ACAS), the Health and Safety Executive (HSE), the Equal Opportunities Commission (EOC), the Commission for Racial Equality (CRE) and the Disability Rights Commission (DRC)

- representatives of employers' organisations and trade union bodies.

You should establish contacts with these learning sources and make use of them to facilitate your learning experience. We shall be making periodic reference to your 'learning sources' throughout this book so, bearing in mind the above list, choose those sources that are going to be of most benefit to you in terms of their knowledge, availability and willingness to help.

In addition to these 'people resources' there is also a range of publications available that provide general guidance and practical help. If you are a member of the CIPD you should already have booklets on the following:

- the CIPD Professional Standards

- CIPD Continuing Professional Development (CPD)

- the CIPD Code of Professional Conduct, any relevant CIPD information notes, Key Facts and Position Papers.

ACAS has also produced a series of advisory booklets that provide invaluable assistance in a wide range of people management activities. We recommend you acquire copies of these booklets either for your personal use or for the whole of the personnel department.

The Internet is now an invaluable source of reference. It is worthwhile becoming familiar with a number of useful sites. If you find your way around favourite sites you will be able to discover up-to-date information on almost any topic of interest.

Further, in order to keep up to date with changes in the world of personnel management, employment legislation and case law, you should encourage your organisation to subscribe to a reputable information service such as that provided by Croner's or Jordan's. Subscriptions cover the initial reference material and a regular loose-leaf and electronic updating service. Addresses are in Further Reading at the end of Chapter 3, pages 77–80.

### The structure

This book has been designed to make it easy for you, the reader, to 'dip in' to chapters and sections that are of particular interest to you. It is divided into nine chapters (including this one). The subject areas represent the major activities associated with personnel work, and the links between these activities are highlighted throughout. Brief details of the contents of each chapter are provided in the Overview section on page 4, including the changes that have been made in writing the third edition of this book.

The next two chapters set the scene for what follows. The internal and external factors that exert an influence on an organisation are examined along with their effect on the work of personnel practitioners.

Each chapter contains the following features, where appropriate:

- learning objectives

- an introduction

- an explanation of why the topics covered are important to personnel practitioners

- the main body of information

- case study material to reinforce key issues and demonstrate points of good and poor practice

- the many and varied roles played by personnel practitioners

- a summary

- activities to encourage the acquisition of knowledge, the application of knowledge in an organisational setting and the planning of work experiences aimed at skills development

- a section covering references, legislative acts and codes of practice, further reading, recommended websites and video titles.

The last two features highlight our desire to change your learning experience from a passive to an active one. You are recommended to tackle at least two activities from each chapter.

In this new edition we have taken particular note of the importance of legislative changes, the changing nature of employment, the changing organisational context of personnel work, the increasing value and use of competency frameworks and the significance of the Internet. These and other changes are highlighted in the Overview.

To encourage you to use the Internet as a source of up-to-date information we have included website addresses where relevant.

## Overview

### Chapter 1 – Introduction

As you will have seen, here we cover our purpose and the types of reader borne in mind when compiling this book, the wide range of learning sources available to you, the book's structure and an overview of its contents and an indication of the main changes in content from previous editions.

### Chapter 2 – The organisational context

We consider the broader aspects surrounding the personnel function, as well as the wide range of activities involved in its execution. We examine the differences between the terms 'personnel management' and 'human resource management'. In this latest edition we have paid attention to the different types of organisation and organisational structures in which practitioners may work, as well as including the concepts of customer care and stakeholders. The effects of the internal corporate culture and the external corporate environment are summarised, noting the types of action that practitioners can take. This latest edition includes a section on human resource planning. Trade unions and their role in formulating collective agreements are explained and there is a brief examination of the role of ACAS, the Advisory, Conciliation and Arbitration Service.

## Chapter 3 – The legal background to personnel practice

Following on from Chapter 2's appreciation of the external factors acting upon the organisation, we address the complex area of legislation. We concentrate on the employment law aspects and provide a summary of the relevant legislation under four main headings:

- civil law and, in particular, contracts of employment

- employment protection rights, concentrating on the important issues of unfair dismissal and equal opportunities

- other statutory legislation, covering the broad areas of health and safety and human rights (data protection is covered in Chapter 4, Personnel information systems and computer facilities)

- trade unions and their role in formulating collective agreements.

Employment law is becoming ever more important to personnel practitioners, for several reasons. Not only is there much new legislation, and more expected, but the new laws are changing the very nature of the employment relationship. Employees have had significant protection for many years, but recent legislation provides more rights for non-employee workers. Legislation covering the rights of part-time workers and the right to equal treatment for men and women has also been strengthened.

An important section on handling redundancy programmes has been added to this latest edition.

Three case studies drawn from law reports reinforce points made in the chapter and give readers an insight into how the law works in practice.

Our aim here is to provide general guidance on the basic knowledge requirements for personnel practitioners, and in this latest edition we highlight recent and expected changes. We also seek to underline the difficulties of gaining a comprehensive knowledge of the legislation and the need to seek expert advice when dealing with specific problems.

## Chapter 4 – Personnel information systems and computer facilities

We emphasise the importance of keeping accurate personnel records. We consider manual and computerised systems (alongside the legal implications), concentrating particularly on the important role of computers, the many benefits they bring and the large number of computer applications relevant to personnel work. The chapter has been updated to reflect changing technology and the increasing importance of the Internet. There are now significant sections on data protection and on e-mail and Internet use, highlighting the implications of these for personnel practitioners.

## Chapter 5 – Recruitment and selection

Now we start the process of homing in on specific groups of personnel activities. Taking into account the legal setting, we consider the processes of:

- recruitment – job analysis (job descriptions, person specifications and competency frameworks) and advertising, including Internet advertising

- selection – collecting information on candidates via application forms, various types of interviews, aptitude and personality tests and assessment centre performances, and assessing and comparing candidates (with specific guidance on good interviewing practice)

- making an offer – conditional offers and employer checks

- induction – of new starters

- evaluation – of the whole process.

### Chapter 6 – Training and development

In this chapter we look at definitions of training and development and then work through the stages of the training cycle, starting with the identification of training needs and proceeding through the stages of planning, implementing and evaluating. We consider important issues such as the range of available training and development techniques and individuals' preferred learning styles. In addition, we consider national training initiatives such as Investors in People (where the updated principles of the Investor in People Standard are reproduced) and National Vocational Qualifications. Some updating was carried out for the second edition of this book to reflect changing technology and the increasing relevance of competencies. In this edition we now cover e-learning.

### Chapter 7 – Performance management

First we examine the differences between performance appraisal and the broader concept of performance management. We use a case study to demonstrate the need for all performance management systems to be closely integrated and directed towards achieving business goals. Performance appraisal is looked at in some detail: its purposes, motivational effects, history and trends, and the various components requiring consideration if one is designing a new scheme. We include a new section on giving and receiving feedback. Payment systems, including financial and non-financial rewards, are also covered, as are the legal considerations and the skills necessary to be an effective appraiser.

### Chapter 8 – Employee relations

In the opening sections of this chapter we examine individual conflicts, looking at disciplinary rules and grievance procedures against the backdrop of relevant employment legislation, with particular reference to the revised ACAS code of practice. We provide tips on good practice in carrying out disciplinary, capability and grievance interviews, and high-light the need for your organisation to follow the correct procedures at all times. We stress that poor handling of conduct or capability cases will increase the risk of claims to employment tribunals of unfair dis-missal and that employee-relations problems may result from the mis-management of formal grievances. A brief section on absence management tools has also been included in this edition. Finally, the importance of employee involvement is stressed when considering trig-gers for potential collective conflicts, in both unionised and non-unionised environments.

## Chapter 9 – Personal effectiveness

This final chapter, incorporating minor revisions, seeks to provide fur-ther guidance on the variety of skills necessary for effective perform-ance in a personnel role. We examine the broad issue of self-development before covering the following skills areas:

- communication – report writing, making presentations and making a business case for introducing change

- negotiating, influencing and persuading – in formal and informal situations

- counselling – for example, in handling redundancies, early retire-ments, sickness absence and personal problems

- time management – in and outside the workplace

- assertiveness – in work-related and personal situations.

Finally, we refer to the emphasis placed nowadays by a large number of professional associations such as the CIPD and the Institute of Administrative Management on the concept of continuing professional development (CPD). The main focus of this concept is the proposition that learning (and the acquisition of knowledge and skills) is not a finite process but one that should carry on throughout our working lives. We have sought to reinforce this message, and hope that it is one you take to heart at this, the beginning of a new learning experience.

## CHAPTER OBJECTIVES

After reading this chapter you will:

● appreciate the type of activities in which personnel practitioners may be involved

● understand the subtle differences between 'personnel' and 'human resources'

● recognise the type of organisation for which you work and the main implications for you as a practitioner

● grasp the main principles of the customer care and the stakeholder concepts

● be able to distinguish administrative, advisory and executive tasks as carried out in the personnel function

● be able to develop links with your management team, your employees and the community

● have a broad understanding of the role of trade unions and be aware of the services of ACAS

● be able to understand the key roles and tasks of the personnel function and its contribution to organisational success

● be more able to anticipate the demand for new employees

● be better placed to find suitable sources of employees in the labour market

## Introduction

Because the personnel function operates within an organisational context, we shall be considering the nature of organisations and the relationships that personnel practitioners need to establish with managers, trade unions and employees. The corporate environment is also important, and this includes the effect of changes that occur in that wider environment.

We believe that the personnel role is the most interesting and exciting one in any organisation. It may be a cliché that people are an organisation's greatest asset, but no organisation exists without people and nothing is achieved except through their efforts. Therefore personnel practices go to the heart of the organisation and potentially have a role in every facet of its activities. As a personnel practitioner, you could conceivably be called on to help solve very personal individual problems. Equally, you could be asked to contribute to major strategic policy decisions in the boardroom. Quite possibly both could happen on the same day.

Because we consider it important for you to understand your role, each chapter will comment on the personnel practitioner's role in the context of the material covered by that chapter. Here we are taking an overview of personnel practice within the context of the organisation.

We will start by looking at the environment in which your organisation exists.

## External environment

We do not need to look far to see tremendous change in our society. Indeed, change is becoming the third great certainty – the other two being death and taxes! Look back over the last 15 years. How many public bodies have been privatised, how many turned into agencies? Reflect on the effect of the Internet and on the implications for your employer, for society and for yourself. Look at the effects of European legislation where regulation of working hours and new rights for part-time employees are just two effects in the employment area alone. How many employees experienced redundancy in the 1990s? To what extent have 'green' issues come to the fore?

The environment in which organisations operate is wide, and change originates from six areas which may be summarised with the mnemonic PESTLE. The areas are shown below:

- *political*: changes brought about by powerful bodies such as governments, the European Union (EU), the trade union movement and regulatory bodies

- *economic*: economic prosperity, interest rates (which affect the cost of borrowing and, potentially, company profitability), unemployment, demand for goods, import tariffs and European monetary union

- *social*: one-parent families, an ageing population, consumer expectations, demographic changes (changes in the structure of the population), lifestyles, consumer attitudes to social, environmental and other issues

- *technological*: developments in medicine, mobile phones, energy sources, the Internet

- *legal*: new laws originating from Acts of Parliament, interpretations of the law by the courts (both domestic and European), international laws (for example, covering disposal of waste at sea)

- *environmental*: climatic change, holes in the ozone layer, pollution.

The sources of change are often interrelated. For example, equal opportunities for women (a legal change) was spurred on by social change (women's liberation).

Some years ago, Peter Wickens, while still personnel director for Nissan, expressed it succinctly for us at a meeting of the (former) Institute of Personnel Management (IPM): 'Change is inevitable – in a progressive organisation change is constant.' If it was true then, it is even more so today.

Managers must anticipate and respond to the effects that such changes have on their organisations, if the latter are to remain viable. Training is often an important response, so we shall look at these areas again in more detail in Chapter 6.

There are some serious implications arising from the changing environment for employees. Flatter organisations mean fewer opportunities for promotion. Thus promotion can be less easily used to increase earnings or as a reward. Less security implies that employees will seek opportunities to develop and grow to ensure they have marketable skills and experience to help them if they need to change employers. They will want experience in activities that are in demand so that they have relevant achievements to put on their CVs.

To be effective in this changing world, you as personnel practitioners need to keep in close touch with changes in the external environment, with employees, and with the community at large. Doing so will help you to anticipate and respond effectively to people issues. Reading the CIPD's magazine, *People Management*, and keeping in touch with current affairs is important. We will look more closely at how you might keep in touch with employees and the community in a later section on 'Building Bridges' (page 30). Here, though, we will first examine the corporate environment in which a personnel function operates.

## Characteristics of organisations

Organisations exist for different purposes and in a wide variety of different sectors. Thus there exist organisations of very different types. The activities and functions you will find in a manufacturing company differ markedly from those in a recruitment agency, for example.

An organisation of any size will be subdivided into different functions. In a traditional shoe manufacturing company, these might include groups of people responsible for purchasing, manufacturing, sales, finance, design and personnel. Raw materials are purchased, shoes are manufactured and they are sold.

Manufacturing activities form a 'line' from supplier to customer – the people working in these functions are often referred to as being 'in the line' and their managers as 'line managers'. Costs associated with these functions are referred to as 'direct' costs.

People working in other functions such as finance, design and personnel are not part of the line because the product does not pass through their responsibilities on the route from suppliers to customers. Often they are referred to as 'staff' functions. Costs associated with these functions are referred to as 'overheads'.

In a recruitment agency, however, some personnel activities such as selection could be regarded as 'line' activities. Indeed, a large recruitment agency may have personnel practitioners in both line and staff functions.

Staff functions are supportive to the main task or purpose of the business. One disadvantage for support staff is that they may be seen as less important because they are a cost and do not bring in business directly. An advantage is that they can often be nearer the heart of the business strategy and are impartial when it comes to conflict between line functions. For example, a personnel practitioner (who is a staff rather than a line manager) should be involved in discussions about how to attract talented candidates. This is close to the business strategy because it can affect business decisions, such as where the organisation locates its operations geographically.

Not all organisations are commercial and one way of distinguishing some characteristics that are important to the personnel practitioner is to look to see where the organisation is accountable, for example to shareholders, to a trust or to a government department. These characteristics will, in part, determine how practitioners should seek to influence others in the organisation.

It has been said that organisations do not have objectives, it is people who have objectives. Because of this it is also important to look at those people who have the greatest influence over the direction of the organisation. The circumstances surrounding them, their motivations and their accountability will exert a marked effect on what is regarded as important within any organisation.

We will look at some examples of different organisations and the accountability of their senior people.

### The small private limited company

The owners of a small private company may well have much of their personal capital invested in the business. While their liability is limited (to the capital they have invested in the business) they may be in considerable financial difficulty if the business fails. In taking such risks they are usually seeking significant financial gain. Inevitably, this will affect how they view activities that may be desirable but which do not produce income. But it does not necessarily mean that wealth creation is the only or even the prime motivation. In such a company the chief executive is likely to have a clear 'vision' of where he or she wants the company to go and to be totally committed to the success of the enterprise.

You need to try to recognise this vision and relate your responsibilities towards achieving it. It will invariably help if you can also relate your activities to profit, productivity, risk reduction and the assistance of business growth.

### The partnership

Partners who have equity in the business (in effect have invested their own capital) may be of comparable standing with each other, especially in a small partnership. This often means that all partners need to be prepared to go along with proposals that you may make. However, in larger partnerships many matters will be delegated to a managing partner, a managing team or similar body. The influence that any individual partner has will be determined by the structure of each particular firm and his or her position in it.

Partnerships are common in the professions. Professional firms seek to maximise fee-earning activities and minimise activities that do not attract fees. It will be important to recognise this. Reducing the time that partners spend on problems associated with people management will be seen as a valuable contribution.

### Public limited company – 'plc'

The shares in a public limited company are usually traded on the stock exchange. This can have a number of effects – for example, the senior members of the company may from time to time be heavily engrossed with how the shares are trading and with all the figures that influence how company performance is viewed. One knock-on effect of this is that you could be under pressure to have very accurate figures about the numbers of employees.

Public limited companies are hugely varied in their characteristics and range in size from small to multinational, but they are all strongly commercial because they have to provide a return for their investors.

You may work for a small subsidiary company of a large plc, or even for a small site within such a company. How much independence smaller units of that kind have depends on the approach of the parent company.

In some cases the chief executive may have his or her own vision and be able to manage the company with a fair level of independence, treating the parent company almost as if it were a banker. Such chief executives are not usually at as much financial risk as private owners. Although the chief executives may have shares in the organisation, they are unlikely to be rendered bankrupt personally if the business were to fail. Nevertheless, failure might bring serious consequences for their careers.

In other cases subsidiary companies may be subject to a strong corporate identity and firm control from the parent company. If this is the case, your chief executive is likely to be concerned with how his or her performance is viewed by the parent company and this may influence how you or your senior managers relate to the chief executive.

Many factors influence the attitudes in any large commercial company: where the company's product might be in its life cycle, its position in its marketplace, the nature of its marketplace (whether it is growing or declining) and its edge, or otherwise, over competitors. In general, the more prosperous and secure the company, the more it is likely to invest in good employee relations. In companies that are less prosperous or suffering declining sales, you will have to work harder to get new ideas adopted and there may be a need to consider more difficult issues such as redundancy.

## Local and central government organisations

Organisations in the public sector can be very different from those described above. Public sector organisations are likely to have a hierarchical structure (see the next section) with more clearly defined jobs and positions than is generally found in the private sector.

The emphasis is on career management and meeting the expectations of the political framework rather than on profit. Government employees prosper by career progress and this arises, in part, by increasing the level and span of their control.

Government organisations exist to implement government policies either locally or nationally. Employees of local authorities are answerable for their performance to the elected councillors, and staff in government departments to ministers. The authority for any actions that employees take is determined by legislation and individuals have much less freedom to act than they may have in a private organisation. For example, a commercial organisation may choose to charge for tours of its factory or head office building. A public sector organisation could not charge for such tours unless there is legislation that specifically allows them to do so.

In addition, all spending is subject to the scrutiny of the Audit Office, which is independent of government and reports to Parliament directly on the effective use of public money.

Public sector organisations have to comply with European directives as failure to do so can render them liable to action in European courts. Private sector organisations have to comply with UK legislation and need to be aware of the obligations of public organisations (such as employment tribunals). However, they do not have to comply directly with European directives until the directive has been translated into UK legislation.

Government organisations therefore exist in a precise environment in which risks are minimised and policies, procedures and actions are well documented.

It is important to be mindful of this as a personnel practitioner. Those to whom you might report are likely to be very conscious of risks, accountability and compliance with legislation as well as their own career progress.

## Other government organisations

Some other public sector organisations are centrally funded but relatively independent of the direct accountability to an electorate. Universities, the NHS, learning and skills councils, local education authorities and various government agencies such as the Benefits Agency all account to the government and Parliament to a greater or lesser degree. Independence is provided by various funding arrangements, but when funds are granted, the grant is invariably subject to conditions that can restrict the level of independence.

Government control is also exercised in a variety of other ways. For example, league tables are used to monitor the performance of the NHS and universities, among others. Inspection authorities are used to assess standards, share best practice and assist continuous improvement – for example, the Office for Standards in Education (OFSTED) monitors performance in schools and colleges. The Audit Office monitors the organisation's activities, and tendering processes are used to ensure services provided by public bodies and agencies are at a competitive level.

In such organisations, it is inevitable that there will be a preoccupation with the measures used to determine performance and thus access to funds. Inspection processes require good documentation. Personnel practitioners need to familiarise themselves with the funding arrangements and control processes that exist in their own organisation if they are to contribute appropriately to meeting objectives.

It should be remembered that costs and the control of costs are still important. It is good management of available funds that, in the end, determines whether the organisation can meet the objectives set for it.

## Other organisations

It is important to realise that we have only scratched the surface here in terms of the types of organisations and the issues they may regard as important. We have not mentioned mutual societies (owned by their members), the charity sector, the armed forces, the police, nationalised industries or public–private partnerships – and even this list is not exhaustive.

---

**Activity 1**

Look carefully at your own organisation. What is specific to your organisation that distinguishes it from other organisations? To whom is it ultimately accountable? What is regarded as important? Discuss your conclusions with appropriate learning sources within and, for comparison, outside your organisation.

---

# Organisation structures

### Hierarchical

In a typical hierarchical structure each member of staff reports to an immediate superior and there are several 'layers' between the most junior and the most senior individuals. As a general rule each person has a relatively small 'span of control' with no more than five or six people reporting to him or her.

If the organisation is large then each job is likely to be specialised and may be closely defined. For example, within the personnel function alone there may be separate departments for employee relations, apprentice training, staff training, management development, recruitment, and compensation and benefits. Such subdivisions will be reflected in other parts of the organisation.

Typically, each person reports to only one immediate superior to whom he or she is accountable for all job responsibilities. In practice, there can be some reporting to another person, often referred to as a 'dotted-line' responsibility because it may be shown by means of a dotted line on the organisation chart. For example, a factory personnel manager might report to a head office personnel director, but have a dotted-line relationship to the factory manager.

Hierarchies are characterised by protocol to varying degrees from the very informal to the strict. Conventions place restrictions on who can talk to whom about what. In a hierarchical organisation with very strict protocols there can be little sideways communication between departments with all disagreements being reported upwards.

In recent years, the need to reduce costs in order to meet international competition has led many companies to downsize their workforce, with consequential de-layering of the organisational structure. As well as reducing both costs and bureaucracy, downsizing and de-layering can often lead to much more effective internal communications. However, companies have to be careful to avoid downsizing to such an extent that remaining staff only have time to deal with day-to-day operational activities and strategic thinking is driven out of the organisation altogether.

## Flatter organisations

This trend towards smaller organisations and flatter structures reduces the likelihood of protracted decision-making. With fewer organisational layers, individuals have easier access to senior decision-makers. However, each person is likely to be in greater demand, with many people reporting to him or her, and people at all levels need to have a wider range of skills.

In a small company the personnel practitioner may need to handle a range of personnel activities. In larger, but flat-structured companies, personnel staff may still have a narrower responsibility (say recruitment) but could find that they have to balance the needs of all the other functions in the organisation (sales and production, for example) rather than relying on one boss to set the priorities. This demands a greater understanding of the organisation's wider operations and its priorities.

In flat organisations individuals sometimes report to more than one boss in what can be called a matrix structure. For example, the personnel manager may be responsible to the factory manager, the sales manager, the distribution manager and the head office head of personnel, all in approximately equal measures.

In this flatter type of organisation personnel practitioners who want to introduce a new application form can talk to all their colleagues directly. When everyone is convinced of the benefits of the change, the practitioners can introduce the new form. By contrast, practitioners in a strict hierarchical structure would have to convince their immediate boss (and if they are lucky) the boss would then convince his or her own boss. Eventually a decision will be taken at a sufficiently high level that all the practitioners' colleagues 'fall in line' and the new application form may be imposed from above.

Here we have looked at two important and relatively common forms of organisation structure. There are other forms and even these two cannot be precisely defined, since they exist to varying degrees in different organisations.

If you want to influence decision-making, you need to understand how your organisation is structured.

---

### Activity 2

If you wanted to introduce a new recruitment application form (to reflect changes in legislation perhaps), how would you go about getting a decision made? Which of the above scenarios most closely represents what needs to happen in your organisation? Is there another scenario that would apply? Discuss your conclusions with an appropriate learning source.

---

# Personnel and human resources

It is time to look at what the members of an organisation expect of personnel practitioners. One useful way of doing this is to examine the subtle differences between the terms 'personnel' and 'human resources' or 'HR'.

### Personnel management

Personnel management can trace its origins back to the early part of the last century when welfare workers were appointed by organisations to exercise care towards employees. Personnel management as a business function assumed prominence in the latter half of the twentieth century.

Within the memory of many people at work today employment meant working for large organisations such as the General Post Office, Imperial Chemical Industries Ltd or the British Steel Corporation: organisations, often nationalised, employing hundreds of thousands of people.

Each organisation would organise the means of meeting its own needs. For example, a canteen in a steelworks, a significant operation in itself, would be organised and run by steelworks employees. Tasks such as software design and programming, site security, stockholding and distribution would all be undertaken by employees of the organisation.

Almost everyone worked full time. Women retired at 60 and men at 65, often from organisations that they had joined from school.

It is from the initial welfare focus and within this employment context that personnel, as a management function, evolved.

Torrington and Hall (1998: 12) offer an excellent description of personnel management as it has traditionally been seen. For many employers it will still be appropriate:

> *Personnel Management is workforce-centred, directed mainly at the organisation's employees; finding and training them, arranging for them to be paid, explaining management's expectations, justifying management's actions, satisfying employees' work-related needs, dealing with their problems and seeking to modify management action that could produce unwelcome employee response... Although indisputably a management function, personnel is never totally identified with management interests, as it becomes ineffective when not able to understand and articulate the aspirations and views of the workforce.*

It is worth splitting this quotation down, because it provides a great deal of pertinent information, although our interpretations may not be exactly those made by Torrington and Hall.

*Finding employees*

This is not just a question of advertising and recruiting, although that may be a major task. Effective practitioners build relationships with relevant local bodies such as schools, colleges, job centres, employment agencies, and the community at large. A good profile in the community helps to attract the best candidates. Finding employees is covered in detail in Chapter 5.

*Training employees*

Occasionally this is a separate, or sister, function, but personnel and development are professionally linked. 'Training and development' does not mean only arranging training courses. As we shall see later, it can include diverse activities such as identifying needs, planning appropriate responses and evaluating the success of these activities. Training is important, for example, in the induction of employees to an organisation, in health and safety and in helping an organisation to respond effectively to change. (See Chapter 6.)

*Arranging payments*

For many staff administrators in small organisations, administering the payroll is the entry route into personnel practice. Paying employees regularly, properly and on time is a contractual obligation backed up by legislation (the Employment Rights Act 1996, for example). Proper authority, accuracy and absolute meeting of deadlines are vital issues for payroll staff. Because of this, a payroll officer should be allowed to work to a regular routine and not be interrupted by other priorities. The demands of working in a personnel office can be slightly different – a point of which those making the transition from payroll to personnel need to be aware.

Personnel aspects of paying employees can, at one extreme, involve clarification of entitlement to individual pay items and, at the other, negotiating pay rates.

It is good practice (to reduce the possibility of fraud) for those who authorise payments (such as personnel practitioners) to have separate reporting relationships from those who pay employees (the payroll staff).

*Explaining management expectations*

Personnel is usually the most appropriate organisational function to explain management decisions to staff. The personnel practitioners can be expected to have the necessary communication skills and are likely already to work closely with trade unions or workplace representatives. Examples of issues which personnel practitioners have experience of explaining on behalf of management teams are: productivity schemes, health and safety needs and disciplinary policies and procedures.

A related area is collective agreements made between an organisation's management and a trade union (on behalf of members employed in that organisation). These agreements determine terms and conditions that apply to the employment contract and should therefore be explained by personnel in co-operation with the trade union, and not left for shop stewards alone to explain.

*Justifying management actions*

Where you need to do this, we hope you will have been able to make a contribution to the decisions themselves. Justifying actions that you may not have chosen yourself is one of the greatest challenges for the personnel practitioner. It is a central aspect of managerial responsibility that, once you have put all your arguments, you accept and implement whatever is decided. That may be stressful, particularly if you have not been able to put those arguments at the right level. Typical actions that personnel practitioners might be called on to justify are: restructuring and redundancy, reductions in fringe benefits, changes within the place of work and relocation. An example is provided in Case Study 1 below.

## CASE STUDY 1

Under the Truck Acts 1831–1940, now repealed, employees had an entitlement to be paid in 'coin of the realm'. The purpose of the legislation was to prevent ruthless employers from paying their workers in products manufactured by the company. A few years ago, a candelabra manufacturer in an east European country paid its workers in product (candelabras) which the luckless workers sold wherever they could (on railway station platforms, for example). The Truck Acts protected workers in the UK from this type of treatment. (They still enjoy this protection under different legislation.)

However, many workers used the legislation to insist that they also had a right to be paid in cash and not through a bank account. Company X already paid office staff and managers through their bank accounts but hourly paid workers could be paid in cash and, indeed, many were keen for this to continue.

Company X found that bringing large quantities of cash into a factory always posed a security and hence a safety risk and the cost of security became disproportionate. The senior managers in the company (including the personnel manager) decided to insist payment be through employees' bank accounts and took the following actions:

- Notification was given to trade union representatives at the annual pay round in April that cash pay would cease on 31 December that year.

- Consultations were held with representatives to identify and discuss any issues.

- Many employees did not have bank accounts. A small incentive (£50) was offered to cover the trouble of opening a bank account.

- The personnel manager made arrangements for the local bank to come on site to discuss opening bank accounts. This took the form of presentations to manageable groups of 20–30 people. The personnel manager also joined the presentations. Care was taken to ensure all shifts had the opportunity to see a presentation.

- Personnel staff helped individuals complete forms where required.

Personal discussions were entered into with those employees who initially did not wish to agree, the emphasis being on persuasion. In the event the project was a success and all employees agreed to be paid through bank accounts by the end of January the following year.

While this may seem a relatively minor matter, such changes can meet significant resistance and even become a *cause célèbre* if handled badly. Here, plenty of notice was given, time was taken to explain and consult, employees were helped and a small incentive compensated for any inconvenience. The benefits were worth achieving.

*Satisfying employees' work-related needs*

These are issues such as health and safety, fringe benefits (company vehicles, for example), welfare matters and long-term protection such as life assurance and pensions. In large companies some of these matters may be dealt with by a separate department.

*Dealing with employees' problems*

Grievances are raised on a huge range of issues. Many of these will be settled by line managers. Those issues that are not will invariably require a relatively 'neutral' broker – a personnel practitioner. We look at this in detail in the chapter on discipline and grievance-handling (Chapter 8).

Other employee problems for which you need to be prepared include early retirement, redundancy, debts and bereavement.

*Seeking to modify management's actions*

An example of a management action may be a move from weekly to monthly pay. The simple modification of providing an interest-free loan may generate acceptability from employees and enable a senior manager to achieve his or her objectives.

Personnel practitioners should be close to employees and be able to judge what will be acceptable to them. They should also recognise what may damage motivation and commitment, what may cause harmful stress and what may lead to industrial action.

The very high levels of stress being experienced by employees today and the increasing likelihood of successful claims against employers in tribunals suggest there is a very serious challenge here. Unfortunately, personnel practitioners are not immune to stress themselves. They may be particularly vulnerable when they fail to modify those management actions that conflict with their own values.

A personnel career, as may have already been pointed out to you, is not a 'soft' option. Confidence, assertiveness, judgement and emotional resilience are qualities needed by effective practitioners. Given these qualities, practitioners are more likely to find that senior managers listen.

We shall look at how you can develop your personal skills in the chapter on personal effectiveness (Chapter 9).

*Understanding and articulating employees' aspirations and views*

Personnel practitioners' capacity to influence management actions depends on their ability to judge the outcomes of those actions. Judging outcomes means understanding the language of the employees; influencing managers means using the language managers understand. Understanding and communicating well with both employees and managers is an important skill for practitioners. You can foster both languages by spending time with each group.

Walking the floor is better than opening the door. Stay in your own office and you will meet only the more confident employees or those with specific issues to resolve, however wide your door may be open. Senior managers have their own language; that of the chief executive, for example, may be different from that of the board members. Management courses and finance for non-financial managers' courses provide some of the vocabulary. You may be able to learn from social opportunities – talking to senior managers at in-company award ceremonies, for example. There may be external opportunities to learn the decision-makers' language by taking on a responsible community role – for example, becoming a school governor or a magistrate.

Employees at your establishment may be represented by trade unions. If so, that is another group with which to develop a good relationship. Our experience has been that those who become involved in trade unions are genuine and articulate people. Their influence can be valuable in resolving differences between employees and management. It is usually easier to resolve a matter with a few representatives than with a whole workforce. Nonetheless, in our view managers must always reserve the right to communicate directly with their own employees.

We have stated that the definition of personnel management above is a traditional one. We now explore a newer term: human resource management.

## Human resource management

Your perception of human resource management (HRM) may be moulded by the organisation for which you work. Some see it simply as an alternative (either US or 'upmarket') term for personnel management, but others note that it can conveniently encompass training and development, health and safety, pensions and other major activities not regarded as pure 'personnel management' work. Sometimes there is a more strategic perception of human resources (HR): a view that it is a tougher, less people-sensitive function, which is much closer to the decision-makers.

It is worth pointing out that employers are now much more likely to design their organisational structure around their core business and to buy peripheral services from outside by 'outsourcing' them. The core of a business consists of the activities directly associated with its central objectives. For a brewery this might be the particular activity of brewing. Distributing the beer might be regarded as a peripheral activity and be 'outsourced' to a transport and logistics company.

The increasing tendency to separate core and peripheral activities makes organisations smaller and more manageable. It also enables managers to concentrate on their core business, for which they will employ core workers who are skilled and knowledgeable in the activities that make that business unique. For some peripheral activities they may use self-employed freelance consultants, workers from an agency or employees of another company such as a computer software provider. Because personnel has been associated with employees, it can be useful to use the term 'human resources' to embrace this larger circle and include those who are not employees.

More and more employees are working part-time: indeed, social trends and legislation are encouraging it. Employment is becoming more transitory; few people now reach the original retirement ages of 60 and 65 without at least one change of employer or of career.

Clearly this has implications for employers' investment in their employees, for both these changes suggest a lower return on that investment. But they also suggest a need for greater communication and training. To communicate effectively with employees who are there only for part of your operational hours needs new approaches. Continual changes over which person does a particular task will increase the demand for more formal training to ensure knowledge and skills are passed on.

It is against this background that the term HRM is evolving. It may explain why some see HRM as focusing on people as a resource no different from materials or financial funds, thereby reflecting the lower investment associated with peripheral, part-time or transitory workers.

The core activities of personnel and HR are not fundamentally different. For example, human resource planning (anticipating the future employee needs of the business), a typical HR role, is also a personnel management activity. Pick up an HRM textbook and you will see activities that are found in personnel management textbooks, too.

We are of the view that the distinction between personnel management and HRM is not a particularly important one. Adoption of the title 'human resources' may gain some temporary advantage in senior management perceptions. This could be important, if it can be built upon. In any event, you will be judged on what you achieve for your employer, not by the title on your door.

So what should you be achieving for your employer? That very much depends on your employer's expectations. Unless you work for a 'sole trader' (someone who is self-employed – see Chapter 3), your employer will be an organisation.

You may notice that in this book we refer to organisations frequently, although we may from time to time use related terms such as employer, business or company where it might be more appropriate. 'Organisation', though, is a convenient term because the points being made will generally apply whether the 'organisation' is a small private enterprise or a multinational, a small charity or a government department.

Nevertheless, each organisation is unique and the models in this book will vary in their applicability to a greater or lesser extent with different organisations. This is one of the reasons why we stress the importance of using learning sources in the first chapter.

It is therefore wise to think through the fundamental nature of the organisation for which you work in order to understand what your employer may expect of you. Two important concepts help.

## The customer care concept

This concept originated outside the personnel function. It is based on the idea that all functions have a responsibility to serve customers. Those functions that do not deal directly with the organisation's customers nevertheless have 'internal' customers. This concept applies a sound discipline to which it is easy to relate: we all experience the customer relationship when we are customers ourselves. In that position we expect to be treated with respect. Indeed, as people travel more, particularly to the USA and the Far East, they develop an understanding of what good customer care really means. In consequence, they also increase their own expectations.

Service-level agreements are an extension of the customer care concept so that it can operate within an organisation. A typical agreement might be one in which the personnel department agrees to fill all staff vacancies within, say, 10 weeks of authorisation. As practitioners, we have found that setting some standards of service goes down well with other functions and motivates us strongly to achieve them. For personnel departments (as with other functions and many professions), the question still arises: 'Who are our customers?' Are they other departments, prospective employees, current employees, senior managers, or all of these? Since the last option is essentially correct, how can we balance conflict between different customers – who will have priority?

One way of understanding the dilemma this poses is to look at the notion of stakeholders.

## The stakeholder concept

In the stakeholder concept these other parties or customers are seen as having a stake in our department's time. Although balancing conflicting interests may be seen as a managerial function, we all have to mediate between the various people who make demands on our time at and away from work.

As an example, consider others who have a stake in your personal time: your partner, your family, your source of income, any voluntary leisure commitments. You need continually to balance the demands of each of these on your time and energy and against each other.

Looking again at the work situation, the stakeholder concept is not restricted to internal departments. The organisation itself needs to consider a whole range of groups that have a stake in its activities. These are likely to include employees, shareholders, trade unions, the government and local communities, as well as customers and suppliers.

Balancing the differing needs of stakeholders demands good communication, understanding, assertiveness and judgement. It is a major challenge for all managers.

---

**Activity 3**

Taking your organisation, or the site within it where you work, identify the main stakeholders. Which groups or organisations benefit from the existence of your employer? Who would lose out if your organisation became less successful or reduced its presence? What implications do these stakeholders have for your work? (As an example, in a small community the local school may be a major supplier of new employees. The implications for you could be that you would wish to foster good relations with the school.)

---

## What activities are you expected to be involved in?

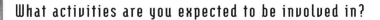

Earlier, we looked at a number of personnel-related activities using the description adopted by Torrington and Hall (1998). Broad though our examination may be, it does not include every activity a personnel practitioner may be asked to do. You will probably identify activities with which you are involved that are only touched upon here, or even omitted altogether. Managing the company car fleet, editing the company newsletter or carrying out health and safety audits are just three examples. Much of the work that falls to personnel departments may not be viewed as strictly personnel-related work. Indeed, management guru Peter Drucker has described the personnel department as the 'trash can' department that takes on almost any activity no one else wants!

It is important to find the balance between customer care activities, when you try to 'delight' customers, and taking on 'trash-can' activities, which will not earn any 'brownie points'. The latter are activities that waste your time and do not gain any credit from the people who have influence over your career. Identifying which is which is not always easy; priorities have to be set. You may want to keep an eye on what activities influential people regard as being most important.

There is a view that many personnel activities should be done by line managers, leaving time for personnel practitioners to concentrate on the medium- to long-term strategic issues. At one of our Certificate in Personnel Practice courses a guest speaker put it succinctly: 'We must avoid becoming embroiled in detailed reactive issues; in essence, more day-to-day personnel activities must be the responsibility of line management.'

## What actions can practitioners take?

We describe several types of action below. In practice, the types of things that you can do arise from a complex mix of the authority vested in you, your persuasive abilities, your credibility with decision-makers, your responsibilities and the norms of your organisation. To these you should add your own capabilities, risk tolerance, emotional resilience and assertiveness.

Generally, you will have to discover for yourself most of the organisational factors in the mix, but we hope that the section on the characteristics and structure of organisations will give you some pointers. Observing and taking counsel from your boss, others in your department and others in the organisation is the way in which you should consolidate this. Personal effectiveness can be increased though self-development, as we outline later.

However, if you are a newly established 'personnel person' within your organisation you will have less advice to draw upon. If you have grown to the position from within the organisation you will already have some idea of the authority you have and your own credibility. If newly appointed, then your manager will probably indicate the boundaries within which you can act. All being well, you will have a job description setting out your main responsibilities and accountabilities (we look at job descriptions in Chapter 5). This job description may indicate your 'authority'; perhaps it specifies a budget, but it is unlikely to be specific about every activity that you will undertake.

One approach is to examine each activity and in each case ask, 'Should I be taking administrative action, advisory action or executive action?' The answer will lie in the factors we discussed above. Let's have a look at each type of action.

### Administrative action

This consists of maintaining procedures and operating systems. For example, a personnel practitioner may be advised of the outcome of salary negotiations and then be expected to calculate new salaries and notify the payroll department. Other examples are the headcount (regularly establishing the number of employees), recruitment activities, maternity leave and issuing letters of appointment. In the case of administrative activities you will usually be given some specific instructions initially and, if supervised, details of how to carry out the task.

The administrative tasks of personnel departments are now 'outsourced' by some organisations – employees of another company perform the tasks and are supervised by that other company. It is then that company (rather than the original organisation's employees) who are responsible for the effective performance of a service contract. In many cases the place of work may remain unchanged, indeed the people doing the work may be the same people. What changes is the reporting relationship.

Outsourcing should not be confused with the use of agency staff. In that case the staff might be employees of the agency but they would be supervised by the organisation's own managers.

Typically, payroll administration has been outsourced by some organisations for many years. Recruitment has also often been outsourced. Further, business services companies are now using their experience of computerised business systems to undertake personnel administration as a business activity.

### Advisory action

This assumes you have some specialist knowledge or information and can provide guidelines for managerial decisions. Areas in which personnel practitioners typically advise are disciplinary procedures and employment law. Clear knowledge and understanding here will enhance your credibility considerably. Keep in mind, though, that this is a difficult area – if in any doubt, seek advice from more senior colleagues or the Advisory, Conciliation and Arbitration Service (ACAS).

In salary negotiations personnel practitioners frequently brief the negotiating team on current remuneration packages or on market rates. They may also be members of the negotiating team.

Some large organisations have set up personnel call centres as sources of advice. These concentrate expertise in a central area and may assist consistency of advice. The organisation's own specialists may staff them or a call centre may be 'outsourced' to another organisation.

### Executive action

This means taking full responsibility for certain tasks, making decisions and taking appropriate action. For example, in some organisations a personnel practitioner may be sufficiently senior, and authorised, to take the decision to dismiss an employee. Similarly, some practitioners take full responsibility for salary negotiations – that is, for reaching an agreement and implementing it. You will not, of course, be taking such decisions unless you have been very clearly authorised to do so.

**Activity 4**

Study the table on activities (Table 1 opposite). Identify activities and tasks that take place in your personnel department.

- Now identify the types of action that your department takes, placing a tick in the appropriate column(s).

- Circle those actions that you might take yourself.

- Discuss the results with others in a similar position in different organisations.

- How do the activities of your department differ from theirs?

**Table 1**   Activities and tasks of personnel departments

| Activity | Task | Executive | Advisory | Admin. |
|---|---|---|---|---|
| Recruitment and selection | Determining methods<br>Defining requirements<br>Advertising<br>Processing applications<br>Interviewing<br>Taking part in decisions<br>Organising programmes<br>Offering jobs<br>Taking up references | | | |
| Industrial relations | Attending meetings<br>Applying agreements<br>Acting as a specialist<br>Advising on law<br>Participating in procedures | | | |
| Direction and policy | Developing policy<br>External relations | | | |
| Health, safety and welfare | Counselling<br>Occupational health<br>Pensions | | | |
| Pay administration | Instructions to pay<br>Initiating transactions<br>Dealing with complaints | | | |
| Manpower – planning and control | Maintaining records<br>Controlling numbers | | | |
| Training and development | Identifying needs<br>Providing training | | | |
| Employee communications | Planning<br>Operating | | | |
| Organisation design | Job descriptions | | | |
| Information and records | Determining needs<br>Providing information | | | |

Adapted from Farnham (1999: 114).

# Corporate culture

As we said earlier, personnel activities take place within an organisation. This means that your role – what you do, and how you do it – are inevitably influenced, or even constrained, by the organisation's nature or corporate culture.

It is valuable to understand your organisation: it will help you decide how to earn those 'brownie points' that we mentioned earlier. It may be that you do not want to advance your career in terms of responsibility. But identifying and performing well in those activities that are valued will enhance the esteem in which you are held, your influence and, perhaps, your salary.

If you have changed employers during your working life then you will appreciate how they differ even within the same industrial sector. The differences between large and small organisations, between the various industrial sectors, and between public and private are even more marked.

Don't assume that the ways in which tasks are carried out in your organisation – say, the way in which job descriptions are prepared – is the only approach or indeed a necessary approach. Many companies, for example, survive profitably without job descriptions.

Within your organisation, observe the characteristics or 'culture' of different departments. In our experience, sales teams are often characterised by positive, outgoing attitudes and a preoccupation with status, targets, performance and reward (for example, the commission scheme).

Production teams are more likely to evidence a 'no-nonsense' attitude, be driven by meeting deadlines, and reject what they see as 'time-wasting' activities (such as writing job descriptions, perhaps).

The predominant corporate culture will depend on the nature of the business. A trading company is likely to be driven by sales attitudes. A manufacturing company is more likely to be characterised by production attitudes. There are many ways of identifying and describing corporate culture. The boxed text, 'Cultural indicators', gives examples of some other differences that characterise culture.

---

**Cultural indicators**

*The nature of reporting relationships*
Does everyone have one established manager or do managers change frequently in response to business needs?

*The management style*
Are employees managed by instruction and control or by consultation and personal development?

---

*Pay*
Is it fixed or linked to performance, grading, or 'merit'?

*Employees*
Are they valued? If so, how is this obvious?

*Customer care*
Are customers valued? If so, how is it obvious?

*Costs*
Do they matter? How does their importance compare with potential income?

*Profit*
Are employees conscious of profit? Is it relevant or important?

*Business objectives*
Do employees identify with business objectives?

*Status symbols*
What role do they play? Are they a substitute for power or remuneration?

*Ethics*
Are ethics important? If so, how is it obvious?

*Risks*
What are the consequences of making a mistake?

There is a series of indicators to show whether an organisation has a positive or negative culture (see the Activities at the end of this chapter).

---

**Activity 5a**

Think about other departments in your organisation, such as purchasing, finance, research and development, marketing, and data processing, as well as the personnel department. What characterises people in those departments in terms of attitudes to, and concern with, the following issues: deadlines, accuracy, documentation, cost, profit, status, ethics and personal financial reward?

---

**Activity 5b**

Reflect on your employer and another employer with whom you are reasonably familiar – perhaps a friend's or your partner's employer. Make a list of the differences in attitude and concerns as outlined in the first part of this activity and any other differences that are appropriate. How do you account for the differences?

Building good links between yourself, your management team, employees and the community is an important task if you are to relate effectively to others in the organisation. How will you do it?

## Building bridges

Spend some time considering the questions below and the discussion that follows each; they should give you some clues as to how you can develop the links we have just mentioned.

- How do employees make contact with you? Interruptions are a major source of inefficiency but, at the same time, you cannot afford to be remote. Is your department close to where most employees work? Is your department found easily? An open door encourages contact, whereas a formal appointment system may discourage it. For a larger department a 'front desk' helps avoid the whole department being interrupted by an enquiry. Intranets, perhaps with a Frequently Asked Questions page, may be an effective way of reducing interruptions while also answering employees' questions.

- How do you make contact with employees? Making time to 'walk the floor' can ensure employees know who you are, foster contact and help you to assess the general mood and spot any changes in mood. It takes time, of course, on your part and on that of employees. Furthermore, not all management teams will welcome direct contacts between you and (their) employees in this way. Another approach is to make a habit of going to see employees directly to deal with matters, rather than telephoning, calling them to your office or issuing a memo. You can inform the employee's manager first, if protocol requires it.

## CASE STUDY 2

A successful 'walking the floor' strategy is demonstrated in this example. With the support of the managing director (who dealt with most protocol issues), the personnel manager blocked out two hours each week to walk the shop floor. During the week he stored up suitable issues with which to approach particular individuals. These were not serious matters (they might otherwise have been handled by a memo or a telephone call) but he found it easier to discuss some relevant issue than simply to make small talk. He also made a note of where he had been each week so as to try to see everyone in the factory over the course of time. If stopped en route by an employee he made time to stop and talk.

He soon found it easier and easier to talk to individuals without having to have a particular purpose and he began to look forward to the weekly exercise. When, at a later stage, major changes were required on the shop floor it was much easier for him to explain the need for the changes and he could expect to be trusted.

- How good are your relationships with trade union representatives? Keeping representatives in touch with issues that concern their members helps build good relationships. You need to be careful what you do discuss, consulting senior management members first if you have any doubts. Nevertheless, making time to talk with the representatives and taking an interest in their viewpoint can be revealing, and you may very probably see your organisation in a different light. Often you will pick up minor issues that you can remedy, or more serious ones in which you can still have an influence. We provide some background on trade unions in the section below.

- Are you in touch with your management team? Using a telephone is efficient and promotes good time management. On the other hand, visiting individuals may be more effective and, crucially, builds relationships. Be mindful of people's time and the pressures on them; nonetheless, most managers enjoy discussing issues face to face. A useful tip is to stand up for informal meetings, thus encouraging contact to be short. The tip also works for telephone calls, because your voice changes when you stand up – it conveys more urgency. Attend relevant formal meetings. Some organisations have a 'meetings' culture, in which case you will probably want to attend as few as possible. Whatever the culture, try to be present at important meetings and go along prepared to make a positive contribution.

- Does the community regard your organisation as a good employer? The manner in which you recruit, respond to unsolicited applications and reject unsuccessful job applicants is often commented upon, especially if you are in a small community. Contact between the community and a major local employer invariably increases the regard in which that employer is held. It may also provide you with valuable information; and liaison between personnel practitioners and local bodies, such as schools or societies, is usually welcomed. If community activities interest you, then you may be able to foster links in the community by being active in, for example, the Chambers of Commerce, or in the various clubs for executive, professional and business people.

- What is the department's profile? The quality of communications can help set the scene. Here we are thinking of examples such as induction information and the staff handbook, notices on the notice boards, clarity of payslips, notification of pay increases and contributions to the company newsletter. How you deal with personal issues will go deeper. Learning good counselling skills helps here. Actions always speak louder than words.

- How will you react to a redundancy programme? Redundancy-handling is one of the most emotive issues with which you are likely to come into contact. Whether you are involved in handling the issues directly or not, you will probably be identified with such programmes by other employees, and you should think through the implications of this. More information on handling redundancies is contained in Chapter 3.

- What else may you have to face? Other personal issues such as bereavements, maternity, AIDS, debts or bankruptcy may well demand your attention. The sympathetic and practical way in which you handle these will reflect strongly on your department's reputation. As with redundancy, it helps in these cases if you think through in advance how you will handle the issues.

You will find help and guidance in Chapter 9 on developing the skills necessary.

# Trade unions

For many personnel practitioners, trade unions are part of the organisational context within which they work. Therefore before leaving the organisational context, we will provide some background to trade unions and the issues that surround working in a unionised environment.

### What is a trade union?

A trade union is an association of members – in which respect it is different from, say, a private company, which has a distinct legal identity. To be a trade union an organisation has to be recognised by a Certification Officer (appointed by the Government) and will usually be a member of the Trades Union Congress (TUC).

Each trade union has its own rules for membership and its own administration and operation. However, there are significant restrictions on union activities brought in by comparatively recent legislation, much of it aimed at 'increasing democracy' within trade unions. For example, at one time, trade unions were able to form 'closed shops' in which only members of particular unions were able to work in particular jobs or companies. This could make it difficult for employees to move jobs unless they carried the right union card. Legislation now outlaws discrimination in employment on the basis of membership or non-membership of a trade union, which effectively prevents closed shops.

### Recognition and collective agreements

Not all employers, of course, welcome unions, and others pride themselves in having such good communications with employees that unionisation has not been desired by those employees. But those employers who recognise a trade union give that union the right to make *collective agreements* with them on behalf of its members. In order for a trade union to form and enter into collective bargaining, there are two requirements: the ability to organise and to be recognised by an employer.

If groups of workers feel sufficient mutual interest for them to wish to negotiate together, they would normally join an appropriate existing trade union. 'Organisation' implies the ability of these workers to meet in one place and formulate some common objectives. This has always been easier in large establishments such as the NHS or BAE SYSTEMS. Industries in which workers are scattered into smaller groups (such as retail shops, hotels and farming) find organisation less practical, and they tend to be less unionised and therefore less likely to have collective agreements.

Where a union has a substantial number of members within a particular group of workers, it may apply to the employer for *recognition*. Employers may then draw up agreements with a union branch to 'recognise' the right of the trade union and its shop stewards to represent its members with the employer. Shop stewards are employees who are also representatives of the trade union at the place of work. Where recognised by the employer, they have legal rights to go about a variety of duties related to their trade union responsibilities.

Where employers do not reach agreements voluntarily then there is a legal procedure under which a trade union may apply to a Central Arbitration Committee (set up by the Government) to have a ballot for recognition. Recognised trade unions have the right to negotiate on behalf of their members in relation to pay, hours and holidays as well as any other matter that may form part of the recognition agreement.

In addition, they have statutory rights to consultation on a number of matters. These include consultation on occupational pensions, on health and safety issues, on redundancy, on the transfer of ownership of the business and on training policies and plans.

A key part of trade union philosophy, enshrined in the word 'union', is that by joining together employees can counter employers' powers to 'exploit' them. Traditionally it was manual workers that most strongly felt this need, but in the latter part of the twentieth century, many white-collar workers became unionised in order to negotiate collectively. The process of negotiating is usually referred to as collective bargaining, and the outcomes of such bargaining as collective agreements.

In negotiating agreements, trade unions have a statutory right of access to the information necessary for the bargaining process. If they are denied access to particular information, they may apply the Central Arbitration Committee for adjudication as to whether they are entitled to access to the information. Collective agreements can cover almost any part of the employer–employee relationship. They may be divided into substantive and procedural.

*Substantive agreements* relate to aspects of the contract between employer and employee: for example, the terms and conditions of employment, the rate of pay or the hours of work. They are often subject to annual negotiation – the annual pay round.

*Procedural agreements* cover the procedures for regulating the relationship, including the method by which they will conduct collective bargaining. An overall procedural agreement is usually made in order to define the areas in which trade union representation is acknowledged. The procedures themselves provide a means of dealing with issues and resolving conflict in fair and consistent ways. Making procedures part of collective agreements effectively means that, so long as the procedure is followed, unions and management will be in agreement on issues or have clear steps to follow in resolving them. Areas covered by procedures may include:

- how trade union representatives are appointed
- disputes, and the arbitration procedure if not resolved
- discipline and grievance-handling
- redundancy.

Procedures also enable the organisation to indicate the flexibility that it will allow individual managers in order to ensure that they do not make decisions that counter organisational objectives.

Procedures usually provide for matters to rise through levels of management if they cannot be resolved at a lower level. Generally, they would require matters to be raised at the lowest appropriate level first and then at other levels later. So, for example, under a disciplinary procedure a supervisor may be empowered to warn an employee about his or her behaviour, but not to dismiss. Where such action is necessary, the supervisor will raise the matter to the next level.

Employers often see the principle of collective agreements as beneficial to them. It is necessary, for example, to consult workers at a factory that is closing. Where employees are unionised, employers can usually negotiate with a few representative individuals and form an agreement that covers all, or at least a whole category of, employees. Without a recognised trade union, an employer is dependent on workers electing employee representatives. Otherwise the employer would need to consult every single employee on an individual basis. In our example that means all the workers at the factory. Those covered by collective agreements will have many, if not most, of their employment terms determined by such agreements. Where these terms are not to their liking, then their first port of call is their trade union shop steward – a practice which, in effect, filters out many minor issues.

Despite the advantages that collective agreements can offer, the consequences of industrial action lead the public, who are often inconvenienced by such action, to question collective bargaining. It is to such action that we now turn

## Industrial action

It can be argued that power requires the ability to hurt another party (and the willingness to do so), even though exercising such power may involve a cost to both parties. The desire to avoid that cost means that much can be achieved by the knowledge that such power exists and the fact that it is in the interests of both parties to avoid the costs of a breakdown. Don't be deceived by media treatment that likes to emphasise the conflict between 'trade unions and management' just because it is more newsworthy – more often than not, the two parties work together very positively. Nevertheless, the fact that employees may decide to take industrial action is a source of power in coming to collective agreements. The power balance, of course, shifts continuously with many factors, such as the changing legal background, the level of unemployment and the market position of an individual employer.

Where employers and employees (represented, usually, by a union) cannot negotiate satisfactory agreements, either party may resort to industrial action. At the extreme, employers may use the 'lock-out' option (literally locking employees out of the workplace) or employees may strike. There are other options available, too. Employers may bring in a new contract and dismiss those who do not accept it. (Such dismissals may, or may not, be fair.) Employees may withdraw their goodwill and take all kinds of actions, of which 'working to rule' (interpreting rules so precisely that little practical work is accomplished) and overtime bans are typical. Significantly, it is possible for skilful manipulation to distort the picture of who is responsible for the breakdown of talks.

## CASE STUDY 3

A residential home for the elderly found it needed to respond to new employment legislation. The Employment Rights Act, Working Time Regulations and the Employment Relations Act (see Chapter 3), among others, had all created the need for more formal working relationships than had been the case in the past. Written particulars had been prepared and annual leave arrangements had been made. Employees were concerned about these changes and had joined a trade union that then sought and was granted recognition. Even so, members of staff were still concerned about the need for written particulars and the management team was uncertain how to deal with this new trade union relationship.

In consultation with a personnel practitioner, the managers drew up an agreement that recognised appropriate rights for the trade union and confirmed the trade union's respect for the charitable status of the home and the aims of the management team. In particular it determined how collective bargaining would be conducted and how any disputes would be resolved.

The approval of the agreement at a meeting with the trade union has provided a framework for tackling employment matters jointly. In particular it has created a co-operative approach to the annual pay review. While other important changes have been taking place, nevertheless, it is acknowledged that a trade union environment has contributed to better working relationships.

It therefore follows that great skill and care is required and that sensitive industrial relations issues will be probably handled by the most senior and the most experienced people in your organisation. You must be aware, too, that complex legislation regulates industrial action, that there is a need for a union to hold secret ballots and that employees can exercise a right not to strike.

If circumstances mean that you cannot avoid involvement in a dispute, always seek appropriate advice. In a large organisation this will be from more senior members of the personnel department. In a small organisation ACAS (see below) or a consultant practitioner may be your most important source.

## The Advisory, Conciliation and Arbitration Service (ACAS)

ACAS is a body set up by the Government but which is required to act impartially in seeking to promote good industrial relations. Its services are available both to employers and individuals, and it receives enquiries from both sources in comparable proportions. It can be called in by parties that are failing to agree on employment matters. It will endeavour to conciliate (essentially getting the parties to talk their problems through), appoint mediators (to suggest solutions to the parties) or appoint an arbitrator, who must have the full consent of both parties. In this latter case the parties agree in advance to accept the arbitrator's decision. The result is that ACAS officials have a huge bank of experience in industrial conflict and are therefore excellently placed to assist in industrial relations.

---

**Activity 6**

Subject to consultation as appropriate with a senior member of your management team, initiate a discussion with a trade unionist, shop steward or convenor. Discover their views about the employment relationship, about trade unionism and about your organisation's corporate culture and objectives. Do they see themselves as partners seeking to work with management for the greater prosperity of the organisation or as workforce representatives whose responsibilities are solely to represent the interests of their members?

---

Before leaving the question of the organisational context in which the personnel function operates we will look at one particular aspect of personnel activities, namely that of planning the human resources of the organisation.

# Human resource planning

There are two components to the process of human resource planning (HRP): managing the demand for human resources and managing the supply. An effective plan will keep the two in balance.

### Demand

One source of demand arises from the organisation's activities requiring more resources. As a general rule managers like to increase their staff. The fact of having more subordinates signifies an increase in power and influence, boosts self-esteem and, quite possibly, leads to a higher salary level or increased prospects. 'Empire building' is a mark of success in both public and private sectors, although a reputation for the activity can be damaging. However, an increase in employment costs invariably leads to an increase in overhead costs. There is a downward effect on overhead costs from shareholders (who expect the organisation to make a profit) in the private sector and from the Treasury, and ultimately the electors, in the public sector. From time to time there can be pressure to reduce overheads and this is particularly likely to arise if there is a reduction in demand for the organisation's products or services. When it comes to cutting overhead costs, the number of options can be limited and a reduction in human resources (usually the greater part of these costs) is the inevitable outcome. Personnel practitioners should keep the long term in mind and seek to curb unwise or unnecessary increases (or decreases) in employment. You might reflect on whether, in your organisation, it would be easier to gain approval to employ another member of staff at £25,000 per year or easier to get an increase of £25,000 in the training budget. The potential benefits of each should be considered in your deliberations.

Another source of demand arises from the organisation's strategy. If it is expanding, opening more branches, opening new hospitals, serving new markets, for example, then it will require more people to staff those activities. There is of course a converse to this, namely downsizing, where it may be closing branches, combining hospital facilities or relinquishing markets. The longer the time horizon on which these actions are planned, the better the personnel practitioner will be placed to respond effectively. This applies just as much whether it be a recruitment drive or a redundancy programme. The key for personnel practitioners is gaining the confidence of the decision-makers so that the personnel function can be involved at an early stage in the decision-making. Often it is necessary to 'prove your mettle' in other areas of personnel activity before you can gain the trust of the strategists.

An easier source of demand to manage is that resulting from the routine turnover of employees or the 'attrition rate'. If this is steady then it provides a guide as to how much recruiting is likely to be required in a year. You need to keep an eye on changes in the rate that might be anticipated, such as the activities of competitors in your labour markets (see the discussion on supply, below) or a glut of retirements.

The labour turnover rate is a useful figure to calculate for this purpose. This is calculated thus:

$$\text{Labour turnover} = \frac{\text{Number of employees leaving in a year}}{\text{Average number of employees in a year}} \times 100$$

Labour turnover rates are also a good measure of the 'health' of an organisation. The best way to make a judgement is by benchmarking organisations in the same sector, industry and locality. You may be able to find the information you require from networking or from industry sources, or from publications such as those from Incomes Data Services.

Very low turnover rates (especially if they reflect the recruitment rate) may be cause for concern. It is important for organisations to get 'new blood' from time to time as part of a process of keeping up to date with skills and experience available in the labour marketplace.

High turnover rates are invariably bad news. Recruitment costs vary but are, typically, 10–20 per cent of the first year's salary. On top of this, the leaver may have left a position vacant while the new employee is recruited. The new employee is likely to need training and time to establish relationships. He or she will not be performing at 100 per cent during this period.

If your organisation is experiencing high turnover rates it is important to establish whether this arises from new recruits leaving the organisation in the first few weeks of employment (the induction crisis) or whether employees with longer service are leaving. The most valuable statistic in deciding this will be the labour stability rate:

$$\text{Labour stability} = \frac{\text{Number of those employees still in employment today}}{\text{Number of employees in employment a year ago}} \times 100$$

A high labour stability rate (combined with a high turnover rate) suggests an induction crisis and therefore attention needs to be paid to recruitment and induction. (See Chapter 5 for further information on both of these subjects.)

A low labour stability rate is even more serious. However, the figures need to be viewed in the context of the industry. In the hotel and catering industry, high turnover and low stability is not unusual. In a specialist research unit, on the other hand, it could mean that valuable skills and knowledge, the lifeblood of the organisation, are draining away.

Both these figures are difficult to calculate because finding and interpreting the raw data on which they are compiled requires persistence, judgement and significant resources on the part of the personnel department. Consequently, they are often not calculated. But the critical point is that they enable the personnel practitioner to assign costs to certain organisational shortcomings. By doing this, the practitioner can raise the perceived value of an effective personnel function.

## Supply

Though the level of control over demand may be problematic at times, it is more difficult to exert much control over the supply of employees. The external environment has a major influence here and anticipating changes can be valuable. It does not always work, however. In the late 1980s organisations were very worried about a 'skills shortage' that was growing and expected to deepen in the early 1990s. In the event there was a major recession and the 'skills shortage' was not a serious problem, though there were still some shortages in very specialist areas. You will find further comment on these and related issues in the introduction to Chapter 5.

What practitioners can do is to increase their knowledge and understanding of their labour markets. Most organisations operate in a variety of labour markets and you should identify and research the ones that are relevant to you. These can be defined using the following factors, which need to be considered in conjunction with each other.

### Geography

Here you need to clarify where your employees travel from in order to work for you. Manual workers and junior staff may be very local and this is where you would seek them. Some of the skills you seek may also be local and this can be an issue if your organisation is considering relocating its activities. Managers and directors may travel from much further especially if you are in a metropolitan area. In addition, when you come to seek senior or well-qualified people the market can be national or international. Your strategy for finding employees will depend in part on where you believe they are living now.

### Economic situations

You should keep in touch with the unemployment rate within the markets in which you are interested. This is particularly necessary if you envisage a recruitment drive in which you are seeking a significant number of employees. Also identify skill shortages that might affect your organisation. Training can do much to avert skill shortages but it takes time, and so anticipating the shortage can be invaluable, economic downturns notwithstanding.

### Occupational types

The UK labour market is very diverse when it comes to occupational types. By thinking widely you may be able to identify sources of employees that others miss. When solving supply problems remember to include possibilities such as part-timers, job shares, shift workers, students, new graduates, outsourcing, home workers, teleworkers, self-employed, agency workers and workers from abroad.

### Competitive positions of organisations

You compete with other organisations not just for sales but also for employees. Some organisations are taking this so seriously as to consider employer brands just as there are product brands. Your organisation may have a monopoly in its product marketplace or its labour marketplace. Its main product may be new and rising in success or you may be in a 'sunset' industry. These factors influence your ability to find and attract employees and emphasise the importance of understanding your organisation in relation to its potential or actual labour markets. If you don't keep in touch, you could find your employees leaving, even for marginally higher rates, very rapidly. Valuable information on labour market competitors can come from local sources, such as Chambers of Commerce, personnel discussion groups and networking. Desk research from sources such as Incomes Data Services can also be very helpful for the wider market. Your local library may be well worth a visit; discuss your research needs with the librarian.

---

**Activity 7**

Look at your organisation, or a manageable portion of it. In the light of the formulae in this section determine how you would go about calculating the labour turnover and the labour stability index. If the data you need is readily available, then calculate the figures and discuss their significance with your learning sources. If not, determine the systems that you would need in place to produce the data necessary to calculate them. You may want to consider putting such systems into action.

---

## Summary

Personnel practice and management offer an interesting and exciting career. Potentially the function encompasses any issue in which the employer, as a corporate body, relates to the employee. Therefore you should have a good relationship both with employees (and their representatives – usually a trade union – where applicable) and managers at all levels, as well as relevant outside bodies.

Practitioners need to be mindful of the type of organisation within which they work so that they can direct their contribution and influence others appropriately.

The personnel function provides a service to the operational functions. It is not in itself profit-earning or a direct contributor to the operational purpose. What it does is to assist others in that role. To be effective it needs to be mindful of caring for its 'customers' and of the various stakeholders, who may have conflicting interests.

The actions that personnel practitioners can take invariably include administrative actions, and frequently they include advisory actions. In many cases, particularly at senior levels, practitioners may have authority to take executive decisions as well. For practitioners to be well regarded they need to be in tune with the corporate culture in which they work: they need to identify what is valued.

In the new millennium practitioners cannot ignore the pace of change and the effects that that has on employers and employees. Anticipating these effects will greatly enhance your performance.

To be well informed, practitioners need to build and maintain good relationships with a variety of stakeholders, particularly managers, trade unions, employees and the community from which their employees come.

Trade unions are relevant for many practitioners and you will have seen that a union is a different entity from a private company, for example. You should now understand the concepts of recognition, collective agreements and industrial action.

HR planning is, by its nature, a complex area – and personnel practitioners need to adopt systems that anticipate future demand and supply, based on comprehensive information gathering. A sound knowledge base also facilitates a flexible approach that will enable you to help your organisation respond quickly and effectively to unforeseen internal and external labour market changes.

---

**Activity 8**

If you are a personnel or training practitioner, prepare a 30-word statement describing the purpose of your job. (If you are not yet in the function then speculate on the purpose of someone who is in such a position in your organisation.) Ask yourself:

- Why do I have a job?

- What would happen if the tasks I do were not completed?

- How might my contribution be measured?

- How might my performance be measured?

---

**Activity 9**

Look at the positive and negative indicators shown in Table 2 on page 42. How does your employer compare with the examples given? Is there a positive or negative culture prevailing? Look back at the section on 'Building bridges' on page 30. Are there any actions you can take that would increase a positive perspective, particularly in the relationship between personnel practitioners, employees, their representatives and the management team?

---

**Table 2**   Positive and negative indicators of corporate culture

| Aspect | Positive indicators | Negative indicators |
|---|---|---|
| Organisational and personal pride | 'Company problems are our problems' | 'What do I care? – I only work here' |
| Performance/excellence | A success orientation | 'It's good enough' |
| Teamwork/communication | Communication is open and two-way | Destructive conflict and unnecessary competition |
| Leadership and supervision | Leaders and supervisors are concerned with people and productivity | Leaders and supervisors see their role as checking and policing subordinates |
| Profitability and cost-effectiveness | People see a connection between profits and their well-being as employees | Opportunities for cost savings and increased sales are neglected or overlooked |
| Relationships with colleagues | People work hard to see that all colleagues are treated with dignity and respect | Company and employees tend to look at each other as having separate interests |
| Customer and consumer relations | Customer satisfaction is seen as vital to personal and organisational success | The customer and consumer tend to be looked upon as a kind of unavoidable burden |
| Honesty and safety | Safety regulations are taken seriously; people place a high value on integrity and support integrity in others | People are careless with company money or products, and neglectful in following or enforcing safety practices |
| Training and development | Training and development are looked upon as an integral part of all that occurs within the organisation | Training is seen as unimportant and barely related to the day-to-day work |
| Motivation and change | People are eager to consider new and innovative approaches | People look at new ways of doing things with unwarranted suspicion or mistrust |

Based on work by Allen and Pilnick and adapted from Edwards (1988).

### References and further reading

BEARDWELL I. *and* HOLDEN L. (1997) *Human Resource Management: A contemporary perspective.* London, Pitman Publishing.

EDWARDS E. (1988) 'Corporate culture'. *Management Accounting.* May. p19.

FARNHAM D. (1999) *Managing in a Business Context.* London, Institute of Personnel and Development.

HACKETT P. (1991) *Personnel: The department at work.* London, Institute of Personnel Management.

TORRINGTON D. *and* HALL L. (1998) *Human Resource Management.* Hemel Hempstead, Prentice Hall.

WEIGHTMAN J. (1999) *Managing People.* London, Institute of Personnel and Development.

You will find useful information on human resource planning matters available from:

INCOMES DATA SERVICES, 77 Bastwick Street, London EC1V 3TT; tel. 020 7250 3434.

### Websites

ADVISORY, CONCILIATION AND ARBITRATION SERVICE (ACAS)
www.acas.org.uk

CHARTERED INSTITUTE of PERSONNEL and DEVELOPMENT   www.cipd.co.uk

*PEOPLE MANAGEMENT*   www.peoplemanagement.co.uk

INCOMES DATA SERVICES   www.incomesdata.co.uk

# 3 • The Legal Background to Personnel Practice

## CHAPTER OBJECTIVES

After reading this chapter you will:

- know which legislation is likely to apply in the main areas of personnel activity

- be able to discuss the expectations of the law in employment matters with managers and legal specialists

- be able to respond to the fundamental legal expectations placed on employers

- recognise the limitations of your knowledge and know where to find further information

- have an understanding of the basic employment legislation affecting personnel practice, including employment contracts, health and safety, equal opportunities and diversity.

## Why is legislation important?

Many personnel practitioners and line managers feel that bringing the law into employment relationships creates rigidity and sometimes makes it difficult for the business to respond to opportunities. Employees, on the other hand, often feel that the law provides a degree of protection from poor management and exploitation. Many other feelings surround the question of law and employment. Some may arise from political beliefs, others from personal experience. The extent to which strong feelings exist, and their relevance to personnel practice, varies from organisation to organisation. Government organisations necessarily attach great importance to legal matters, whereas some entrepreneurial business people may seek to minimise, or try to disregard, the impact of the law on their employment practices. Other employers adopt employment practices that are in excess of any minimum provided by the law. They aspire to practices that are the best that can be found, embracing the spirit as well as the letter of the law. One example, in the equal opportunities area, is the development of a truly diverse workforce in which every worker's dignity is genuinely respected.

Whatever an employer's intentions are, it is likely that there will be times when an employee feels that he or she has been unfairly treated. If that employee believes that the employer has acted unlawfully, then he or she may make a claim to an employment tribunal. If the tribunal upholds the claim it will, in most cases, award compensation. Such compensation may be thousands of pounds or, in some types of claim, an unlimited amount. Whether the claim is upheld or not, substantial preparation work is involved if the employer decides to fight the claim. Such work makes no direct contribution to business objectives, and adverse publicity may even damage achievement of those objectives. In some cases, trade unions can challenge the employing organisation by taking actions that disrupt its activities, damage its relationship with customers and threaten its profitability. Therefore a knowledge of employment law is a key requirement for personnel practitioners.

However, employment law is not an area where issues are necessarily clear cut. Indeed, even at an employment tribunal with a legally qualified chairman, one party involved may not agree that the law has been correctly interpreted and may appeal against the decision reached. The matter will then be referred to a higher court for it to advise on interpretation of the law. In some cases it falls to the House of Lords or the European Court of Justice to decide this. One consequence is that, quite frequently, the precise way in which the law is interpreted changes.

So, although we shall explain the basic principles that you need to know, you are likely also to need advice from more senior colleagues, the Advisory, Conciliation and Arbitration Service (ACAS) (see later in this chapter), or legal specialists.

---

**Activity 10**

Think about your own organisation. How do managers and workers view the effect of law on employment? Do managers use it to control or manage people? If so, how? Do employment rights reassure employees? What do you think of the attitudes in your organisation? Write down your thoughts and discuss them with one of your learning sources, as described in the Introduction to this book.

---

### A note on employees and workers

You will notice that we have already used the terms 'employees' and 'workers'. Legally the term 'worker' includes employees. Much recent legislation is aimed at workers rather than employees (see 'What is an employment contract?' on page 49). But the term 'worker' is sometimes used more narrowly to denote manual, or blue-collar, workers. In this chapter we have tended towards the legal interpretation. So in our text, as an example, trade unions have generally represented *employees* (including white-collar employees) rather than *workers* (which in the legal sense could include self-employed people).

### Acts and Regulations

You will see these words quoted throughout this chapter and occasionally elsewhere in this book. Acts (Statutes) are major pieces of legislation debated and passed by Parliament. Regulations (Statutory Instruments) are prepared to regulate how the legislation operates in practice and invariably contain specific details. In reading more widely, you will frequently see cases quoted. Case law indicates how courts and tribunals have interpreted the law in the past and a decision by a court is binding on all lower courts and tribunals.

The purpose of this chapter is to give you background information. Reference to Acts and Regulations is sufficient to achieve this. However, most of the case studies in this chapter are based on actual court cases and these demonstrate how the law has been interpreted.

## Employment legislation

It is useful to see employment legislation in three groups: civil law, employment protection rights, and other statutory legislation.

### Civil law

This group deals with relations between two parties. Contracts are an example; breaches of them entitle one party to sue the other (litigation). Typically, in employment, this would be for failure to give proper notice (an example of wrongful dismissal). Most breach of employment contract claims are heard by employment tribunals.

Another example of civil law is the duty of care. This is implicit in all employment contracts. So an employee may sue his or her employers for damages if, for example, he or she is injured at work and believes the employer to be responsible. In doing so the employee may cite breaches of regulations – for example, not being informed of safety procedures. Personal injury claims are currently a matter for the County Court or High Court.

### Employment protection rights

The major employee right is the right not to be unfairly dismissed, and this applies irrespective of the employee's contracted hours of work. The length of service an employee usually requires before acquiring this right is 12 months. The other main area of protection is the right not to be discriminated against. This comprises laws that protect equal opportunities, covering such areas as maternity rights and equal pay, reasonable adjustments for the disabled and the employment of ex-offenders. Redress in employment protection matters is sought by a claim to an employment tribunal. The onus is on the aggrieved party to make this claim. This body of employment protection legislation is a major area for employers and one with which personnel practitioners need to be familiar.

### Other statutory legislation

Many obligations are placed on the employer by other statutory legislation. In contrast to civil law and the employment protection legislation (where claims are made for damages or compensation), many breaches in this area leave employers (principally directors, but also managers and in some cases workers) open to criminal prosecution, fines and (in some extreme cases) imprisonment. In Northern Ireland, such legislation includes the question of religious discrimination.

There are also legal requirements placed on the records that employers need to keep, and also on what they should not keep. Working Time Regulations 1998, the National Minimum Wage Act 1998 and the Data Protection Act 1998 are examples of Acts that place specific requirements on the records employers have to keep. The Health and Safety at Work Act 1974 (HASWA) and the Control of Substances Hazardous to Health Regulations 1999 (COSHH) are another two highly important pieces of legislation. Health and safety is a major area of legislation, especially for employers in the industrial sector, and one with which those who have health and safety responsibilities must obviously be familiar.

We shall look at the key issues in each area, starting with civil law.

## Civil law

### What is a legal contract?

When one person agrees to do something for another, a contract exists. It may be binding in honour only, as for example when we offer to buy a drink for a friend (and he or she accepts our offer). In this example, if we suddenly discover we have left our money at home (and therefore cannot fulfil the contract), we do not expect to be sued! Nonetheless, an informal contract was made and, in failing to fulfil it, we would have broken that contract.

Legal contracts are more binding and, if we break them, the other party is entitled to damages. A failure to agree on what damages are due entitles the aggrieved party to seek redress in a civil court or, if it is an employment contract, in an employment tribunal. Legal contracts can be made by people or by 'legal entities' such as a limited company.

An employment contract is a particular type of legal contract. But let's first look at the conditions needed for a contract to be legally enforceable.

- *Agreement*  An offer has to be made and accepted. You might offer to buy someone's car for £5,000, but no agreement is reached until the offer is accepted. In employment, offers are often 'subject to' issues such as references, a medical or verification of qualifications. In such cases, agreement is not reached until all the 'subject to' issues have been resolved. In the case of the car, you might make your offer 'subject to' a satisfactory engineer's report.

- *Consideration*  There has to be an exchange of benefits – the car in return for your £5,000, for example. In employment it could be wages in return for work. 'Voluntary work' can be a grey area but, unless something tangible is given in return (genuine expenses, perhaps), there will be no legal contract. Incidentally, if work is not genuinely voluntary then the national minimum wage applies (see page 66).

- *Intention*  Both parties must intend to form a legally binding contract. This may be presumed, as in employment contracts, or should be recorded in writing, as in agreements between friends and relatives. Buying cars from friends can be problematic. If your friend gets a better offer while you are at the building society, it may be legally as well as practically difficult to enforce the contract. For self-employed people, employing friends and relatives can be problematic unless a specific legal contract is made.

- *Certainty*  It has to be clear what the parties have agreed so that the contract can be established with certainty. Oral agreements, though having the status of legal contracts if clearly made, can be difficult to enforce. If it proves difficult to establish with certainty what was agreed, then the contract may be void. For this reason it is good practice to put employment contracts into writing.

- *Consent*  The parties must come together freely and not under duress. In practice, unemployed people will often feel under pressure and can easily agree to terms they dislike. Unfortunately such 'duress' is regarded as a normal fact of life. It does not invalidate the contract.

- *Legality*  Contracts can be formed for legal purposes only. This has implications for illegal activities, such as drug dealing. In instances where disputes cannot be resolved by recourse to law, they are often settled by use of violence.

- *Capacity*  The person making the contract on behalf of an organisation must be properly authorised to do so. This is very important for you as a personnel practitioner. If you offer an employment contract without proper authority, your organisation could disown the decision. This would place you in a most invidious position and almost certainly leave you liable to disciplinary action. If the rejected employee had already accepted your offer, and handed in notice in his or her current employment, he or she may seek damages.

Notice that contracts do not have to be in writing. Many offers are made and accepted over the telephone. If it can be established that the above conditions have been met, then an enforceable contract exists. Telephone offers are quicker and therefore reduce the danger of losing a good candidate while a written contract is being prepared. They can make negotiations easier so long as both parties are prepared for them and you have clear authority to reach an agreement. In the longer term, written offers and acceptance have the advantage that both parties know exactly what has been agreed. Therefore there is less room for confusion (if references prove to be unsatisfactory, for example). Care has to be taken to be sure that an interview candidate is not led to believe an offer exists (by agreeing a pay rate, for example) when that is not the intention. Word such as 'if we were to offer you. . . .' are important to help avoid confusion.

You need to find out whether your organisation has a policy on how offers should be made, or whether you are expected to make use of your best judgement.

Offers made by post may be accepted by post. Offers can also be accepted by a person's behaviour: for example, arriving for work would indicate acceptance. It may be helpful to place a time limit on an offer, or formally to withdraw it if it is not accepted within a satisfactory time-scale.

### What is an employment contract?

It is important to understand whether someone who is doing work for you is an employee, a worker or a business.

You may wish to offer work to a person who claims to be self-employed. One difficulty, if you reach an agreement on that basis, is that the Inland Revenue may not be willing to treat that person as self-employed. In that case you, the employer, will probably have to pay tax and National Insurance contributions to the Inland Revenue for the person (even if he or she has already been paid without deductions).

On the other hand, if a person is an *employee*, then he or she has a wide range of employment rights, including the right not to be unfairly dismissed. The claim to be an employee could come after a contract has ended, in order to assert employment rights. So, let's have a look at the distinctions.

If you have your house decorated you do not, usually, employ a decorator; what you do is make a contract for service. Your decorator is likely to be a business, it may possibly be the person's own business. The person you meet may be an employee of the business but he or she will not be an employee of yours. However, if your organisation retains an individual person as a decorator to decorate its premises, then that person could be an employee or a worker.

Employees have a contract of employment. They may receive other benefits such as sick pay. Workers are people who do the work for you, or your organisation, personally (ie they cannot subcontract the work to others); usually they are supervised, and work specified hours. Employees are workers, but workers can also include freelance people and those from agencies. So all employees are workers, but workers are not necessarily employees. Workers are usually paid on a scale that is determined by the employer and may pay tax by PAYE. Workers have some employment rights, such as protection from discrimination. However employees have additional rights, including entitlement to written particulars of employment and protection from unfair dismissal.

Genuinely self-employed people and businesses usually provide their own equipment (such as paint brushes in the case of decorators) and will almost certainly work for others as well as your organisation. They submit invoices and will probably be VAT-registered. They may contract to do a particular task (as opposed to working set daily hours), and any profit or loss in doing the work accrues to the business rather than your organisation. So as not to be held liable for any tax or National Insurance contributions, anyone contracting work from the self-employed may be wise to see a supporting letter from the Inland Revenue or a contractor's certificate.

If self-employed people do work for you and claim to be a business, make sure the set of conditions in the last paragraph is satisfied. If in doubt, you are usually safer to employ them on a contract of employment, deduct tax under PAYE, and accept that they will have employment rights. If you choose not to do so, you could find yourself liable for their tax and/or discover they are claiming employment rights nevertheless.

Genuine businesses would also be free to give the work to one of their own employees or workers. Both self-employed workers and businesses have the right to turn work down if they choose and the organisation contracting with the business or worker is not obliged to offer work. Employer and employee do not have this freedom; there is instead what is called 'mutuality of obligation' where one party is obliged to provide work and the other is obliged to do it.

Despite the differences explained here, it is very important to realise that the distinction is not always clear-cut and that you may need to seek advice. Courts and tribunals can come to differing conclusions on seemingly similar situations and are not bound by decisions made by other bodies such as the Inland Revenue. The terms worker and employee are discussed in detail in an article by Aikin (1999) in the CIPD magazine *People Management* – see page 77 below. Remember that, if a contract of employment is made, a statement of written particulars should be provided within two months.

---

**Activity 11**

Consider the people who help accomplish your organisation's objectives. Are they all employees? If not, how would you categorise them? Carry out some appropriate research into the nature of their relationship with the personnel function. For example, you might want to investigate what records are kept for them and what employment rights they have and reflect on how the responsibilities of the personnel department differ for these people and your employees. Discuss the issues with your learning sources.

---

## Contracts of employment

The contract sets out the legal basis of the relationship. Therefore it should include those matters on which you wish your employee to be legally bound and matters on which you, as an employer, will be legally bound. For example, you may want legally to bind an employee to your office hours. If there is a clear written agreement specifying this as part of the contract, then the hours become contractual.

Typically, disciplinary and grievance procedures are not part of the contract and it is advisable if only the minimum details required are referred to in the written particulars. You may have good reason to use judgement in operating disciplinary and grievance procedures. If such procedures are contractual, then a failure to follow them to the letter can result in a breach of contract claim. For example, if grievance procedures are part of the contract, and you refuse to use them when an employee raises a grievance, then the employee might claim that you have dismissed them by breaking the contract (known as *constructive dismissal*). In this case the employee could sue for damages such as entitlement to notice pay. He or she would be claiming *wrongful dismissal*, that is dismissal in breach of the contract. The employee might also claim *unfair dismissal*, if he or she is entitled to do so. We will look at constructive and unfair dismissal again later. It is important to remember that contracts cannot be changed unilaterally. To change a contract, both parties have to agree.

It is impossible to predict every possible employment situation that can arise. Therefore in areas where judgement or discretion is needed some matters as far as possible should not be contractual. Typical examples might be bonus scheme rules, job descriptions and procedures. For the employer, gauging the degree of flexibility that should exist in the employment relationship is an important decision and requires careful judgement, although the final decision as to whether a particular term is contractual or not may rest with the courts.

Just to clarify the issue further, let's take the example of job descriptions. If you include a job description in an employment contract, then every variation in the duties of the job can, potentially, become a legal issue. For this reason it is advisable to specify only the job title when making a contract (indeed, technically even this could be left for the written particulars). Similarly, there is no requirement to include a job description in the written particulars. Indeed, there is no legal need to have a job description at all.

The degree of formality involved in job descriptions affects an employer's flexibility to a significant degree. At one extreme, a lot of formality (job descriptions signed, or included in the contract) tends to encourage disputes over duties. Such disputes can focus on wording rather than the purpose of the job or the interests of the parties concerned. At the other extreme, complete informality (no job descriptions) may aid early resolution but can make it much more difficult if relationships do eventually break down. In informal situations it is easy for the employer to have one expectation about the employee's responsibilities and for the employee to have another.

Certain matters are implicit in an employment contract and are not usually written down. They apply whether the parties specifically agree to include them or not. They are:

- statutory requirements, such as those in the Health and Safety at Work Act 1974 (HASWA)

- common law duties (such the duty of care and co-operation with the employer)

- custom and practice (such as tea breaks, in cases where they are established).

Other matters that are clearly agreed between the two parties are explicit parts of the contract. If you want a matter to be contractual you need to be very careful in drawing up the contract, because it will not be easy to vary it later. For example, the place of work is usually part of the contract, so state it clearly and accurately.

However, you can put into the contract reasonable rights to vary aspects of the contract. So, in the case of the place of work, you might include a mobility clause. Indeed, you can put into the contract (and written particulars) variation clauses for any right that you may wish to vary, so long as the variation is justifiable and reasonable; but if you are providing for something that might happen sometime in the future, you should still consult the employee(s) concerned when the variation is required.

Finally, it is important to include the notice period for termination of the contract by either party. Alternatively, the statutory minimum notice periods (based on length of service) may be stated.

### Written particulars

Written particulars are provided for information only and represent the employer's view of the terms of the relationship; where they conflict with contractual terms, the contract will prevail. New employees, employed to work for one month or more, have the right to receive written particulars of their employment within two months of starting employment. Today these rights are provided for in the Employment Rights Act 1996.

Look at the boxed text below that describes the required content of written particulars. Think through why the law provides these rights and what benefits they confer.

- Is it fair and reasonable for employees to know where they stand?

- Do written particulars protect employees from maltreatment? If so, how?

- Is a better understanding between employer and employee likely to arise as a result of putting particulars in writing?

- Why do you think many employers still do not provide written particulars? Is it:

  - through lack of knowledge of the law?

  - to save administration costs?

  - for power, gained by keeping employees ignorant of their rights?

---

**Written particulars**

The following are required in one document, termed 'The Principal Statement':

- names of employer and employee

- date when employment began

- date when continuous employment began

- scale or rate of remuneration or method of calculation

- intervals at which remuneration is paid

- terms and conditions relating to hours of work (including normal working hours)

- holiday entitlement (including any entitlement to accrue holiday pay)

---

- job title or brief job description

- place of work.

The following may be provided in separate documents:

- terms relating to injury, sickness, and sick pay

- pensions and pension schemes

- period of notice each party must give to terminate the contract

- where the employment is temporary, how long is it likely to last, or the termination date for a fixed-term contract

- collective agreements which directly effect terms and conditions

- disciplinary rules and steps in the disciplinary and grievance procedures, specifying the people with whom, and how, an employee can raise a grievance or apply if dissatisfied with a disciplinary decision.

Certain additional details are also required for employees sent to work outside the UK for more than one month.

Compiling written particulars demands care. Simplicity can give rise to anomalies because simple solutions do not recognise different sets of circumstances. An example of this might be an employer who gives 25 days' holiday a year plus all public and bank holidays. This is a simple rule, but how do you interpret it for an employee who works only Monday and Tuesday each week? You could 'pro-rata' the 25 days to 10, but how do you handle public and bank holidays, which often fall on a Monday?

On the other hand, complex systems can lead to confusion and often mistrust. For example, a system could be devised where we add up how many holidays have been taken and then pay the part-time employees for only some of them. Of the 25 days' holiday plus the 8 public and bank holidays we might pay 13.2 days (two-fifths of 33 days) as one day per month plus one every 10 months. The employee could accumulate payable time at that rate and be paid the amount of entitlement that they had accumulated when they took a holiday. Such a scheme might be precisely fair.

You may have found this explanation hard to follow. So, we hope you will agree that it is complex and difficult to understand. It could create distrust or even lead to outright dispute in some particular instance. You need to learn how to strike a balance between the simple and the complex.

There are many guides available for preparing particulars, for example in *The Personnel Administration Handbook* or in Jordan's Employment Law Service (see Further Reading, pages 77–80).

You might like to know what the consequences of not providing written particulars are likely to be. Bear in mind that Government officials will not arrive to check their existence, and neither you nor your employer is going to be prosecuted for such failures. However, if you fail to provide written particulars within the time limit, an employee can apply to an employment tribunal, which may then determine particulars of employment as it sees fit.

You may feel this is unlikely to happen. Although it is clearly not good practice to neglect written particulars, so long as relationships with employees remain fair, you might be right. However, redundancies, dismissals or even resignations increase the chances of aggrieved employees making employment tribunal claims. Complaints that you have failed to provide written particulars will substantially weaken your case at tribunal. So you would be wise to encourage the managers in your organisation to accept good practice. Indeed, most managers like to be thought of as 'good employers'.

---

**Activity 12**

Look into how contracts are made and written particulars are prepared in your organisation. Compare the written particulars for a typical appointment with the details here. Discuss any queries with a suitable learning source.

---

Let's look next at employment protection rights, starting with dismissal.

## Employment protection rights – dismissal

### The right not to be unfairly dismissed

As an employee you will be investing a good proportion of your life in the work of your employer. Most probably you will feel that you make a valuable contribution and represent a good investment, not least because of your ongoing desire to learn and improve your performance. All being well, your employer will be of the same opinion. Unfortunately it is not always the case that employers and employees share the same views. What the employee may see as conscientiousness, the employer may see as being exceedingly pedantic. Single-mindedness may be praised or seen as tunnel vision. The list could continue. So employers and employees do not always measure performance in the same way.

Let's take another example. An employee may need to leave early for a doctor's appointment. If the employee forgets to clock out because of being preoccupied with concern over the appointment, he or she may see this as a simple oversight. The employer may see the same action as an attempt to defraud the company.

These conflicting views highlight a point: it is not acceptable, at least in the case of an employee who has been with the employer for some time, for the worker to be dismissed without some serious attempt to resolve conflict.

These are only two examples. There is a whole range of areas where employers and employees may have different perceptions of each other and of what is expected. Here are a few more:

- the reliability with which the employee attends work
- the quality of the work that is completed
- the language that is used at work
- the achievement of targets
- the attitude to authority
- what constitutes reasonable treatment of the sexes
- what constitutes reasonable treatment of minority groups.

There are other, more serious, areas where behaviour is totally unacceptable (gross misconduct) and where summary dismissal (ie dismissal without notice) may be justified:

- pilfering
- unauthorised absence
- violence
- fraud
- drunkenness.

The danger is that in any of these areas it could be that the employee is falsely accused. (Incidentally, dismissal without notice does not mean 'instant dismissal'. All cases of gross misconduct must be thoroughly investigated before a decision to dismiss is taken.)

Dismissals occur for other reasons, too. An employee may become ill and unable to work; a heavy goods vehicle driver could lose his licence; a job may no longer be required; or a reorganisation may lead to fewer jobs even though the same amount of work is being done.

Prior to employment protection legislation, when the decision to dismiss an employee was taken the prime considerations were moral ones. There was no legal obligation to be fair or reasonable. How fair or reasonable dismissal decisions were, in such circumstances, is a matter for conjecture. The consequences for employees then, as now, could be severe. Even though there was low unemployment in the 1950s and 1960s a stigma attached to losing one's job and re-employment could be difficult. At that time the main protection rested in trade union membership, and industrial action in support of dismissed workers did occur. It was not a very satisfactory way to seek redress for unfair dismissals.

As we have already mentioned, the qualifying period for the right not to be unfairly dismissed is now 12 months' service. For an employee to be dismissed fairly there must first be a fair reason for the dismissal and the employer must act reasonably in arriving at the decision to dismiss.

### A fair reason

There are only five potentially fair reasons for dismissal (although the fifth is quite broad):

- *capability* – the inability to perform the type of work for which the employee was employed. This can include health factors.

- *conduct* – failure to meet reasonable expectations. This can include failure to carry out reasonable instructions, bad time-keeping and attendance, as well as gross misconduct, such as theft from the employer.

- *redundancy* – the work for which the employee was employed has ceased or diminished. Here the selection of a particular individual has to be shown to be fair.

- *legal restrictions* – this may apply, for example, when the employee becomes disqualified from driving and the only work available requires the employee to drive.

- *'some other substantial reason'* – this area is established by precedents in case law. An example might be a reorganisation, so long as there is a sound business reason for it. This reason may be used when an employer cannot afford to continue paying on current terms and conditions, dismisses employees for sound business reasons and offers them a new contract.

Whenever a decision to dismiss is taken, it is wise to determine which of the above reasons is the true one. Dismissed employees have the right to ask for written reasons and the reason, or reasons, chosen may need to be defended in a tribunal.

### Acting reasonably

Employers may also have to show that they act, or have acted, reasonably and the best way to do this is to follow a fair procedure. In particular the employer has to show that he or she has acted reasonably in reaching the decision to dismiss. Various ACAS publications cover these procedures in detail, and you should consult the advisory handbook on *Discipline at Work* which contains the ACAS *Code of Practice on Disciplinary and Grievance Procedures*. (See the list of reference sources at the end of this chapter.) During 2003 the law is expected to make minimal dismissal and disciplinary procedures a statutory obligation. To dismiss without following the minimum procedure may become automatically unfair.

## CASE STUDY 4

Mr Polkey was one of four van drivers employed by the respondent company. In the summer of 1982 it became necessary to reorganise the van drivers' duties with the result that the four van drivers were replaced by two van salesman and a representative. Only one of the four drivers was considered suitable for transfer to the new duties and accordingly the other three were made redundant. The first that Mr Polkey knew of the situation was when he was called into the branch manager's office and told that he was being made redundant. He was immediately driven home by one of the other drivers who was himself then dismissed on his return.

*Polkey* v *A.E. Dayton Services Ltd* [1987] IRLR 309. Reproduced by permission of the Butterworth Division of Reed Elsevier, UK Ltd.

Since there was no consultation with Mr Polkey he complained to an industrial tribunal that his dismissal was unfair. Potentially the dismissal was fair because redundancy can be a fair reason. However, if there had been consultation then it is conceivable that an alternative to redundancy might have been found. As there was none, the tribunal could not put itself in the position of deciding what would have happened if there had been. Following appeals, the House of Lords determined that 'it is what the employer did that has to be judged, not what he might have done'. Behaving reasonably means following a fair procedure unless it would be 'utterly useless' to do so. In practice, it means that dismissing an employee without following a procedure is not likely to be found fair by a tribunal.

Different procedures will be appropriate in different circumstances. Having disciplinary and grievance procedures makes sense for all employers because they provide a framework for resolving conflict fairly. Ill-health issues are more effectively tackled by a specific ill-health or capability procedure. What is a reasonable course of action when behaviour is within an employee's control may no longer be reasonable when illness is involved. (See Chapter 8 for more information.)

Reasonableness is the key to fairness. What may be seen as reasonable procedures for a small employer may be considered to be inadequate procedures for a larger employer. To illustrate this, let's now consider case studies 5 and 6 on pages 59 and 60.

Workers also have the right to be accompanied by a fellow worker or trade union representative at disciplinary hearings. For the purpose of this right, any hearing at which you contemplate taking some action in relation to the employer is a disciplinary hearing. So, for example, if you are discussing the employee's ill health (and that could result in a demotion), the employee has the right to be accompanied.

It is worth noting that fairness will be judged in the light of information available *at the time the decision is made*. An employer must carry out a thorough investigation to gather as much relevant information as is reasonable. He needs to have grounds for his beliefs, eg for believing that an employee is stealing. However, he may make the decision on the balance of probabilities; he does not need proof beyond reasonable doubt. Subsequent, more conclusive, evidence of guilt or innocence is not relevant to the fairness of the decision.

## CASE STUDY 5

After establishing grounds for believing an employee to be guilty, a sole proprietor with 10 employees decides to dismiss the employee in question for fiddling his bonus. The proprietor may have been the only person to have investigated the allegation, may have been the only person to assess all the evidence and may have taken the decision to dismiss without consulting anyone else. He might be expected to consider questions such as: Were other employees fiddling their bonus too? Did the employee know, or was it reasonable to expect him to know, that bonus fraud was gross misconduct that could result in dismissal without warning? Although the employer can be expected to have answered such questions, he may nonetheless have to make the final decision without being able to consult anyone else.

In an organisation of 2,000 employees, such a course of action could not rest with one person. More would be expected in terms of the degree of thoroughness. Were the questions posed above properly answered? Was the accusation thoroughly investigated by appropriate people? Was the decision to dismiss taken at a senior level in the organisation? Was an appeal heard in front of people who had not been involved in the original decision?

The guidelines contained in the ACAS Code of Practice are very important. The extent to which they are followed, or not followed, will be taken into account when a tribunal judges fairness.

### Dismissal

Dismissal takes place when the employer terminates the contract with notice, without notice or because of actions that effectively breach the contract. Fixed-term contracts that expire without renewal are also dismissals.

There are times when a dismissal is disputed. For example, a supervisor may 'blow up' at an employee, perhaps humiliating the employee in front of his or her colleagues. The employee decides 'enough is enough', goes home, and does not return to work. Has the employee been dismissed or has he or she resigned?

The employer might argue that the supervisor carried out a reprimand, that it was justified and that it was carried out respectfully – although it may be conceded that colleagues should not have witnessed it. The employer could maintain that the employee has simply resigned. There is therefore no question of dismissal, fair or unfair. Conversely, the ex-employee may produce evidence of previous mistreatment and seek to show that the reprimand was clearly humiliating and very public. He or she might contend that it would be quite intolerable to continue to work in such circumstances. Therefore, because of the actions taken, the employer has dismissed him or her – and unfairly at that.

Were this case to come before an employment tribunal, the question of dismissal or resignation would be examined very thoroughly. For example, the words used in the reprimand (or emotional outburst), evidence of previous maltreatment and any protests the employee may have made in the past could all be taken into account. In some cases a tribunal may decide that the employee resigned. In others, it may feel that the employer's treatment of the employee meant that trust and confidence had broken down and the employment contract had been broken. This would be 'constructive dismissal', entitling the employee to presume, from the employer's actions, that he or she had been dismissed. That is, that the employer had broken the contract.

Whether such a dismissal would be unfair might depend on the reason for the reprimand, on whether there had been a thorough investigation, on whether the employee had been formally warned beforehand and on a range of other factors.

From the employer's viewpoint, sets of circumstances that could lead to an employee claiming constructive dismissal are to be avoided. Once the individual has left the premises, control of the circumstances passes out of the employer's hands. A dismissal may be claimed even if it was not intended. Unless the employee can be tempted back, it becomes too late to ask the employee to explain his or her alleged misconduct. Furthermore, it is too late to carry out an investigation, because the decision has already been taken. The issue has become the employer's misconduct.

Once again, the main relevant legislation here is the Employment Rights Act 1996. The Employment Relations Act 1999 has relevance to accompaniment at disciplinary hearings.

## CASE STUDY 6

The United Bank Ltd had employed Mr Akhtar for approximately 11 years at its Leeds Branch. His written particulars contained a mobility clause: 'The bank may from time to time require an employee to be transferred temporarily or permanently to any place of business which the bank may have in the UK for which a relocation or other allowance may be payable at the discretion of the bank'. Citing the mobility clause, the bank gave him a few days' notice to move to Birmingham and offered no relocation expenses. When he requested a postponement for personal reasons, it was turned down. A series of exchanges led to the bank stopping his pay and Mr Akhtar claiming the bank had dismissed him.

A tribunal held that, despite the mobility clause, reasonable time and expenses should have been given to enable Mr Akhtar to comply with their request for him to relocate. The bank's conduct was such that the employee could not be expected to put up with it. He was entitled to consider himself dismissed. There is an implication in an employment contract that an employer will not act in such a way as to destroy trust and confidence between employer and employee. The dismissal was found to be unfair.

*United Bank Ltd* v *Akhtar* [1989] IRLR 507. Reproduced by permission of the Butterworth Division of Reed Elsevier, UK Ltd.

---

**Activity 13**

Many tribunal cases are reported in newspapers. Look through a quality daily paper for a report on a dismissal case. Review the case in conjunction with the text here. What was the reason for dismissal? Can you see, from the newspaper report, whether the employer acted fairly? While it is useful to complete this exercise, remember that newspaper reporting is not necessarily precise or particularly comprehensive – a whole week in a tribunal might be described in a few hundred words.

---

## Employment protection rights – discrimination

Here we shall be looking at a wide range of areas of potential discrimination; first we examine some broad principles.

Although it may be argued that it makes sound business sense to recruit people solely on their ability to do the job, that judgement is easily influenced by beliefs that are not, in truth, relevant. Even those committed to recruiting on ability can find themselves victims to prejudice that they did not realise they had. More disturbingly, there are still managers who will admit, privately, to unlawful discrimination. For example, they may have prejudices about what constitutes 'men's work' or feel unable to relate to people of a different culture from their own. Unfortunately, in bringing such prejudices to the workplace, they mistakenly believe they serve themselves and their employer better because of it.

As a personnel practitioner you may need to examine your beliefs carefully. It is helpful to read relevant articles in *People Management*, which show how personnel practitioners are positively tackling equal opportunities issues. You could also with benefit look at the principles of 'Opportunity Now', which addresses equal opportunities in the public sector. Make sure you know your own organisation's policy and its true attitudes towards women, ethnic minorities and other groups. These policies should be designed to encourage equal opportunities by educating workers and decision-makers, and by positive actions to address inequality wherever it exists. The spirit or intention of equal opportunities legislation, as well as the letter of the law, is important.

Good management practices are well described by the principles of diversity (see Chapter 5). In any event, unlawful discrimination is an area of developing law. For example a code of practice on age diversity in employment (see Further Reading, page 79) already exists and legislation against such discrimination is expected by 2006.

Notwithstanding the merits of your employer's policies, men and women, ethnic minorities, disabled people and many ex-offenders (those who have been sentenced to time in prison) have protection against discrimination. In Northern Ireland it is also illegal to discriminate on religious grounds. So you need to be aware of the legislation.

Keep in mind that applicants as well as workers can be discriminated against. Everyone who is applying or undertaking work personally is eligible for these rights: there are no length of (employment) service requirements. So applicants as well as new workers can take a claim to an employment tribunal. Furthermore, there are no limits to the amount of compensation that an employment tribunal can award in cases of discrimination.

### Sex discrimination

The social unacceptability of sex discrimination has encouraged appropriate legislation, but much of it has been encouraged in particular by membership of the European Union, in which the Treaty of Rome 1957 provides for equal treatment of men and women.

Discrimination on the grounds of sex or on grounds of people's married status is unlawful, except in certain special circumstances. However, employers and designated (ie by the Secretary of State) training bodies can take positive action to promote equality. For example, they can set up management courses for existing women workers only, if women are underrepresented at managerial levels. Another positive action would be to encourage applications from one sex. But do note that discrimination is not allowed in the actual selection decision.

Both direct and indirect discrimination are illegal. Direct discrimination means allowing gender to influence employment decisions, eg in passing a woman over for promotion in favour of a less-qualified man. Indirect discrimination occurs if conditions that effectively create discrimination are applied. These could be certain criteria on job specifications or advertisements if they tend to preclude women or men. For example, the Civil Service used to restrict direct entry to executive grades to those under 26 years old. It can no longer do so because this would discriminate against women who return to work after bringing up families. An additional point about this example is that it shows that age discrimination can amount to sex discrimination in certain cases.

There is a number of *genuine occupational qualifications* (GOQs) that do allow some sex discrimination. Such GOQs cover reasons of privacy, decency, welfare and authenticity (eg modelling clothes), certain accommodation circumstances, certain single-sex establishments (eg prisons) and, to some extent, work in private homes.

There is an Equal Opportunities Commission (EOC) that works towards eliminating sex discrimination. As part of this work the Commission publishes a code of practice to assist employers. If you are to be well informed, you should obtain a copy. Public-sector bodies and progressive employers have responded by preparing equal opportunities policies, as recommended in the code. The legal status of the code may be compared to the highway code. Breaking either code does not constitute an unlawful act in itself, but the codes are to be used as a guide to appropriate driving or behaviour. So failure to follow the EOC code may be taken into account by employment tribunals in deciding whether to accept claims of discrimination on grounds of sex or married status.

### Maternity rights

Since the 1970s, women have had maternity rights. That is, they have the right not to be unfairly dismissed because of pregnancy, the right to maternity pay, and the right to return to work following maternity leave. Over the years, legislation and case law have strengthened and enhanced these rights. Dismissal on maternity-related grounds is now automatically unfair, irrespective of length of service or hours of work. All women have the right to 18 weeks' maternity leave and maternity pay. The practical administration of maternity rights and pay is subject to much detail. If you are called on, as well you might be, to administer rights and pay, then there are Government publications and other sources, such as updated reference books, which you can use for guidance. Note: maternity rights are due to increase in 2003.

### Equal pay

Men and women are entitled to claim equal treatment in respect of pay and conditions. One of the chief areas where equal pay legislation has been effective is the case of part-time workers (see below).

In practice, operation of equal pay is complicated by measurements. Equal treatment requires determination of like work, of work rated as equivalent and of work of equal value. Equally, of course, what constitutes equal treatment is not easy to measure. Tribunal cases arising under the Equal Pay Act 1970 have frequently led to appeals, proving very expensive for employers. Therefore, despite the complications, every endeavour should be made to ensure equal treatment of men and women.

### Burden of proof

In the event that an applicant or employee can provide evidence of probable discrimination, then it is the employer's responsibility to prove they have treated men and women equally. This means that you need to keep good records of all employment decisions so you can show such decisions did not discriminate on unlawful sexual grounds.

The main legislation of which you should be aware relating to sex discrimination includes:

- Sex Discrimination Acts 1975 and 1986
- Equal Pay Act 1970
- Employment Rights Act 1996
- Employment Relations Act 1999.

### Part-time workers

Until the mid-1990s part-time employees were often the 'poor relations' of full-time employees. Frequently they received lower pay and less sickness benefit and they rarely received pension rights. During the 1990s, rulings by the European Court of Justice (ECJ) about what constitutes 'pay' effectively gave part-timers the right to equal treatment with full-timers. This meant they acquired unfair dismissal and redundancy pay rights after the same periods of service as full-timers. Equal treatment covers a range of pay elements such as pensions, severance pay, access to promotion and training opportunities and sickness benefits. Failure to recognise the right to equal treatment can now give rise, at an employment tribunal, to claims of discrimination or to claims for equal pay. The relevant legislation is in the Part-time Workers (Prevention of Less Favourable Treatment) Regulations 2000.

### Racial equality

Many larger and progressive organisations provide good examples of best practice in equal opportunities. Diversity is particularly visible in the retail sector, which recognises that substantial sectors of the community are of minority ethnic origin, disabled people want to shop for their own goods and that old as well as young people make good workers. You can see that recognition in the range of goods offered on supermarket shelves, catering for cultural diversity, and in the maturity of staff in certain stores.

Cultural diversity has often developed more slowly in other sectors. Downsizing industrial operations has sometimes limited the opportunities to recruit new workers from other groups. Ethnic minorities still tend to be more prevalent in low-pay occupations and in less prosperous industries.

Whether diversity is driven by a desire to be morally right, by commercial pragmatism, or by the law, there exists legislation to underpin racial equality in employment and other areas. The legislation is similar to that provided to eliminate sex discrimination. Direct and indirect race discrimination are both outlawed, as is the victimisation of an individual who brings a complaint. There are legislative exceptions for genuine occupational qualifications, but in this case only reasons of authenticity and welfare qualify as genuine occupational qualifications. Positive action, such as the provision of training, to redress an imbalance of particular racial groups is permitted. There is also a Commission for Racial Equality (CRE) which has provided a code of practice; this encourages *ethnic monitoring* to help identify and eliminate race discrimination. You should obtain a copy of the code. The relevant legislation in this area is the Race Relations Act 1976.

### Disabled people

It may be difficult to come to terms with the fact that a disability has no practical implications for job performance, and yet in many circumstances that is precisely the case. Accomplished blind and deaf musicians are one reminder that disability need not be a barrier to achievement. We have to be very wary of 'mind-sets' that lead us to make unjustified assumptions about others.

In Britain comprehensive anti-discrimination legislation protects disabled people. It is unlawful to treat a disabled person less favourably because he or she is disabled, unless there are very good and relevant reasons in a particular case. Employers are also required to make reasonable adjustments to premises so that disabled applicants or workers are not put at any substantial disadvantage. The employment provisions of the Act apply to employers with 15 or more employees. From October 2004 the 15-employee limit will cease and no employers will be exempt.

There is a code of practice and, again, you should obtain a copy of the code. There is a Disability Rights Commission (DRC), with powers of enforcement similar to those of the EOC and the CRE. Relevant legislation is in the:

- Disability Discrimination Act 1995

- Disability Rights Commission Act 1999.

### Employing ex-offenders

Unless people who have served prison terms can be rehabilitated into employment, it logically follows that they are likely to resort to crime again. So there is some legal protection for those who have received sentences of not more than 30 months. They have the chance to 'wipe the slate clean' after a certain time. The time required varies according to the original sentence. 'Spent' convictions do not have to be disclosed and, even if disclosed, cannot be taken into account in employment decisions. There are, however, exemptions where the work involves access to vulnerable groups such as young people or those with handicaps. The relevant legislation is the Rehabilitation of Offenders Act 1974.

---

**Activity 14**

In your capacity as a personnel practitioner, assume you are invited to assist a manager at an interview. You fear that the manager has no intention of accepting a woman for the vacancy, despite two of the five interviewees being women. Write down what you would do. Discuss your intentions with one of your learning sources

---

## Other statutory legislation

First we take a brief glance at Northern Ireland, where legislation outlaws religious discrimination, then we look at the Working Time Regulations, National Minimum Wage and human rights, before considering the philosophy behind the health and safety legislation introduced over the past few decades and referring to the legislation on trade unions.

### Religious discrimination – Northern Ireland

Fair employment legislation is further-reaching than any other anti-discrimination law. It demands that employers strictly monitor their workforce and applicants. It may require employers to take affirmative action to redress imbalances. Several aspects of the legislation are backed by criminal law. The Fair Employment Commission publishes a code of practice that, if your responsibilities cover Northern Ireland workers, you should obtain.

The relevant legislation is the Fair Employment (Northern Ireland) Act 1989.

### Working Time Regulations

These introduced a maximum working week of 48 hours as averaged over one of three possible periods, 17 weeks, 26 weeks (certain special cases) or 52 weeks by workforce agreement. They provide restrictions on the maximum length of night shifts, and provide for rest periods, work breaks and statutory annual leave of four weeks.

Workers can opt out of the 48 hours voluntarily, but leave must be taken: it cannot be paid in lieu.

The regulations place specific requirements on records that need to be kept in relation to the 48-hour week and night shifts, and records will, of course, be needed if there are disputes over any of the other provisions.

The working time regulations are complicated, so you would be wise to take advice if they have implications for decisions you have to make.

The legislation is the Working Time Regulations 1998 and the Health and Safety (Young Persons) Regulations 1997 providing additional protection for young workers.

### National minimum wage

You will be aware that this provides for a minimum wage for all workers. The way in which the wage has to be calculated (with particular pay and hours elements) is quite specific and employers have to be able to show that they are complying.

It is necessary to calculate a wage for all workers and to be able to provide the necessary information to the Inland Revenue. Individuals are also entitled to statements on request. Failing to keep records is a criminal offence.

The relevant legislation is the National Minimum Wage Act 1998.

### Human rights

The abuse of human rights by state agents during the Second World War led, in 1950, to the development of a European Convention of

Human Rights. This is an agreed set of fundamental human rights. The intention was to restrain governments from abusing the rights of their citizens in the future. Government employees are also citizens and this is one reason for its relevance to personnel work. Such employees can take action against the Government for infringement of their rights.

Before the Human Rights Act citizens who considered that their Government was abusing their rights were obliged to pursue their case in the European courts. However, most of these rights (defined by Articles in the Convention) can now be taken up in the UK courts. Courts and tribunals are also agents of the Government. They therefore have to take account of human rights in considering the issues brought before them.

Privacy is an important area. This could be invaded if an organisation monitors the use of the telephone, the Internet or e-mail for personal (private) purposes. Similarly, the use of drug, alcohol and medical tests in selection or employment would intrude into privacy, as could locker or body searches. However, some of these actions are inevitable for a variety of sound reasons. To avoid these actions compromising rights, it is crucial to have clear and well-communicated policies as to what will be done in the name of the organisation and what employees can and cannot do.

Freedom of expression also impacts on employee relations. For example, can you specify what your employees wear? There can be good reasons for doing so. Image is an important part of business and it is reasonable, in customer-facing jobs particularly, to insist on standards. Again the answer is carefully developed policies on dress code, appropriate language (in some cases) and on other matters of personal expression that could impact on the business.

Finally, citizens should enjoy freedom from discrimination on a wider range of grounds than current UK law. What practical effect this will have still remains to be seen.

All the above are areas where the law is still developing through case law, so it would be wise to keep up to date with the latest developments.

The relevant statutory legislation is the Human Rights Act 1998.

---

**Activity 15**

Choose a piece of legislation that has been enacted in the last few years. Investigate what practices have changed as a result. You could look at application forms, staff handbooks, induction and other training documents, disciplinary procedures and other staff records. Is there anything that should have changed in response to the legislation but still needs attention?

---

## Data protection

This has implications for personnel information systems and details of this are provided in Chapter 4.

### Public interest disclosure

This has implications in relation to grievance procedures and is covered in Chapter 8.

### Health and safety

At the (then) IPD's Harrogate Conference in 1995, a speaker, Henry Olejnik of Motorola, told how his father lost two fingers in an employment accident in the 1950s. He related how, at that time, such an incident was almost regarded as acceptable. It was seen as 'just the way things are'. The point he went on to make is that we tend to accept the psychological damage (ie stress) that we do to people today as 'just one of those things'. He questioned what judgement future personnel practitioners might make of our current attitudes.

The principal issues here are that, first, we no longer find it acceptable that workers should receive physical injuries at work; second, we still tend to accept emotional and psychological injuries as not being the direct responsibility of the employer. But there is continuous progress in attitudes because a mature society, and a caring employer, will look after its people with great care physically and emotionally. In Britain we have seen an increasing legal underpinning of physical and emotional welfare since the early 1960s. The responsibility of the employer to take reasonable steps to manage stress is increasing as a factor in civil court and employment tribunal cases and settlements.

Early legislation related chiefly to premises and concerned working conditions, toilets, first-aid boxes, record-keeping, and fire precautions – the need for fire escapes and for employee training so that people knew what to do if there was a fire. These provisions are now contained within more recent statutes.

## CASE STUDY 7

Mr Walker worked for Northumberland County Council as a social services officer from 1970 to 1988. Throughout that time the workload placed on him increased dramatically. He told his superiors on several occasions that his department was understaffed. He threatened to leave unless he was given support. He suffered a first nervous breakdown in November 1986 (then aged 49) and he went on sick leave. By February 1987 he had recovered sufficiently to contemplate a return to work. His doctor had informed him that he should only consider this if he was provided with more staff to relieve his work burden. His employers agreed to supply him with an assistant. On his return to work he was not given any extra assistance and he suffered a second nervous breakdown in September 1987. In February 1988 he was dismissed by the Council on the grounds of ill-health. The Court decided that the Council was in breach of its duty of care when they failed to provide support when he returned to work. This was the first time that the High Court recognised that an employee could sue for work-related stress.

*Walker* v *Northumberland County Council* [1995] IRLR 35 as summarised in Jordan's Employment Law Service.

*Health and safety legislation introduced in the 1970s*

The main relevant Acts were related to factories and then to 'offices, shops and railway premises'. Hazards, though, are different in different industries. In 1974 legislation required employers to produce health and safety policies for their organisations. Because hazards vary from organisation to organisation, the policy is expected to reflect the circumstances of each. This provision is contained in the Health and Safety at Work Act 1974 (HASWA), which requires employers to safeguard the health and safety of workers 'as far as reasonably practical'. It covers *all* workers, as well as members of the public who may be exposed to hazards from the employer.

Health and safety policies are a statutory requirement for all employers with five or more employees. A central part of the policy is the general statement. This needs to identify responsibilities for health and safety both at different levels and for specific matters. It has to explain how workers are involved and their acceptance gained. The main policy requirements are summarised in the box below.

---

**Health and safety policies should:**

- reflect the plant, equipment, and substances used in the organisation

- address particular hazards

- indicate arrangements for emergencies

- clarify how safety is communicated to employees and visitors on site

- indicate training, safety provision for new workers, etc

- register the regular checks and inspections that are needed.

---

**Activity 16**

Look at your organisation's health and safety policy. Is it readily available? Compare it to the guidelines provided in the relevant section above – does it address each area? Is it up to date? Make a list of any matters that you think should be addressed.

---

As well as the requirement for a written health and safety policy, HASWA made managers personally responsible for safety. It also placed a legal obligation on employees to comply with their employer's safety policies. Trade unions were given the right to appoint safety representatives and employers obliged to consult them. Factory inspectors were given powers of enforcement, enabling them to issue improvement and prohibition notices. An improvement notice means that a safety aspect has to be improved within a set time. A typical improvement notice might be to reduce the level of dust in the working atmosphere. Prohibition notices mean that equipment or premises cannot be used until changes have been made. A typical prohibition notice may prohibit use of a cutting machine until a guard has been placed on it.

Health and safety at work is overseen by the Health and Safety Commission (HSC), which reports to the Secretary of State and has wide powers to enforce health and safety. It issues a code of practice which, again, you should obtain. The Health and Safety Executive (HSE) enforces the law where responsibilities are not covered by other bodies such as local authorities. All enforcing bodies can appoint inspectors. As well as being able to issue improvement and prohibition notices, inspectors can enter premises without notice and can prosecute employers *and* workers.

The relevant legislation is the Health and Safety at Work Act 1974.

*Health and safety legislation introduced in the 1980s and 1990s*
To improve enforcement, new reporting requirements were introduced in 1985. These required employers to report 'injuries, diseases and dangerous occurrences' to the HSE or, where appropriate, to the local authority. They also required the keeping of records and an accident book. Factories and all employers with 10 or more people must ensure that all accidents, however minor, are recorded in an accident book.

It had been known for many years that substances encountered at work (eg coal dust and asbestos) caused illness. Research has continually been adding other substances known to cause cancer. So, in 1988 and again in 1994 new Acts required employers to assess health risks that arise from hazardous substances in their work activities. Employers must provide controls that will be effective in protecting workers and anyone else who may be affected by such work. The main obligations on employers are shown in the box below. The relevant legislation is the Reporting of Injuries, Diseases and Dangerous Occurrences Regulations 1995 (RIDDOR) and the Control of Substances Hazardous to Health Regulations 1999 (COSHH).

---

**Controlling substances hazardous to health**

The main obligations on employers are to:

- assess the risks and the measures necessary for control of exposure

- prevent or adequately control exposure to hazardous substances

- ensure control methods are used and maintained in efficient working order

- monitor the work environment

- carry out health surveillance on employees where appropriate

- provide information, instruction, and training on risks and precautions.

---

The European Commission is now a major force in British health and safety legislation. Such issues are decided by majority voting in which no nation can exercise a veto. Member nations are obliged to bring domestic legislation into line. The result is a strengthening of existing legislation. The main features of health and safety at work regulations are summarised in the box below.

Health and safety should be managed like other functions, with clear reporting relationships, planning, control and monitoring. Workers need comprehensive and relevant information and proper training. The regulations require an assessment of the risks to health and safety that arise from the employer's activities. This is to guide the employer as to measures that may need to be taken to comply with statutory requirements. Anyone employing five or more employees is required to record the findings of the assessment.

New minimum standards for the workplace have been set covering such issues as maintenance of equipment, ventilation, temperature, cleanliness, traffic routes, the potential for falling objects, washing and changing and rest facilities.

Work equipment needs to be suitable, properly maintained and its operatives trained. Controls for starting and stopping machinery have minimum requirements, as do isolation procedures to prevent, for example, equipment starting up while maintenance is being undertaken.

---

**Health and safety at work regulations**

The following areas require attention by the employer:

- managing health and safety (eg assessing risks)

- workplace health safety and welfare (eg working environment, housekeeping)

- provision and use of work equipment (eg tools to be suitable for their purpose)

- manual handling (eg avoiding or assessing needs and methods)

- protective equipment (eg ensuring it is properly used)

- display screen equipment (eg satisfying certain minimum requirements).

---

More than a quarter of reported accidents are associated with manual handling, so regulations provide for a particular procedure to assess such risks. There is an obligation to avoid activities where there is a risk of injury, perhaps by automation or mechanisation. Where avoidance is not completely achieved, measures have to be implemented to minimise risks so far as is reasonably practical.

Personal protective equipment should be seen as a last resort after all other methods of improving safety have been considered. Regulations cover its quality, suitability, use, and the requirement for proper training.

Display screen equipment stipulations cover not only computer screens but other forms of display, such as microfiche readers. A variety of risks need to be assessed, including positioning, posture and the work environment. Those who use such equipment are entitled to free eye tests and to basic costs of glasses to correct vision defects associated with using the equipment.

You can find risk assessment forms in a variety of publications such as *The Personnel Administration Handbook* (see Further Reading, page 77).

Extensive guidance and codes of practice are contained in a series of brochures issued by the HSE. They are important to obtain if you have responsibilities in the areas covered. Pertinent legislation includes the Management of Health and Safety at Work Regulations 1999; the Health and Safety (Display Screen Equipment) Regulations 1992; the Manual Handling Operations Regulations 1992; the Health and Safety Young Persons Regulations 1997; and the Provision and Use of Work Equipment Regulations 1998. There is also a variety of other regulations specific to particular work or industry sectors.

---

**Activity 17**

Pick a topical health and safety issue in your department or organis-ation: for example, the use of computer screens. Research the appropriate legislation and good practice. Compare the legislation and good practice with what actually happens. Make a note of suitable improvements.

---

## Trade unions and redundancy

The legislation that regulates activities of trade unions is complex. But understanding how trade unions fit into the employment framework is important for personnel practitioners. They need to know what a trade union is, what shop stewards do, understand the significance of trade union recognition and of collective agreements and be aware of the power of trade unions as manifested in the threat of industrial action. Awareness of ACAS and the services it offers is also important. All these matters are covered in Chapter 2.

The legislation that regulates trade unions and their activities is the Trade Union and Labour Relations (Consolidation) Act 1992 as amended and the Employment Relations Act 1999.

### Redundancy

When an organisation has more employees than it needs for its activities it invariably has to look to reducing the number of employees. Employees are a major cost and an organisation whose income is reduced (by the loss of a major order, for example) may not be able to continue affording to pay all its employees. The process of reducing the number of employees when they are dismissed for this reason is known as redundancy. In legal terms there are two slightly different definitions of redundancy. The Employment Rights Act 1996 s139 refers to:

- a reduction or cessation of work of a particular kind or

- a reduction or cessation of work of a particular kind at the place where the employee is employed.

The Trade Union and Labour Relations (Consolidation) Act 1992 (TULR(C)A) s195 refers to redundancy as being dismissals where the reason(s) for dismissal are not related to the people being dismissed. Although it may seem inconvenient to have two meanings, in practice one refers to the employees' rights and the other to the need to consult.

There is a duty under TULR(C)A s193 to give notice to the Secretary of State (a form is available from the Employment Service) where there are a number of redundant employees.

The law protects redundant employees in a number of ways.

*Consultation*

Firstly there has to be consultation and there are precise rules on the length of consultation required according to the numbers to be made redundant (see Jordan's Employment Law Service, for example, Further Reading, page 80). Consultation has to be with a trade union or with employee representatives (if there is no recognised trade union) and with the individuals themselves. The consultation has to seek to avoid redundancies. Therefore, we will discuss some of the alternatives to redundancy. Where the reduction in work could be temporary it should be possible to reduce the labour cost by means of reductions in overtime, by short-time working (working less than normal hours) or by lay-offs (periods of time where employees do not work and might not be paid).

In circumstances where the reduction is not expected to be temporary, one of the most popular alternatives to declaring redundancies is to use 'natural wastage'. This refers to the fact that in any organisation people will tend to leave 'naturally'. They may retire, find other jobs or leave for personal reasons such as a partner moving their job location. Indeed, organisations facing redundancies may seek to encourage wastage by means of early retirement packages, reduced promotions or steady wage levels. During the consultation process there may be requests to allow natural wastage to take its course or for early retirement packages to be enhanced.

Allied to natural wastage is a 'recruitment freeze'. In these circumstances the organisation places a ban on recruiting more employees.

Trade unions may call for a recruitment freeze partly because it puts pressure on the organisation.

This pressure encourages consideration of other alternatives such as redeployment (to alternative work) and re-training. It is not unusual for an organisation to be recruiting in one area of its activities and making redundancies in another. Organisations have a high level of investment in employees in terms of their experience of the organisation's culture. Redundancy is also expensive in terms of payments to individuals as well as the disruption it causes to the day-to-day activities and the senior management time that is invariably involved, so redeployment and re-training may be a cost-effective option.

Relocation to another place of work, a form of redeployment, can also be an option in some cases. While redundancy may be a cessation at a place of work, it may be reasonable to offer alternative work some short distance away. How far is reasonable is best based on advice. There are several past cases that give guidance.

Voluntary redundancy may be an alternative to compulsory redundancy. Here employees who might have been considering leaving or retiring are offered a financial package (usually a favourable one) to encourage them to leave voluntarily. During a consultation process there may be requests to improve the package to encourage volunteers.

Outplacement, career assistance or other means of assisting employees to find other work are often provided. Since the employer is seen as a party with a vested interest, these services are often provided, at the employer's expense, by outside consultancies. They may be provided before an employee has been declared redundant, to assist natural wastage, or afterwards.

Because demand for employees can fluctuate, some employers keep employees on after they no longer need them, ie they keep a surplus pool of employees. Opportunities may arise later and the employee is there, ready to take the position. In addition, natural wastage can take effect over a longer period. Surplus employees are sometimes seconded to charities. This can keep their skills up to speed, give the charity some benefit and avoid a demotivated employee remaining on site. It is an expensive option, though, generally taken up by large employers with substantial resources only.

When all else fails an organisation will be forced to declare 'compulsory redundancies'.

*Fair redundancy*
For the employee, their next line of protection is that their selection for redundancy has to be shown to be fair. One of the most popular means of establishing fairness is a simple rule such as 'last in, first out'. Here the employees most recently recruited are the first ones on the list if redundancies are declared. This does not always serve the employer's

interests. For example, recent recruiting may have been a response to a skills shortage. Therefore, employers will often use alternative procedures to determine who is to go first. The essential point of any procedure is that it must be demonstrably fair. Dismissing those who lack essential skills may be fair. Dismissing on the basis of a performance rating may also be fair. However, if the rating is a subjective one, perhaps involving ratings where different employees have been rated by different people, that would be very questionable.

Ideally, the rules for determining fairness will have been laid down at an earlier (less emotional) time, ie a redundancy policy and procedure will have been agreed. Consultation, therefore, is likely to centre on application of the rules ensuring that they are indeed applied fairly.

Unfortunately, this is not always the case. The rules, formulated in an earlier time, may no longer be appropriate. Or there may be no rules at all. In these circumstances there is little option but for the determination of the rules to form part of the consultation process.

### Redundancy pay

Finally, a redundant employee, aged over 18 with two years' service, has a statutory right to redundancy pay. The precise details of this are in reference books, but the amount ranges from one week's pay to thirty weeks' pay depending on the employee's age and length of service.

The main relevant legislation is the Trade Union and Labour Relations (Consolidation) Act 1992 and Employment Rights Act 1996.

## The role of personnel practitioners

In employing you in the personnel function, your organisation will be looking to you and your colleagues to help keep its activities in line with legislative requirements, if not to go further and help it to adopt best practices. But don't be surprised if, from time to time, colleagues outside the function do not seem as committed to such premises as you might expect. Let's have a look at your likely roles.

### An advisory role to line managers

To be effective you need to know and understand the basics of employment law and to know where to go to find more detailed information in specific instances. This chapter has outlined the main aspects of employment law but it can only provide general guidance. Minor details of law can become very important in specific instances, so always check the detail if you have decisions to make. Follow the law, not your intuition. Remember that the legal situation changes continually both in response to legislation and in the way in which it is interpreted. To help you, there is a wide range of reference books available; those that are regularly updated are particularly valuable. Such books are usually available on CD-ROM which makes it easy to access particular topics or information.

You will also find Acts and Regulations dating back to 1988 available on the Internet at the HMSO website (see page 80). However, it is crucially important that you do not overestimate your understanding of the law, so, if you are in any doubt, always seek further advice. This would normally be from senior colleagues or from bodies such as ACAS. They have offices in all regions of the United Kingdom except Northern Ireland, where similar services are available from the Labour Relations Agency.

### A decision-making role

From time to time you may be called on to make decisions that require an understanding of employment law. As an example, you might be involved in the decision to move employees from one place of work to another. While you must act within a legally defensible position, be wary of invoking the law with employees in a direct fashion. It would be inappropriate, for example, simply to demand that an employee moved his place of work just because, five years ago, he signed a contract which included such a clause. However, much can be achieved by consultation and negotiation. Remember that you are expected to act fairly and reasonably and, in this context, that would mean consulting with the employee about the issue. So, acting fairly and reasonably is not just a moral requirement but a legal necessity. Therefore, as a personnel practitioner, you may often find the law supporting you in your desire to 'do the right thing'.

### An overseeing role

If you maintain regular contact with your colleagues by 'walking the floor' in workshops and offices or through other network activities, then you will often become aware of potential legal problems or potential disputes that can be 'nipped in the bud'. Some overseeing roles may need to be more formalised, such as equal opportunities monitoring. Health and safety audits also need to be formal, although if you have specific responsibilities in this area you should seek further appropriate training.

### An administrative role

This may be your key role, ensuring good accessible records of contracts, and keeping equal opportunities records, health and safety records and disciplinary records. Your diligence in this area may attract scant attention, and even a little resistance. But when problems arise these good records can afford real protection for employers and managers who may need to defend their actions at a tribunal or in other courts.

### A training or educational role

If line managers are to take true responsibility for personnel matters – a direction in which many organisations are progressing – then they too will need an understanding of employment law. The very process of passing on your own understanding will force you to become more familiar with the subject and should reinforce your own role as 'the expert' in your organisation.

## Summary

In this chapter we have outlined the main areas of legislation that have relevance to personnel activity. We have explained the difference between civil law, employment protection legislation and other statutory legislation, discussed the essential components of contracts and described the main characteristics of contracts of employment, written particulars, employees as opposed to workers and the nature of business relationships.

In looking at employment protection rights, we examined the question of unfair dismissal and looked at the need for a fair reason and a fair procedure and the requirement to establish dismissal in alleged constructive dismissal cases. We indicated the main areas of protection against discrimination so that you will know where to take care in decision-making. When looking at statutory legislation we included some of the most recent additions to the legislature – Working Time Regulations, Minimum Wage, the Human Rights Act and the main legislation in health and safety.

Finally we considered redundancy and the personnel practitioners' main responsibilities in this area.

You will by now be familiar with the terms used and know which legislation is likely to apply in the main areas of personnel activity. References, further reading and website addresses are provided at the end of this chapter for your information, and Activities have been suggested throughout. You are encouraged to complete some, if not all, of these activities in order to reinforce and apply your learning.

---

**Activity 18**

Visit an employment tribunal as an observer. You will find observing a tribunal case puts much of the practice discussed in this book into a real context.

---

### References and further reading

AIKIN A. (1999) 'Working titles'. *People Management.* 3 June. p25.

BONE A. *and* SUFF M. (1999) *Essential Employment Law.* 2nd edn. London, Cavendish Publishing Ltd.

FORSAITH J. *and* TOWNSEND N. (1997) *The Personnel Administration Handbook.* London, Institute of Personnel and Development.

FOWLER A. (1994) 'How to produce a health and safety policy'. *Personnel Management Plus.* January. pp24–25.

GENNARD J. *and* Judge G. (1999) *Employee Relations.* London, Institute of Personnel and Development.

LEWIS D. (1997) *Essentials of Employment Law.* 5th edn. London, Institute of Personnel and Development.

PICKARD J. (1996) 'The legal fight for workplace justice'. *People Management.* 29 August. pp32–35.

TORRINGTON D. *and* HALL L. (1998) *Human Resource Management.* Hemel Hempstead, Prentice Hall.

See also the CIPD's *Legal Essentials* series:

HAMMOND SUDDARDS EDGE (2002) *Contracts of Employment.* 2nd edn. London, Chartered Institute of Personnel and Development.

HAMMOND SUDDARDS (2000) *Data Protection.* London, Institute of Personnel and Development.

HAMMOND SUDDARDS (2000) *Disability Discrimination.* London, Institute of Personnel and Development.

HAMMOND SUDDARDS EDGE (2001) *Dismissal.* 2nd edn. London, Chartered Institute of Personnel and Development.

HAMMOND SUDDARDS (2000) *Maternity Rights.* 2nd edn. London, Chartered Institute of Personnel and Development.

HAMMOND SUDDARDS EDGE (2002) *Redundancy.* 2nd edn. London, Chartered Institute of Personnel and Development.

HAMMOND SUDDARDS (1999) *Sex and Race Discrimination.* London, Institute of Personnel and Development.

HAMMOND SUDDARDS (1999) *Transfer of Undertakings.* London, Institute of Personnel and Development.

HAMMOND SUDDARDS (2000) *Working Time Regulations.* 2nd edn. London, Institute of Personnel and Development.

See also the following CIPD title:

EARNSHAW J. *and* COOPER C. (2001) *Stress and Employer Liability.* 2nd edn. London, Chartered Institute of Personnel and Development.

ADVISORY, CONCILIATION and ARBITRATION SERVICE. (Revised 2000 ) *Advisory Handbook on Discipline at Work.* Leicester, ACAS. [This includes the *Code of Practice on Disciplinary and Grievance Procedures.*] These and other advisory handbooks and booklets are available from: ACAS Reader Ltd, PO Box 16, Earl Shilton, Leicester LE9 8ZZ; tel. 01455 852 225.

The following codes of practice are available from The Stationery Office (mail, fax, and telephone orders only), PO Box 276, London SW8 5DT; tel. 0870 600 5522; fax 0870 600 533. See also their website.

*Code of Practice: Equal opportunities policies, procedures and practices in employment.* (1985) London, The Stationery Office.

*Code of Practice: For the elimination of discrimination in the field of employment against disabled persons or persons who have had a disability.* [1996] London, The Stationery Office.

The following is available from the Equal Opportunities Commission, Overseas House, Quay Street, Manchester M3 3HN; tel. 0161 833 9244:
*Code of Practice on Equal Pay.* [1997] London, EOC.

*The IPD Guide on Managing Diversity.* Available from Plymbridge Distributors, tel. 01752 202 301.

See also:
*Disability Discrimination Act 1995. Industrial Relations Law Bulletin.* No. 535, December 1995.

The following is available from Central Books, 99 Wallis Road, Hackney, London E9 5LN; tel. 020 8986 5488:
*Code of Practice: For the elimination of racial discrimination and the promotion of equality of opportunity in employment.* [1984] London, CRE.

The following is available from: DWP Publications, Sherwood Park, Annesley, Nottingham NG15 0DJ; tel. 0845 60 222 60.
*Age Diversity In Employment: A code of practice.*

See also:
*Fair Employment (Northern Ireland) Code of Practice.* [1989] Belfast, Department of Economic Development. Available from the Equality Commission, Andras House, 60 Great Victoria Street, Belfast; tel. 01232 240020.
*A Guide to the Working Time Regulations.* London, Department of Trade and Industry (DTI).
*A Detailed Guide to the National Minimum Wage.* London, Department of Trade and Industry (DTI).

The following are available from the Health and Safety Executive, HSE Books, PO Box 1999, Sudbury, Suffolk CO10 6FS; tel. 01787 881 165:
*An Introduction to Health and Safety (INDG 259).* [1997] London, HSE Books.
*Everyone's Guide to RIDDOR 1995 (HSE 31).* [1996] London, HSE Books.
*Five Steps to Successful Health and Safety Management: Special help for directors and managers (INDG 132).* [1992] London, HSE Books.
*Getting to Grips with Manual Handling: A short guide for employers (INDG 143).* [1995] London, HSE Books.
*Health and Safety Regulations: A short guide (HSE 13).* [1995] London, HSE Books.

*HSE Small Firms Strategy (MISC100).* (1997) London, HSE Books.
*A Short Guide to the Personal Protective Equipment at Work Regulations (INDG 174).* (1992) London, HSE Books.
*Working with VDUs (INDG 36).* (1998) London, HSE Books.
*Workplace Health, Safety and Welfare: A short guide for managers (INDG 244).* (1997) London, HSE Books.
*Writing a Safety Policy Statement: Advice to employers (HSC 6).* (1990) London, HSE Books.

See also CIPD Publications (available from Plymbridge Distributors, tel. 01752 202 301) and CIPD Infosource documents on employment issues available on the CIPD website (www.cipd.co.uk/Infosource).

There is also a variety of publications of general relevance to employment law and personnel work available from Croner Publications Ltd, Croner House, London Road, Kingston on Thames, Surrey KT2 6SR; tel. 020 8547 3333.

For those who need knowledge in depth there is an updated Employment Law Service produced for the CIPD by Jordan Publishing Ltd, 21 St Thomas Street, Bristol BS1 6JS; tel. 0117 923 0600.

## Websites

Arbitration, Conciliation and Advisory Service (ACAS)
www.acas.org.uk

Department of Trade and Industry
www.dti.gov.uk

Health and Safety Executive     www.open.gov.uk/hse/hsehome.htm

Incomes Data Services     www.incomesdata.co.uk

Chartered Institute of Personnel and Development
www.cipd.co.uk

Law Rights     www.lawrights.co.uk/emp.html

*People Management*     www.peoplemanagement.co.uk

HMSO     www.hmso.gov.uk

The Stationery Office     www.tso-online.co.uk

TUC     www.tuc.org.uk

UK Government site     www.uk.online.gov.uk

One Click HR     www.oneclickhr.com

# • Personnel Information Systems and Computer Facilities

## CHAPTER OBJECTIVES

After reading this chapter you will:

- be aware of the importance of keeping accurate personnel records

- be able to contribute to a discussion on the benefits of computerised personnel systems

- to be able to discuss suitable computer applications for use in the personnel function, including the role of databases and spreadsheets

- know the main principles involved in reviewing a computerised system

- be able to respond to the main legal requirements for confidentiality, data protection and security of data

- recognise the implications of Internet and e-mail use in an employer organisation.

## Why are personnel records important?

There are four main reasons why records are important: to satisfy legal requirements; to provide the organisation with information to make decisions; to record contractual arrangements and agreements; and to keep contact details of employees.

### To satisfy legal requirements

Employment protection rights demand that we keep records to protect ourselves, as employers, from claims that we have discriminated against or unfairly dismissed employees. Health and safety legislation demands that records are kept of accidents, exposure to hazardous substances, training provided and much more. Employers must be able to demonstrate responsible management of health and safety issues. Additionally, Government departments, including the Inland Revenue, can demand information on how many people you employ, what they are paid, what they have been paid over a number of years and how many hours they have worked.

Legal requirements are increasing. The Working Time Regulations and the National Minimum Wage Act, both introduced in the late 1990s, each require certain specific records relating to hours of work and, in the latter case, pay.

When employees feel their rights have been infringed, they may make claims to employment tribunals. Expectations on employers are increasing. For example, although equal pay and protection from sex discrimination has applied for some time, since June 2001 employers may have to prove specifically that they have treated men and women equally. Defending a case in an employment tribunal places heavy demands on the quality of personnel records.

A glance at Chapter 3 will highlight some of the many legal requirements on organisations.

### To provide the organisation with information to make decisions

Knowledge and information are the lifeblood of good decision-making for organisations. For individuals, access to accurate, factual and dependable information that can be used for arguments and influence is a vital factor in their ability to achieve. In the past, financial information has been highly regarded and available to considerable levels of sophistication. Personnel information has been harder to obtain but, as computer software is becoming highly developed in this arena, such information is becoming much better and more readily available.

It is also significant that in an era of high technology, products of all kinds are quickly and easily imitated. Consequently products are becoming increasingly similar and therefore business is beginning seriously to value service. It is now frequently service that differentiates one supplier from another. This leads to business decision-makers appreciating their employees' value more, because of this need for them to give good service to customers. In a healthy organisation 'good service' includes internal customers (ie fellow employees). In turn this places more emphasis on good personnel information. For example, if you want to know the level of staff turnover in different departments, a good computer system will allow you to assess it relatively easily. Having such information may aid identification of problems.

### To record contractual arrangements and agreements

Agreements that are recorded are clearer and also easier to insist upon. It is not only a legal requirement to provide written particulars of employment, it is simply good practice to provide them. Employment problems are less likely to arise when all parties are clear about what has been agreed. Records are needed for reference purposes in the case of disputes and, as we have already highlighted, for defence if, for example, claims are made to an employment tribunal.

### To keep contact details of employees

The simplest and most obvious reason for this is so they can be paid. It is not difficult to see other reasons, such as the need to call someone in at short notice to provide relief cover.

Good organisation of records is the key to efficiency and effectiveness.

---

**Activity 19**

Have a close look at the records in your department.

Identify what is recorded, what duplications occur, what information is routinely sought, what information is aggregated.

Is data recorded that is never used?

How much time does it take to record the data?

How easy is it to obtain information when it is needed?

What routines exist to ensure that data is kept up to date? Do they work?

How do systems cope with current information required (such as number of employees) before current data has been recorded (such as new appointees)?

---

## Manual and computerised records

You can see from the above that many records are kept and that many of these will be manual records, ie written or printed on sheets of paper. Increasingly, application forms, copies of qualification certificates and everyday correspondence received about an employee are being computerised. Such documents can be scanned into computers and their image stored as a computer file. The advantage of having scanned documents on computer is that they can then be accessed by means of a computer screen rather than by going to a filing cabinet. Indexing of the documents can be computerised, making them easier to find. They can also be assigned an expiry date so they are not kept longer than necessary. However, unlike other data, their contents cannot be easily processed or indexed unless first converted to text.

### Databases

Much personnel information does lend itself to computerisation, and increasingly so. To understand why, envisage this experiment: look up your own telephone number in the directory. So long as you have an entry, you will find that quite easy. Now change one digit at the end of the number. Can you find whose number that is? Theoretically it is possible, but it would be an inordinately difficult task, and the number may not even exist. By comparison, if the directory was on computer disk, the task takes a fraction of a second. That is because a computer database can search on a whole variety of different indexed fields. Once a database has been set up for employees, you may be able to find who is due for a long-service award, who will retire next year, whose probationary period ends next week, whose salary exceeds £30,000 – just by a few clicks of a mouse. Proprietary computer systems use databases in such fast and subtle ways that you may not even be aware of the search processes or the structure of the database.

The speed of access to data is only one example of the power of the computer. So what other benefits are there?

## Benefits to personnel of computers

Computers make the management, and in particular the analysis, of information much more efficient. In doing so they offer new opportunities that (as we have just seen) would not be practical with manual systems. To be valuable, information should be meaningful and should assist decision-making. For example, an employee's attendance record might provide information that makes a disciplinary warning appropriate. Providing valuable information in a timely fashion is very important for the credibility of the personnel function.

Computers enable administrative tasks to be monitored and completed more effectively. A good recruitment system, for example, will acknowledge applications, prompt timely action, keep track of the progress of individual applications, facilitate letters of invitation to interview and prepare the letters of rejection. Finally it can transfer details of successful candidates to the main record system. Word processing of standard letters, or standard paragraphs, and the mail-merging of addresses make essential communications easier, and it becomes practical to personalise far more correspondence.

The use of processing facilities in databases and spreadsheets enables what would be laborious calculations to be completed in a timely fashion. This can assist in wages and salary negotiation, the calculation of increased salaries, redundancy pay calculations and many others. In wages bargaining, for example, what-if models can quickly calculate the cost to the organisation of an extra penny on shift allowance or an extra 1 per cent on the basic salary rate.

Don't lose sight of the reasons for your wants! Computers in the personnel function are not an end in themselves but a means to better business performance. Try to distinguish between what you need (the software to produce organisation charts, perhaps) and an item you would like (the latest communication technology, for example) but which will not enhance performance.

Before looking at the many applications of computers in the personnel function it is worth considering the benefits in more detail.

# Benefits to the business of computers in personnel

### Timeliness

As the pace of change in organisations continues to increase, decision-makers are demanding more information more quickly than in the past. By way of illustration, think about negotiators in the annual pay round. If the cost of a particular settlement option can be assessed quickly and thoroughly, then time spent in negotiation will be reduced. If supervisors are to be effective in tackling poor attendance, it has to be identified and acted on quickly. Computers make it possible to have 'trigger levels'. Trigger levels mean that as soon as a particular employee's 'number of days absent' exceeds a set level the matter is flagged up and a supervisor can be prompted to assess the situation.

Always remember, of course, that for the computer to produce timely information (flagging up the poor attender in our example) it has to have the 'raw data' in the first place. Thus staff time (even data input clerks, perhaps) will be needed for the attendance records to be input to the computer first. If the input is not timely the computer will be of no help. Ideally the data could come from another computer source; in our example that might be the payroll. Putting any data onto a computer system once only is an ideal to strive for. Unfortunately, effective computer links between payroll and personnel systems can still be difficult to make. Both use current and unchanging data (eg name, date of birth). But payroll relies on a weekly or monthly cycle whereas personnel often seeks events (eg last disciplinary warning, retirement date) or secondary data where information is cumulated over specific groups (eg average length of service in different departments).

### Accuracy

Once a correct piece of data is put onto a computer system, unless it is changed by a deliberate (or accidental) process, it stays correct. It can be used for calculations or transferred to other applications without change. Dates of birth are just one example. In the personnel department they can be used to calculate age (updating it continuously) or transferred to another application, such as pensions administration. Similarly, once a calculation has been set up using the correct logic, it can be performed easily and accurately every time. For example, redundancy calculations usually require a date of birth, the date on which service commenced, and current earnings (the raw data). The calculations are often complex. Nonetheless, once set up on a computer, accurate data can be accessed and consistent redundancy calculations completed with confidence and timeliness. Don't forget the importance of the original data being accurate! Equally, the logic of any processes performed on the data has to be correct.

Again, accuracy depends on the operator and (for the calculations) the programmer. However, the computer can assist by rejecting or asking for confirmation of what might be errors. As an example, it could reject (by means of messages on the input screen) a date of birth that suggests an employee is too young or ask for confirmation if the employee is over retirement age.

Increasingly data can be transferred electronically from other sources. Here checks are advisable to ensure that data has been placed into the right fields (not date appointed in the date commenced field, for example). Scanned documents can be converted to text that can be processed by word processors. Here proof reading of the document, in the word processor, is still needed in most cases.

### Presentation

We all tend to believe the printed word in preference to hand-written notes. Indeed, in formal business correspondence presentation generates credibility. Just reflect on how much paper flows onto your desk with the morning mail. How do you decide what to read? Leaving aside essential communications, visual impression is a major factor. You are more likely to read a document that is visually interesting. Often it is only parts of a document that may be relevant to you, so you will want to be able to identify what is important to read. You will probably distrust the authority of material that is riddled with spelling mistakes or grammatical errors. Are you impressed with material that uses old-fashioned or inappropriate type styles? What impression is given of the writer by lack of attention to detail or to style?

We hope you will agree that in seeking to influence others, presentation is a major factor. Crucially, personnel practitioners have many people to influence. Think about the senior manager who has requested information, the promising candidate assessing whether she wants to work for you, the neighbour who has written to complain about noise from your factory.

Modern printers produce quality that rivals commercial typesetting with colour, diagrams and photographs. Word processors have scaleable fonts and can incorporate attractive features. PowerPoint is one of the most popular applications and can be used for sophisticated presentations that include almost any computer feature for projection onto a screen. Desktop publishers have so many features that they can be used for attractive brochures, newsletters and projection of slides.

There is some movement in the opposing direction. Hand-written material is more personal and there may be instances where it could be more appropriate; in a letter of condolence, perhaps. The humble flip chart still has a place in the interactive training room.

Remember too that these facilities demand an investment in learning, and the result still depends on the skill of the operator. In general, the more sophisticated the presentation, the more investment is needed in learning and the more time is required to produce the final document.

So keep the standard of presentation in line with your purpose. As course tutors, we sometimes see written assignments with distinction-level presentation but barely passable content. You cannot influence by presentation alone!

### Flexibility

Sophisticated systems allow a great deal of flexibility in how information is analysed and presented. Often they make it practical to carry out tasks and information that would be too laborious to collate, analyse and present by using manual systems. For instance, it is now very practical to calculate the actual cost of a particular salary review settlement on a what-if basis.

The main source of inflexibility in computer systems is the difficulty of incorporating variations. Computers lend themselves rather better to inflexible, standard processes than to flexible, ad hoc responses. As an example, you might reflect on letters of 'rejection' where applicants and candidates are turned down. Standardisation in such a letter will often be obvious to the candidate, and yet standardisation (where the same activity is repeated again and again) is an area in which computers are highly valuable. Although computers are increasingly flexible you may, on occasion, have to strike a balance between efficiency and impression.

### Administrative efficiency

Fortunately, much administration is repetition of an activity again and again. As an example, consider the recruitment and selection process. From the point an application form is sent out, the applicant's address will be used several times: to send out the form, to acknowledge the application if it is returned, subsequently to decline the application or to invite for interview, then to decline or offer an appointment, and perhaps finally to go on the employee's records file. Many of the communications will need to be standardised, especially in a major recruitment exercise, and you will also need to keep track of how each applicant progresses. Nonetheless, one recruitment exercise is, in administrative terms, fundamentally the same as another. Not surprisingly this is an area in which computerisation saves considerable time. The value to the organisation is reduced time for filling the vacancy and lower administration costs.

Remember that time is needed to learn the system and, as already highlighted, over-standardisation is not ideal in the sensitive area of recruitment.

### Accessibility of personnel information

Computers make information accessible. It is now possible to have virtually every piece of information stored on a single desktop computer, or on a central server with a keyboard and screen on your desk. It makes it easier and faster to respond to ad hoc enquiries. Salary enquiries are one example. Traditionally, in manual systems, a salary card with salary history was held for every employee in an individual wallet and stored in a filing cabinet. Obtaining one salary was a minor inconvenience. Thirty salaries would have been a major interruption. On a computer screen neither is a serious problem and it is easy to print out 'hard copy', ie print the salaries onto a sheet of paper. This is less prone to error than copying figures from salary cards.

Of course, salaries are typical of information that we need to keep confidential. Indeed, the principles of the Data Protection Act 1998 regulate the disclosure of information. Passwords, careful placing of computer display screens (so visitors cannot pry), and simply locking the computer, and office, at night are appropriate precautions. Many personnel practitioners resist networked computers with unrestricted access, where security becomes dependent solely on passwords. Unfortunately, the value of interchanging data, with accounts systems for example, is a counterforce. It creates pressure to share company-wide networked systems.

## CASE STUDY 8

In a medium-sized manufacturing company not many years ago, maintaining the records for and calculating a redundancy payment for an employee was a laborious process. The employee's earnings were held on a salary card contained in an envelope in a filing cabinet. Salary cards were updated annually after the pay settlement or when an individual's salary changed. This card (which had to be removed from the envelope) did not contain the date of commencement or date of birth of the employee. This latter information had to be looked up in a book of forms that maintained a list of employees in alphabetical order. When an employee joined, a new form with their details was inserted and when one left the form was removed to a 'past employees' book.

Length of service and age had to be calculated mentally from the respective dates. A week's pay was calculated from the salary. Statutory entitlement in terms of the number of weeks' pay (subject to a statutory maximum) could be determined from a 'ready-reckoner' and the correct weeks' pay calculated from the salary. There were also company enhancements that depended on service

and age and on a week's pay but without the statutory maximum limit.

For reasons of confidentiality and responsibility, each calculation was performed by the Personnel Manager and for accuracy was checked by the Personnel Director. Typically, 20 minutes' work went into each calculation and almost as much again into the checking. The final result was written longhand on a paper form for discussion with the individual.

With hundreds of redundancies during the 1980s and early 1990s, much time and resources were devoted to this relatively simple task. If it was necessary (as it occasionally was) to know the costs of a proposed redundancy programme, only an estimate could be made, as a precise figure would not produce the information in sufficient time.

Today the information (even for closing the whole company!) can be determined in seconds by the use of a few keystrokes on a computer keyboard and it can be confidential, timely, accurate, well presented and administratively efficient.

## Multiple access

There are advantages, indeed, in less restricted access. For example, where line managers can access information about their subordinates without directly involving personnel staff they are more likely to do so. Better management decisions are likely to result. Interruptions in a personnel office are a major source of inefficiency. Therefore a networked system that allows enquirers to answer their own queries will help personnel practitioners make greater contributions in other areas of expertise.

In terms of the politics in an organisation, knowledge and information are power. Not all personnel practitioners are comfortable with making this more easily accessible. It may reduce their own ability to influence others because it reduces the opportunity to divulge information selectively!

## Staff performance

Reference information on matters such as employment legislation and training material on almost any business subject is readily available through the Internet and through organisations' intranets. This means better-informed personnel staff. When used for training, such material creates the potential for greater performance from all employees in their job areas. Wider availability means that decisions and plans for the future can make much greater use of factual information.

Various time and work organisers can help you to work more efficiently and effectively. They can increase efficiency by enabling you to carry out activities more quickly and increase effectiveness by reminding you of activities that need to be completed, for example.

---

**Activity 20**

If you have a personnel computer system, carry out a simple evaluation of it. Take a scale from 0 (the system is worse than a non-computerised system) to 10 (you cannot envisage that it could be better) and rate it for the following:

- Timeliness

- Accuracy

- Presentation

- Flexibility

- Administrative efficiency

- Accessibility of information

- Access by people outside the personnel function relative to the desired level of access

- The overall effect on staff performance.

Discuss any low ratings with one of your learning sources. Decide whether you could, or should, do anything about improving the benefit.

---

### Speed of communication

We look at e-mail and the Internet shortly and these are good examples of the improved speed of communication made possible by computer systems. Another is video conferencing, which reduces the need for individuals to travel for face-to-face communication. As bandwidths increase, and so allow clearer images, people may take advantage of this opportunity more and more. Call centres that enable telephone queries to be routed to the right person via menu systems are another example of improved communications saving business time.

### Benefits from particular applications

We have attempted to identify the main benefits that might be expected from computers but there are thousands of different applications, many of which can assist your work in personnel and your organisation. A route planner would be but one example. So at this point we will set out just some of the main applications and also a few particular ones of which we are aware. The world changes so quickly now that new ideas are developing as we write. A really good way to identify useful applications software is to talk to others; use those learning sources that we advocate throughout this book.

## Application software on computers

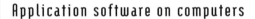

You will have noticed that we have referred to the use to which a computer is put as an 'application'. Thus, drawing an organisation chart may be considered an application, and there is a variety of proprietary software available to meet this purpose. Often applications are contained within other applications. For example, a word processing package will probably include an organisation chart facility. For clarity, this software is usually referred to as 'applications software'. Matching organisation needs to applications software demands knowledge of both the needs and the software. So this section is where we look and see what applications software is available to meet potential business needs. In doing so we may discover other needs that we would like to satisfy.

There is always a trade-off between the benefits available from a particular piece of software and the investment in time required to learn all the possibilities it provides or input all the data it needs. Some priority-setting is likely to be necessary.

### Word processing

This was probably the first computer application for many personnel departments. As well as being more productive than typing, it lends itself well to the standard correspondence typical of the personnel function. By use of facilities such as mail-merge and standard letters or paragraphs, considerable efficiencies can be achieved. The various facilities for improving presentation that word processing provides may also be important to the department's credibility. If you do a lot of word processing, this is an application where it may be well worth exploring all the options available within the application. For example, in compiling later editions of our book we have been able to make invaluable use of the review and revision facilities available in our word processing package.

### Using databases for primary employee records
This is another popular first application and is often a necessary first step. The data here would typically be personal details such as name, address, date commenced work, date of birth, National Insurance number, payroll number and salary. It could be used in its raw, unprocessed form to send out a letter, for example. In addition it could be processed to identify who is due to retire or to calculate salary costs for a department. Aggregating data for reports to managers is a valuable computer task. Databases are frequently used for this purpose. Separate databases for past and present employees are common. Usually a computer routine transfers details from one database to the other.

### Absence recording and analysis
This is another popular early application. Because tangible financial savings can be identified from reductions in absence level, it is easier to make a cost case for this application. Only actions taken by managers and supervisors can bring the absence level down, but good records can help them to do that job. The personnel department can also monitor the situation to see that the job is being done.

### Administration
Much of the literature concentrates on computerised personnel information systems whereas, in fact, personnel departments are equally interested in reducing administrative burdens. Computers can help with many aspects of administration, of which recruitment administration is a particularly good example.

### Spreadsheets
These are a handy application and can be used to check pension calculations, prepare redundancy calculations and be used for what-ifs in negotiations. They are most useful when rows and columns of figures need to be used for a series of repetitive calculations. However, for many personnel requirements, such calculations can be done within processes in other applications. A database may display a person's age on the computer screen, for example, by running a process that calculates age. Processes within applications tend to supersede spreadsheets. Nonetheless, many personnel people find them useful for special applications pertinent to their work. For example, they may be useful to check pension calculations in certain circumstances.

### Diaries, organisers and workflow
These applications can bring to your attention all the tasks to be done

each day. They can identify which probationary periods need chasing, what long-service awards are due, when retirements are pending, which salary reviews are due – indeed anything that they are set up to identify. Records can be kept automatically of activities with the date of completion, forward activities can be planned and all your work and filing centralised.

Organisers can bring together the diaries of different managers, making it much easier to identify dates and venues. This can be invaluable for discovering when, for example, all members of a recruitment panel might be available. Such a facility might be put onto an intranet or even the Internet, with appropriate security, of course.

These applications can improve workflow around the organisation, ensuring tasks are passed smoothly from one individual to another and keeping all people in the system informed of the progress of items, subject to any access restrictions.

## CASE STUDY 9

Personnel secretaries in the past lived by their diaries. Every recurrent task would be entered as to when it was to be done. Task lists would be prepared so as to check that all the activities, for a new starter for example, were completed and each activity would be ticked off as it was done. Typical tasks could be to confirm salary, send out an offer, check contract accepted, confirm this to the manager, notify payroll, notify security, prepare a salary card, etc. Probationary reviews, stages in the pay review process, retirements (employees used to retire at 60 or 65), long service awards due are all examples of the information that would be entered. Irregular day-to-day activities would also be added. Great diligence was needed to ensure all activities were entered, all procedures followed and everything ticked off correctly when it was done.

Today's secretary can rely on a personnel database as an organiser. Task lists are less necessary because the system will do most of them automatically. Ones that require manual action can be set up as an automatic list of actions to be prompted. New information will still need to be entered but actions can be brought to the secretary's attention in advance. Tasks with relevant telephone numbers and addresses can all come onto the screen at the appropriate time. Actions not completed can be deferred to a later time. Memos, letters and e-mail can be written direct from the database and a record kept on the employee's file, cross-referenced to the memo, letter or e-mail itself. History records, with notes, can be easily kept for future reference.

### Payroll

Some people see this as the first personnel-related computer application. It contains much of the information held in primary records and for this reason there is a great temptation to amalgamate the two. Unfortunately, payrolls are designed for weekly (or monthly) calculations and for 'pay history' purposes. As explained above, they do not usually lend themselves well to the task of providing or analysing other personnel information. It is feasible to 'link' payroll and personnel systems, and the software that makes this possible is becoming more sophisticated.

### Time and attendance

Systems such as these help manage flexitime and, when linked to payroll, pay. Clocking systems are linked to a central computer and can make considerable administrative savings. Care is needed over who controls the system to ensure there is no abuse.

### Organisation charts

Drawing organisation charts by hand is a long and tedious task and one that soon needs repeating if they are to be kept up to date. People outside the personnel function often ask why personnel practitioners never seem to be able to cope with what they see as an easy task. Fortunately, a variety of software now exists to make the task more manageable.

### Candidate selection systems

These are a very different form of application, but there is an increasingly wide variety available. A number of purveyors of psychometric testing provide their own software; others sell selection systems to help identify suitable candidates from your own employees. They tend to be more relevant to larger organisations. See the cautionary notes on page 100 about the logic in automatic systems.

The Internet is also being used for candidate selection. There is a wide variety of systems, some of which give the applicant immediate feedback as to whether they are a suitable candidate.

### Specialised processing applications

Placing primary employee records onto a computer database provides in itself no more than a computerised reference system, valuable though that might be. Adding processing applications offers benefits by facilitating routine calculations. Complex calculations such as those for redundancy pay, pensions, labour turnover, salary trends and time to fill vacancies can be set up and easily and routinely calculated. Furthermore, what-if calculations can be invaluable in assisting decision-making.

### Training records

The key to effective training records is to identify what information is likely to be required and to code it effectively. Long descriptions of course titles are not helpful, and qualifications are very diverse and consequently difficult to code. Coding used to be important because merely searching to see who has been on a personnel course would not have identified a course entitled 'Recruitment and Selection' or even, necessarily, 'Human Resource Management'. Today the low cost of memory means in many cases, descriptions, as opposed to codes, can be used. Sophisticated searching applications can be programmed to recognise

Personnel and Human Resources as if they were the same. Care may be needed but, at one extreme, it makes it possible to find who might entertain an important French-speaking visitor and at the other it facilitates the planning of an organisation's training strategy.

## Other record systems

There are many other records that lend themselves to computerisation. Company vehicle records, Control of Substances Hazardous to Health records, risk assessments and equal opportunities monitoring are just a few such. With interrelational databases they can usually be cross-referenced to the primary employee records and to each other.

## Communication facilities

Computers offer the opportunity for much greater availability of information through e-mail, the Internet and web pages, bulletin boards, conference facilities, intranets and computerised fax. These enable communication with many (or selected) employees by means of single actions. Intranets and bulletin boards make it easy to refer to reference material such as the disciplinary procedure. With e-mail and workflow you can trace whether your communication has been read and, with all these facilities, manage your communications. It makes it possible to refer back easily to what was said, to whom, and when, and, in some cases, to discover whether the person did anything about it! Newsgroups and conferences allow sharing of experience and information.

## The Internet

Not exactly an application as we have described it, but this makes information available from huge quantities of data. The benefit to you, for your studies, is described in Chapter 1 but as a source of reference it is huge. Increasingly the information you want is there and even more importantly, you can find it! As mentioned in Chapter 3 there is a huge reservoir of legislation available and, as the readability of computer screens improves, there is little need to print it out.

## Electronic reference sources

Reference books such as some of those published by Croner are now available on disk, making it easy to search for any subject by using a key word. If you have a CD-ROM facility on a home computer you will have already have come across ENCARTA™. This is an encyclopaedia available on a CD disk and may be read through your CD-ROM drive. Although more expensive than CDs at your local music store, many business and professional reference works are available on CD-ROM. As already mentioned, they are very helpful for anyone needing information on employment law and related subjects.

## Expert systems

As specialised versions of reference information, expert systems can guide inexperienced individuals (by means of question-and-answer sessions) through otherwise complex decisions. One area they are used is in medical diagnosis. In personnel, such systems can be used to guide managers through disciplinary action and legal requirements, for example.

### Interactive learning

Similar in principle to expert systems, these often use the Internet, CD-ROM and laser disks to enable learning. Typically, users choose answers to questions posed and the system takes the user through learning points appropriate to the answers they give. Systems use text and a variety of illustrations, and often incorporate substantial amounts of video illustration. Many larger organisations and training centres have set up learning centres where these facilities are available to their employees and often also to outsiders. They seem to be more successful when a learning centre manager proactively promotes them rather than when they are just left available for employees themselves to explore.

We look at e-learning in Chapter 6.

### Self-service

Many large organisations are beginning to allow staff to access the information held in their personnel records from their own workstation and to update their own personal details, such as change of address. Clearly this frees the personnel staff from much work of a minor nature and helps to meet many aspects of subject access, required under the Data Protection Act.

### Other applications

Our list is not exhaustive: there are route planners, presentation tools, video conferencing facilities and many other applications that can help you and your department perform well. But, as we said earlier, for personnel practitioners these are the means to an end. It is important not to lose sight of the end itself!

---

**Activity 21**

Meet up with some of your learning sources; those from outside your organisation may be most valuable. Discuss these applications with them. Do they have any applications that they (and therefore you might) find especially useful?

---

## Reviewing your current system

It is likely that your organisation already has a personnel computer system. If so, then we suggest you study it carefully. Find out how it measures up both to the advantages and disadvantages described above. How many of the applications are available? Would you like to see any of the above applications introduced? Does your computer system have other applications that are not described above? Does it meet your needs for information in the formats that you need?

### Where to start

If you are contributing to the choice of a computer system or reviewing the effectiveness of the current one, start with your ability to meet your organisation's needs. For what information are you continually asked? To what discussions and decisions does your department regularly contribute? What would you like to influence? Establishing your needs is a crucial first step. The better you can establish these, the less likely you are to be disappointed subsequently.

Organisations are at different stages of progress in personnel computer systems and the options for future development are increasing all the time. Some systems are designed for multinational organisations; others would be appropriate in a small private company. Observing a demonstration, always an uncertain approach, will do little more than scratch the surface of any worthwhile system.

Personal networking would be an invaluable step in answering questions and for looking at options. Talk to others in your personal network group and find out what they do. Perhaps they will let you visit them, talk you through the system they have, and explain how it meets their needs. Looking at literature or visiting exhibitions, such as the Computers in Personnel exhibition, could be a wise step.

### The next steps

Once you have some feel for systems, it would be wise to stop and give further careful thought to what you would want a system to do for your department or organisation. Have a look back through the benefits and applications above and relate them directly to the needs you identified earlier. Choose that application or those applications that are likely to realise most benefits. Read through suitable literature on computer systems, especially computerised personnel systems. A single chapter in a book, such as this one, can only give you 'pointers'. Think through the politics of computer systems in your organisation. Do you have an information technology (IT) department? Who will be able to make the decision? Who will need to be convinced? Will your computer system need to integrate with other systems such as accounts, the payroll or a central server? It could be that, given substantial computer capacity in the organisation, a stand-alone system is not appropriate.

Now you know something about the subject, you will want to talk to appropriate people in your organisation. We assume you will have influence in any decision but that the responsibility to purchase will be taken by a more senior person. Your influence will be greatest if you are quite clear about the benefits, the costs and the type of system needed. Do recognise the importance of ease of use, especially if you are the person who will be using it!

### Security

This covers not just password protection and the other issues we looked at under accessibility, but also long-term protection of data. The major threats are computer failure, viruses, fire and even sabotage. The main protection against all these is a regular programme of back-ups. If this is to be done, then the back-up system must be easy to operate. Make sure your supplier addresses this issue with an approach that is not unduly time-consuming or cumbersome. Keep the following in mind:

● Back-ups must be capable of being restored to a different machine to cover machine failures.

● Viruses usually come from software that originates from an uncertain source, such as pirated software or software down-loaded on the Internet.

● Discipline in using only proprietary software helps, but anti-virus software is widely available and must be used.

● Back-ups are very important in virus protection because if a virus does get through it may corrupt your data. In that case your only hope could be your last uncorrupted back-up.

● Fire and sabotage can be covered by using a fireproof safe for back-ups or by an off-site back-up (password-protected) at another location. If you are a 'belt and braces' person you will do both!

● Hacking is also a risk to your data. Linking your computer to other departments creates a slight risk. But if connected to external e-mail or the Internet then you are also at risk of an outside party accessing your computer. Take advice from a reputable supplier on 'firewalls' that minimise the risks.

---

**Activity 22**

Imagine that there was a serious fire at your place of work. Your office, archives and computer system were completely destroyed. What would happen? Are critical pieces of data protected? If no data would be protected then what should be? Even if back-ups were secure in a fireproof safe, would you be able to get access to key information (such as contact details) if access to the site was denied? Put forward recommendations to rectify any shortfalls.

---

# Data Protection Act 1998

This Act applies to personal data that is held in a 'relevant filing system'. This means that it applies to personal data held in manual filing systems as well as to newer technology such as e-mail, taped telephone conversations or websites. You must have legitimate grounds for processing such information. A code of practice now exists.

The Act places restrictions on the processing of personal data. Obtaining, recording or simply holding data is equivalent to processing it. A data controller needs to be specified. Your organisation also needs to be registered with the information commissioner. If your organisation does not appear to be registered, discuss the need with appropriate people in your management.

Certain data is defined as sensitive information. This includes anything that relates to a person's racial or ethnic origin, political opinions, religious beliefs, trade union membership, physical or mental health or sexual life. Processing of such data requires the explicit consent of the individual, unless for ethnic monitoring purposes or unless the individual has himself or herself made it public.

It is also important to realise that data gathered for one purpose cannot be used for another. So, for example, if you gather information about union membership to deduct union dues (with explicit permission, of course) you cannot then use it in negotiations unless, again, you have explicit permission to do so. Workers (and others on which you might hold data) will be entitled to know the purpose for which data on them is held.

### Staff handbooks

Employers are responsible for ensuring that they, and their staff, comply with the data protection principles. It would therefore be a good idea if the staff handbook and policy provided guidance so staff will know how to comply with the data protection principles. Staff and managers can only lawfully have access to personal data where there is a legitimate need.

Disciplinary rules need to indicate examples of misconduct and gross misconduct in relation to data protection. For example, you would be wise to make it a disciplinary rule that references must only be given by a specified level in the personnel department.

Your handbook could be a useful place to indicate what information is held on individuals, how it is obtained, how it is processed and to what purposes it is put. This would help to avoid staff requesting this information individually and creating a serious administrative burden. If your handbook is on an intranet, it will be easier to keep up to date. If you allow employees to access their own records this will enable employees to check the information held on them.

### Data protection principles

As a data-user you have to comply with a set of principles that are designed to protect individuals from the misuse of data. These are summarised in Table 3 and are described in detail in a student pack that is available from the commissioner; see the further reading (page 106) section at the end of this chapter.

We shall not comment on these principles in detail, as guidance can be found in the further reading section. But some key points may be worth your attention, as will the Code of Practice.

You will note the need for data to be adequate, accurate and, where necessary, kept up to date. Obviously this has implications for the information you keep on employees and the principle is not likely to be met without careful procedures being designed and used.

**Table 3**  The data protection principles

---

1  Personal data shall be processed fairly and lawfully and, in particular, shall not be processed unless
   (a)  at least one of the conditions in Schedule 2* is met, and
   (b)  In the case of sensitive personal data, at least one of the conditions in Schedule 3* is also met.

2  Personal data shall be obtained only for one or more specified and lawful purposes, and shall not be further processed in any manner incompatible with that purpose or those purposes.

3  Personal data shall be adequate, relevant and not excessive in relation to the purpose of purposes for which they are processed.

4  Personal data shall be accurate and, where necessary, kept up to date.

5  Personal data processed for any purpose or purposes shall not be kept for longer than is necessary for that purpose or those purposes.

6  Personal data shall be processed in accordance with the rights of data subjects under this Act.

7  Appropriate technical and organisational measures shall be taken against unauthorised or unlawful processing of personal data and against accidental loss or destruction of, or damage to, personal data.

8  Personal data shall not be transferred to a country or territory outside the European Economic Area unless that country or territory ensures an adequate level of protection for the rights and freedoms of data subjects in relation to the processing of personal data.

*  Conditions cover consent (explicit consent in Schedule 3) and legitimate interests as well as a number of specific conditions such as the administration of justice. So long as certain conditions are met, sensitive data may be kept for ethnic monitoring purposes.

---

For example, not keeping data longer than necessary may be simple when such data is kept on a computer and cross-referenced by date. However, manual records can pose a problem. An example of this is leavers' files. These may be more conveniently filed in alphabetical order than in order of leaving. That will make it more difficult to remove files of employees who left a particular time ago. Cross-referencing manual files to a computer system could provide an interim solution. Phasing manual files out may provide the long-term answer.

One particularly relevant provision is that appropriate technical and organisational measures must be taken against unauthorised or unlawful processing of personal data and against accidental loss or destruction of, or damage to, personal data. Personnel departments need to be particularly careful about disclosure where it may be unlawful. Personnel computer screens should not be visible to visitors to the department. Keep in mind that telephone calls from people purporting to be building societies, future employers or other plausible bodies may, in fact, be from private investigators.

Of course you will want to respond to genuine written enquiries. Therefore the intention to make such disclosures should be recorded in your data protection entry and perhaps in your staff handbook. It is also important to remember that having an entry does not oblige you to make a disclosure.

Data can be destroyed accidentally and we looked at the need to take security measures to protect computer data in an earlier section of this chapter. Other forms of data recording are not so easily duplicated, so there is a need to consider appropriate protection where manual data is held. So, for example, fire-proof safes may be appropriate.

### What are the legal implications?
It is a criminal offence to hold personal data without registering it, and your employer could be prosecuted. The same applies if the data is used outside the terms of its registration; in this case you as an employee could be prosecuted. However, this applies only if you have done this 'knowingly and recklessly' – but be careful!

Individuals have rights under the Data Protection Act 1998. They include the right to have access ('subject access') to the information you hold on them (although not to any intentions, such as promotion, that you may have). This access includes details of the data being processed, to a description of the data being processed, the purposes for which it is being processed, any potential recipients of this data and information as to the source of the data.

Where the data is processed automatically, and is likely to form the sole basis for any decision significantly affecting the data subject (such as a psychometric test used for short-listing purposes), then the individual will also be entitled to know the logic involved in the decision-making. It is your responsibility to supply the logic to any enquirer, so you will need to be careful to obtain it from test suppliers. You would also be wise to check that the logic is valid. Validity is described in Chapter 5 but checking the validity of a test, even relying on data from the supplier, requires some understanding of statistics. If you need to do this yourself, we suggest you read Roland and Frances Bee (see further reading, page 106).

Failure to comply means that the individual can complain to the commissioner, who has a range of powers. Individuals can also request information to be corrected or deleted, and they can also sue for damages if they suffer financial loss (or physical injury) as the result of incorrect data.

This is an important Act. As we warned in Chapter 3, employment law is not an area where issues are necessarily clear cut. Quite frequently, the precise way in which the law is interpreted changes. This is likely to be particularly so with relatively new legislation.

So, although we have explained key principles, you are likely to need further advice from more senior colleagues, the Advisory, Conciliation and Arbitration Service (ACAS) or legal specialists.

**Activity 23**

The information commissioner provides a series of guidelines, a code of practice and a student pack. You might find it useful to obtain these and use them to check how your organisation is complying with the Act. You should be able to obtain a copy of your registration from within your organisation. If necessary, you can gently remind the person responsible that the registration entry is in the public domain.

## The personnel implications of e-mail and the Internet

### E-mail

The use of e-mail has increased enormously in the last few years. Today it is almost impossible to conduct business without having e-mail addresses for staff.

By contrast, business styles for correspondence evolved over decades, if not centuries. Etiquette grew up. Business letters start with 'Dear . . .' and finish 'Yours faithfully, or 'Yours sincerely', even if the writer might not be very faithful or sincere, or indeed the recipient very dear! Care is still taken over whether to use 'Dear Madam', 'Dear Mrs Smith' or 'Dear Emma'. Yet business e-mails starting 'Hi Sarah' are quite acceptable in many quarters.

E-mail etiquette is evolving quickly and some note needs to be taken of the conventions emerging and the implications of using this medium. The accountability for responsible use may not be as well defined as it should be. A lot depends on well-written policies and communication with employees about appropriate behaviour. It is reasonable to assume that much responsibility will rest with personnel practitioners. You will need to work with information technology specialists who may share the burden of accountability.

Guidance needs to be given to employees. They need to know the policy on use for personal purposes (mirroring the Internet guidance below), be clear about any rules on content (not attaching offensive material for example), and make use of suitable disclaimers. Employees also need to know what disciplinary actions might be taken against them for breaches of the policy. Below are some examples of where personnel practitioners, among others, need to be vigilant:

1    E-mail has the equivalence of a company headed paper. It is traceable and recorded on both your computer and the receiver's computer (as well as possible intermediate servers). Employees need to realise the implications of this. For example, contracts, including employment contracts, could be established unintentionally by careless use of e-mail.

2    E-mail addresses can be easily disclosed. Simply circulating e-mail to everyone in your address book, as some virus warnings advise, could disclose the address of each of your contacts to everyone else in your address book, including (perhaps conveniently) the person who sent you the warning! An e-mail address is also personal information and this would be likely to breach privacy and to make unregistered disclosures. Data protection principles apply to e-mail just as they do to any other form of storing personal data.

3    E-mail started as an informal process and this has led to communications that are not always carefully phrased. And yet, as already said, it is recorded and traceable. E-mail should never be used for processes, such as discipline, in which the parties must see each other. Where e-mail has to be used for difficult subjects it is advisable to read, delay, re-read, delay and re-read before sending the message. Strong language can have a devastating effect on the recipient and prompt serious reactions. It should not be used. Once an e-mail is sent the 'die is cast'.

### Internet

No serious researcher can work without the Internet. As we have already outlined, this facility makes a wealth of information available at the desk of everyone connected to it. But, like e-mail, employees need guidance. Here are a few specific issues that personnel practitioners may need to consider.

A policy should specify the limitations and conditions of any use for personal purposes. Some organisations allow business-only use, others accept personal use in the employees' own time (after normal hours for example) and a third alternative is to allow limited private use in work time (as might be allowed for private telephone calls for example). Many organisations do not allow their employees to view Internet recruitment sites. It is important that employees know the rules and also, especially if use is to be monitored, that they know that private matters may not remain private.

Some of the material obtainable is very offensive, in rare cases illegal. Fortunately, most of the worst material can now be filtered out by technology, but some may get through. Equally, many employees may consider soft pornography relatively harmless. Guidance is needed on what is acceptable to view or circulate. Just as rules are established about what may be pinned up in an office, so they need to be established for Internet usage. Almost all organisations make downloading of pornographic material a disciplinary offence, or even a gross misconduct offence. The law may still be evolving here but a well-communicated policy provides the best basis for justifying action.

What can be downloaded may need to be restricted further. Copyright is an issue to consider both in respect of software and in respect of other material that might be printed or forwarded. Material from uncertain sources may contain viruses or assist hackers in gaining access to the organisation's systems. Information technology specialists should be involved in preparing guidance on downloading material.

## Monitoring

Employers often have reason to want to know what their employees are doing. For example, they want to maintain standards of service (for example on customer care lines), they want to know if disciplinary rules are being broken, they may want facts to support a disciplinary action and they may want to be sure that commercially valuable information is not leaking out of the organisation.

At the same time, employees do not want their privacy invaded or personal data disclosed. This desire has legislative support.

You will find appropriate references in the further reading section to help with preparing policies. However, what employers can monitor, and how, is an area of evolving law and it is essential to obtain up-to-date advice if a new policy is being implemented or an existing one questioned. The Data Protection Act 1998, the Human Rights Act 1998, the Regulation of Investigatory Powers Act 2000 and the Code of Practice on Data Protection are all relevant.

## CASE STUDY 10

In January 2000, Income Data Services published a study on Internet and e-mail policies. Company policies vary considerably in their scope and detail, but the following provisions most often feature in codes:

- personal use is either prohibited or allowed on a limited basis

- confidential information should not be transmitted by e-mail, unless it is encrypted

- external e-mail messages should have appropriate signature files and disclaimers attached

- employees should be familiar with general housekeeping good practice (eg the need to delete e-mail messages regularly)

- employees should use appropriate etiquette when writing e-mail messages; the use of capital letters, for example, is considered to be the equivalent of shouting

- inappropriate messages are prohibited including those which are sexually harassing or offensive to others on the grounds of race, religion or gender

- employees should not send potentially defamatory e-mail messages which criticise other individuals or organisations

- employees should not access or download inappropriate material, such as pornography, from the Internet

- employees should take care not to infringe copyright when downloading material or forwarding it to others

- employees should ensure that any information which is posted on a corporate website is accurate and updated regularly.

---

**Activity 24**

Discover whether your organisation has an e-mail and Internet policy. If so, then study it and compare it to what is written above. If your organisation does not have a policy, then draft one and discuss it with an appropriate learning source.

---

## The role of personnel practitioners

Personnel information systems are tools that you use to support line managers and to assist with your other personnel roles and activities. We can look at your role in four categories:

### An administrative role

This involves keeping well-organised records and providing information. It is seen by some as the dull area of personnel activities. However, the flow of information around an organisation is vital to effective decision-making. Providing the management of the organisation with quality personnel information (ie pertinent, clear, timely and accurate) represents a major contribution to the business. At the same time, it is a substantial job for personnel practitioners, and one that can be underestimated far too easily.

### An influencing role

In this role you are meeting the challenge of providing quality information that enhances the credibility of the personnel function in your organisation. Credibility leads to greater access to decision-makers. That makes your job more rewarding and may provide the opportunity to extend your role and influence into other interesting areas.

### A user role

This concerns the user of computerised systems. Here you may become the customer of an IT department or of an external supplier. You will have a part to play in ensuring that the systems meet your needs for providing your 'customers' with the information they in turn need. Making sure that computers and the available software applications assist rather than hinder this objective is a substantial task in itself.

### An advisory role to line managers

It is quite possible that the issue of data protection in your organisation will fall to the personnel department. In addition the increasing use of e-mail and the Internet means you may be called on for advice on policy issues and the actions required if there is abuse of these facilities. If so, you need to know and understand the basics of the relevant legislation and to know where to go to find more detailed information. We have already cautioned you in this chapter about the complexity of the legislation and when we looked at a similar role in relation to other employment law. It is crucially important that you do not overestimate your understanding of the law, so if you are in any doubt, always seek further advice.

## Summary

We have looked at the need to keep records and at the benefits of computer systems both to the personnel function and the organisation. You should now have a broad idea of the range of applications to which a computer can be put and of what is involved in reviewing the facilities available on a computer system. We have also considered the requirements of the Data Protection Act 1998 and considered the implications, for personnel practitioners, of e-mail and Internet use.

Personnel practitioners need to be familiar with computer software opportunities, the Internet and the communication of information, in order to assess how these facilities can help them in their personnel responsibilities.

You should take time to keep up with the trends in improved software, Internet opportunities, new applications and communications facilities.

---

**Activity 25**

1   Visit an exhibition such as the CIPD Computers in Personnel Exhibition held in London each year and persuade exhibitors to show you their systems in a free demonstration.

2   Seek out a simple personnel system and ask for a demo copy. Explore the facilities it offers.

3   Log onto the Internet and go surfing! If it is a new world to you, we suggest you start with your organisation's intranet or with some of the web pages suggested in this book. But keep an eye on the clock as time can go quickly!

---

**References and further reading**

BEE R. *and* BEE F. (1999) *Managing Information and Statistics.* London, Institute of Personnel and Development.

EDWARD A. *and* ROBINSON D. (1997) *The IPD Guide on Implementing Computerised Personnel Systems.* London, Institute of Personnel and Development.

EDWARD A. *and* ROBINSON D. (1999) *The IPD Guide on Choosing Your Computerised Personnel System.* London, Institute of Personnel and Development.

HOGG CLARE (2000) *Internet and E-mail Use and Abuse.* CIPD Good Practice Guide. London, Chartered Institute of Personnel and Development.

HUMAN RESOURCE MANAGEMENT LTD. (1994–95) *The HR Manager's Guide to Human Resource Information Systems.* London, Human Resource Information Ltd.

THE INFORMATION COMMISSIONER. *Student Information Pack and Code of Practice.* Available from The Information Commissioner's Office, Wycliffe House, Water Lane, Wilmslow, Cheshire SK9 5AF.

ROBINSON D. *and* EDWARD A. (1999) *The IPD Guide on Using Your Computerised Personnel System Effectively.* London, Institute of Personnel and Development.

*Internet and e-mail policies*, IDS Study 682, January 2000

Articles in *People Management* (www.peoplemanagement.co.uk):

| | | |
|---|---|---|
| 'Caught in the Web' | Jane Amphlett | 3 February 2000 |
| 'Insider information' | Olga Aikin | 23 November 2000 |
| 'On peeking terms' | Olga Aikin | October 2000 |
| 'Uncertain freedoms' | Audrey Williams | September 2000 |
| 'How to monitor e-communication' | Ellen Temperton | 22 June 2000 |

# Recruitment and Selection

## CHAPTER OBJECTIVES

After reading this chapter you will:

- understand why it is important to adopt sound recruitment and selection practices

- be able to identify the constraints (and opportunities) imposed by legislation in this area and be prepared to keep up to date with forthcoming changes

- appreciate the need for rigorous job analysis as a starting point for the whole recruitment and selection process

- be able to choose appropriate sources of recruitment and methods of selection, depending on the nature of a vacancy, and be willing to evaluate the outcome of your decisions

- be able to identify the factors needed to ensure an effective induction process that meets organisational and individual needs.

## Introduction

Many personnel practitioners spend a great deal of their time engaged in the activities associated with the recruitment and selection of staff. Major recruitment campaigns may be carried out to recruit and select replacement staff, staff with specialist skills, trainees, graduates etc. Thus personnel practitioners often gain a great deal of experience in the administrative and interviewing activities associated with staffing the organisation. In larger organisations specialist recruitment officers may be appointed, whose main role is to ensure that (to borrow a time-honoured expression) they employ 'the right people in the right jobs at the right time'. Other personnel practitioners have little involvement in recruitment and selection, however, as often these activities have been devolved to line managers or outsourced to specialist agencies and the in-house practitioners may only get involved in overseeing the process.

With regard to evaluation, often the process stops at the point of entry to the organisation as everyone just breathes a sigh of relief that, for the time being, the staffing level is correct. We shall see in the concluding stages of this chapter that evaluation should continue for a period of up to 12 months after appointment in order to ensure that the whole process is as cost-effective as possible. (In the case of some appointments such as graduate recruits the evaluation process may last considerably longer.)

The employment situation over the years shifts from a seller's to a buyer's market and back again. However, this effect is not evenly balanced across the employment spectrum. In some areas there are skills shortages, which often result from new technology or changing markets. In fact during the 1990s the economic climate dictated that most organisations did not expand but downsized, so that the emphasis changed from the 'input' side of the staffing process, ie recruitment, to the 'output' side, ie effecting terminations of short-term contracts, redundancies and early retirements. We have seen many organisations move towards the 'flexible firm' model proposed by Atkinson (1984). Essentially this means that employers retain a core group of primary workers who are likely to be full-time permanent employees. Numerical and functional flexibility is then provided by employing a range of part-time, temporary, casual, fixed-term and agency workers as well as out-sourcing activities to other companies and self-employed individuals.

As a consequence we have seen a shift in the proportion of the labour force who are in full-time permanent employment towards more flexible arrangements including self-employment. In any event, the same level of care and attention needs to be paid to the recruitment and selection process (of employees and other 'workers') in order to ensure that the organisation's human resource (HR) requirements are satisfied in as cost-effective a manner as possible.

Further, whatever the economic climate, the HR planning process is by no means simple. Organisations need to predict their HR requirements (eg numbers, skills and levels of responsibility) in accordance with future corporate objectives. Even if it is obvious that fewer staff will be required in the future than currently, it is highly unlikely that a recruitment freeze could be effective for an extended period of time if the organisation is to remain viable. There are many factors to be taken into consideration (eg existing skills, training and development provision, career progression and labour turnover), and it would be an unusual – and fortunate – employer that did not need to look at the external labour market to 'buy in' new skills and abilities for key posts.

We shall now explain why the interlinked activities of recruitment and selection are so important, before outlining the relevant legislation and the practical issues involved in the recruitment and selection of staff. We shall be covering the key recruitment stages of job analysis and advertising, selection (candidate data collection, interviewing and other selection methods), assessment and comparison. Finally, the induction and evaluation processes and the various roles played by personnel practitioners will be considered.

## Why are recruitment and selection important?

It is crucial that selection choices result from a thorough and systematic process. As personnel practitioners, you will need to be knowledgeable about the wider issues involving recruitment and selection decisions, such as legislation and good practice, and the range of recruitment sources and selection methods, as well as being skilled in interviewing and assessing potential employees.

Examples of poor practice in recruitment and selection decisions and their possible outcomes are listed below:

- When a job becomes vacant, failure to question whether it ought to be redesigned by making changes to, say, the level of responsibility, remuneration package, hours of work, working methods and reporting lines – or even whether it should be filled at all (ie where the work could be absorbed by existing members of staff) – will have cost implications, because the job has not been designed to suit current needs and the possibility of potential savings has been ignored.

- A hurried attempt to meet an advertising deadline in the local paper may result in inaccurate copy which, at the very least, misleads potential applicants and, at worst, discourages them from applying.

- Failure to carry out effective research into advertising media for a specialist post resulting in a lower standard of applicants than envisaged, and therefore the necessity to re-advertise in, say, a specialist journal, will project a poor image of the personnel department or of whoever was responsible.

- Untrained interviewers projecting a poor public relations image of the organisation to prospective employees and the use of inadvisable lines of questioning (eg family circumstances) may lead to claims of sex discrimination.

- Untrained and inexperienced observers used to assess too many candidates against too many criteria in a lengthy group exercise during an assessment centre may lead to invalid results.

- A decision to offer posts to candidates who performed 'best on the day' even though they fell short of the requirements defined as essential for performing the job satisfactorily (see the person specification section on page 115) may result in their leaving or being dismissed in the short term or requiring more training than was envisaged in the long term.

We could go on! The important factor to note is that all of the above examples of poor practice result in unnecessary costs to the organisation. Advertising alone is expensive, but once you move beyond a wasted advertising opportunity to the salary costs of an unsuitable employee or the potential cost of a lost employment tribunal case, then you may be facing the loss of thousands of pounds (and the wrath of higher management).

# The legislation

Before moving on to look at the mechanisms of recruitment and selection, we are going to outline the relevant legislation before considering the important issue of good practice. The legislation is referred to and commented on throughout this chapter as well as being specifically referred to in Chapter 3. You should be aware of the impact of the following main pieces of legislation:

- Sex Discrimination Acts 1975 and 1986

- Race Relations Act 1976

- Disability Discrimination Act 1995

- Part-time Workers (Prevention of Less Favourable Treatment) Regulations 2000.

In simple terms, the above legislation makes it unlawful for organisations to take into account a person's gender, marriage, colour, race, nationality, ethnic or national origin or disability in employment decisions. Here we are specifically concerned with decisions at the point of access to the organisation. Thus you should ensure that you take account of equal opportunities at all stages of the recruitment and selection process, from job analysis and advertising, the choice of selection methods and the making of selection decisions through to induction into the organisation. You should note that this protection from discrimination covers pre-, during and post-employment, so training, promotion and termination decisions are also covered and part-time workers now have specific protection in this respect.

The enforcement agencies associated with the promotion of equal opportunities in the workplace are the Commission for Racial Equality (CRE) and the Equal Opportunities Commission (EOC) for race and sex discrimination respectively. They have both issued codes of practice giving guidance to employers on how to comply with the legislation (see the legislative acts/codes section at the end of this chapter). For instance, it is recommended that employers have written equal opportunities policies, procedures for making complaints and monitoring arrangements, and that they take positive action to redress any imbalances in the make-up (gender or race profile) of their employees by, for example, wider advertising, special needs training, flexible working hours arrangements and help with childcare.

As for the disability legislation, there is a Disability Rights Commission (DRC) with the same powers of enforcement as the EOC and CRE. There is also a code of practice designed to help employers get to grips with this wide-ranging legislation.

So far we have considered only those groups of employees who are covered by legislative provisions. Many leading organisations in the equal opportunities field have policies that include reference to groups not specifically covered by the legislation. This good practice shows that they 'cast the net' wider to ensure that employees or potential employees are also not discriminated against because of their age, religion, sexual orientation etc. During the 'life' of this book, more legislation is expected in this area to provide overt protection against discrimination for other minority groups and the full effects of the Human Rights Act 1998 are likely to become more apparent. You are strongly advised to read the CIPD Infosource documents referred to at the end of this chapter under further reading (page 143) for more guidance on best practice in the fields of recruitment and selection, equal opportunities and managing diversity. We will now take a few minutes to examine a case study on this subject and an associated activity.

## CASE STUDY 11

An organisation in the environmental field publicises itself as an equal opportunities employer on all of its job vacancy notices. Last year the equal opportunities policy was replaced with a Diversity Statement which reads as follows:

'To fulfil our vision of a better environment for present and future generations, we will develop an organisation where all employees are actively supported in giving their best contribution to corporate aims and objectives. This means attracting people from all parts of the community, valuing the differing skills and abilities of all our employees and responding flexibly to the needs of individuals in achieving organisational goals.'

The organisation recently lost an employment tribunal claim in which the applicant claimed race discrimination. The tribunal chair commented that there was little evidence that the organisation was an equal opportunities employer or embraced diversity in its workforce.

---

**Activity 26**

1   What are the differences between equal opportunities and managing diversity? If you are not sure, then discuss this question with one of your learning sources or look it up on the CIPD website.

2   List at least four things the tribunal chair would have looked at in considering whether the organisation employed good equal opportunity or diversity management practices.

Compare your responses with the feedback provided at the end of this chapter.

---

# Overview

Continuing on the theme of good practice, we are now at the stage of considering the practical issues relevant to recruitment and selection. We shall, for simplicity's sake, be considering these two processes separately, but it is obvious they are closely interlinked, as demonstrated by the simple flow chart in Figure 1 below.

**Figure 1**  Recruitment and selection flow chart

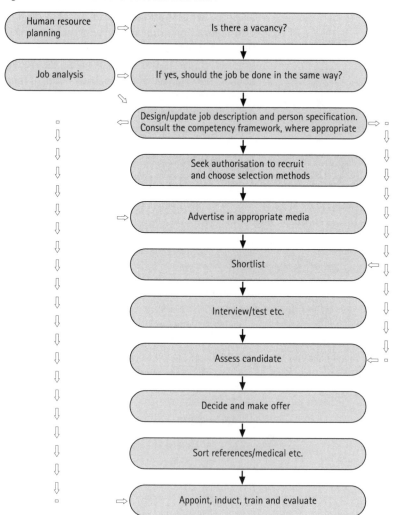

The black arrows indicate the sequence of events and the white arrows indicate where information from one stage is fed into another. For instance, the scrutinising of job applications for shortlisting purposes should not be carried out as a separate event but should be based on the information provided by the person specification on the characteristics and qualities that are being sought. In fact, application forms, if used, can easily make a judgement as to whether applicants possess the characteristics or qualities that are deemed to be essential.

NB: It is important to examine at each stage areas where discrimination could occur and take preventative action.

# The recruitment process

There are two major stages involved here: job analysis and advertising. We have already looked at examples of the potential pitfalls of inactivity, hurry or sheer carelessness at these and other stages. Both job analysis and advertising will often fall within your activities as a personnel practitioner, and you should ensure that you take a proactive stance here. With regard to job analysis, however, you should seek to ensure that line managers retain responsibility and ownership for this activity for their own staff, and do not view this purely as a personnel function. Regarding advertising, the design and placing of advertisements is usually handled centrally, ie by personnel practitioners, to maximise control and minimise costs. We will consider the two stages below.

### Job analysis

We will be concentrating here on the role of job analysis in recruitment and selection but it is worth pointing out that it is also relevant to work design, organisation structures, job evaluation, the identification of training needs and performance management issues, especially the setting of objectives.

**Table 4** Job analysis techniques

| Technique | Main advantages | Main disadvantages |
| --- | --- | --- |
| Observation | Comprehensive information can be gathered about observable activities. | Very time-consuming. Those observed may act differently from the norm. |
| Interviews | Skilled interviewers can probe areas that require clarification. | Interviewees may seek to impress the interviewer by 'talking up' the job. |
| Group discussions | Provides more balanced information than an individual interview as exaggeration by job-holders will be discouraged. | Time-consuming and logistically complicated to arrange. |
| Critical incidents | Forces interviewees to focus on specific occurrences rather than to generalise. Helps to identify the types of behaviour which lead to success. | A complex and a time-consuming process. |
| Questionnaires | Objective, efficient and straightforward way to gather a wealth of information. Less opportunity for interviewer-bias. | If not carefully designed, the information gathered may be difficult to analyse. |
| Work diaries | A systematic way of gathering comprehensive information. Most suitable for higher-level jobs. | Very time-consuming for the individual and, if not structured, may be difficult to analyse. |

There are three elements in job analysis:

- field study
- job descriptions
- person specifications.

We shall take each in turn.

*Field study*

In order to acquire information about a job and the skills and qualities required of a person suited to that job, we need first to carry out a thorough analysis of the job and its organisational environment. There are various techniques for so doing, and these include observation, interviews, group discussions, reviewing critical incidents (where interviewees are asked to focus on aspects of their behaviour which make the difference between success and failure), questionnaires and work diaries. Each has its own advantages and disadvantages as demonstrated in Table 4 on page 113.

Please note that, while the above techniques can be used on their own, the outcome of the job analysis will be more reliable if a combination of techniques is used.

The aim of job analysis is to answer the following questions:

- What is the job-holder expected to do?
- How is the job performed?
- What skills are required and what is the level of those skills?
- Should the job be reorganised (eg change to hours, level of responsibility, duties incorporated into other posts)?

The field study stage should provide information that can then be formulated into 'user-friendly' documents, ie the job description and the person specification.

*Job description*

In simple terms, this describes the job. Organisations usually have their own standardised formats for job descriptions and, though they vary enormously, generally they include the following sections:

- *identification data*: job title, department, pay grade, main location
- *organisational data*: responsible to and for, other working relationships (this could be visually presented as an extract from the organisation chart)
- *job summary*: a brief statement of why the job exists
- *job content*: an explanation of the principal duties with brief summarised descriptions
- *miscellaneous*: covering unusual arrangements such as shift-working, a need to be mobile, casual car user allowance plus a reference to any other documents, eg collective agreements, which provide further details.

Recent years have seen a move away from this traditional approach to job descriptions with some organisations questioning whether they are necessary at all as increased flexibility and empowerment mean it is difficult to summarise many jobs. Further, some organisations now use generic job descriptions for job groupings rather than drafting job descriptions for each job type. There is a strong argument that detailed job descriptions are still necessary for effective recruitment, training and performance management purposes (to name but a few). It is essential that the unique features of the job, particularly shift patterns and the need for mobility, are spelled out to job-holders and potential recruits in written particulars, if not in a job description.

We are also seeing the use of terms such as Key Accountabilities and Role Profiles in place of job descriptions. Both documents cover the information listed above but the former also emphasises performance measures for each job (admittedly performance standards have been included by some organisations for their more senior posts for many years). The latter tends to combine the information required for job descriptions and person specifications and often makes use of competencies (see below).

*Person specification*
Other commonly used terms are the 'personnel specification' or 'job specification'. All three are used to describe 'the ideal person for the job'. (We would recommend that you use the term 'person specification' or 'personnel specification' but avoid the term 'job specification' as this has different meanings across organisations.)

Once again, person specifications vary in content and format depending on the 'house style'. We see, in examples of person specifications, the terms 'skills', 'experience', 'qualifications', 'knowledge', 'personal qualities' and, increasingly, 'competencies' used, but basically their purpose is the same: to set down the minimum requirements that an applicant must possess before being considered for a vacancy. Further, most person specifications go beyond stating the minimum (essential) requirements and also state other (desirable) requirements, as demonstrated in Table 5 on page 116. (In this example, you will see that the methods of assessment are also suggested. Please note that these are not the only choices and, as a note of caution, the application form would have to be very well designed to ensure that sufficient information was available for assessment against all these criteria. Further, references too have their limitations.)

Thus a successful candidate will be expected already to possess all the essential requirements and to be capable of, or have the potential to be trained to, an acceptable standard in the desirable ones. You should take note that *all* the requirements must be *realistic* and *justifiable*. An example where this would not be so is as follows:

**Table 5**  Example person specification form

| Company name | | | |
|---|---|---|---|
| **Job title:** Personnel Manager<br>**Department:** Personnel | | | |
| | **Essential requirement** | **Desirable requirement** | **Method of assessment** |
| Qualifications | Graduate calibre (ie at least two good A levels). CIPD-qualified. | Graduate in relevant subject. MCIPD. | Application form and certificate check. |
| Experience | Minimum of three years' experience in generalist personnel work at personnel officer level. | Five or more years' relevant experience in a unionised environment. | Application form, interview, and references. |
| Knowledge and skills | Up-to-date knowledge of employment legislation. Organisational skills. Financial awareness. Computer-literate. | Knowledge and skills in employee relations and negotiating. Experience of working with XYZ personnel information system. | Application form, interview, and role-play plus references. |
| Personal qualities | Good communicator – written and oral skills, good judgement, confident, persuasive, approachable, dependable, uses initiative, average numeracy. | | Application form, interview, group exercises, tests, and references. |
| Motivation and expectations | Desire to develop personnel function. High expectations of self and others. | | Application form, interview, and references. |

- A stipulation that candidates for a supervisory position be fluent in Urdu, Bengali, Welsh and English and be physically strong enough to handle sheets of lead for sustained periods of time would be unrealistic: there are simply not enough people meeting those requirements out there in the labour market (particularly for the salary on offer!).

- The above requirements would also be unjustifiable if in reality the job did not involve communications in all the specified languages or did not entail the need to lift heavy items for sustained periods. (It would also undoubtedly be safer to provide special lifting equipment.)

In any event, care must be taken to ensure that person specification requirements do not discriminate either directly or indirectly on the grounds of race, sex or disability.

---

**Activity 27**

Taking into account best practice, study your own job description and person specification (if they exist) and draft out accurate, up-to-date and comprehensive versions after carrying out a systematic analysis. Discuss their contents with one or more of your learning sources. You will be surprised at how much you do!

---

We shall now consider the role of competencies in this area.

### Competency frameworks

Competency frameworks provide a common set of criteria across a range of HR activities. They are multi-purpose and essentially assist managers in:

1   recruitment and selection decisions

2   performance appraisal discussions

3   career development planning

4   the distribution of rewards.

The shortfalls of person specifications such as the example provided in Table 5 have resulted in a growth in the number of organisations using competency frameworks for job analysis purposes.

So what are the shortfalls of traditional person specifications? It's quite simple – we tend to use expressions such as 'good communicator' and 'effective leader' and expect that everyone will know exactly what is meant. It is obvious that this is not the case and these terms need to be precisely defined so that interviewers and assessors, in particular, have a common understanding and will be able to assess candidates accordingly. Thus competencies are used to describe the typical behaviours that we would expect to see when we observe a good performer, eg a good communicator or an effective leader. This area is a complicated one and you will find some excellent reading in Whiddett and Hollyforde (1999). They provide the example in Table 6 (page 118) of a competency framework, showing the various levels of competency applicable to different jobs.

In summary, assuming that we have decided there is a vacancy to be filled and we have permission to do so, we must ensure that:

•   we carry out a thorough job analysis and design our working documents (job descriptions and person specifications)

**Table 6**   Typical content of a competency framework

Competency framework

**COMPETENCY CLUSTER**
Working with people

COMPETENCIES *with levels*

- **Managing relationships**
  Level 1: Builds relationships internally
  Level 2: Builds relationships externally
  Level 3: Maintains external networks

- **Teamworking**
  Level 1: Is a team worker
  Level 2: Supports team members
  Level 3: Provides direction for the team

- **Influencing**
  Level 1: Projects a positive image
  Level 2: Influences the thinking of others
  Level 3: Changes the opinions of others

**BEHAVIOURAL INDICATORS**
(for managing relationships)

| **Level 1: Builds relationships internally** | **Level 2: Builds relationships externally** | **Level 3: Maintains external networks** |
|---|---|---|
| - Adapts personal style to develop relationships with colleagues.<br>- Adapts form and presentation of information to meet needs of the audience.<br>- Identifies and maintains regular contact with individuals who depend on or who influence own work. | - Takes account of the impact of own role on the needs of external contacts.<br>- Maintains regular two-way communication with external contacts.<br>- Identifies and nurtures external contacts who can contribute to the business. | - Takes account of different cultural styles and values when dealing with external organisations.<br>- Actively manages external contacts as a business network.<br>- Identifies and makes use of events for developing external networks. |

© Whiddett and Hollyforde (1999)

- we consult the competency framework, where this is available, to determine exactly what sort of behaviour signifies good performance on the job.

Armed with this information, we must choose appropriate selection methods before we are ready to advertise the vacancy.

### Advertising

Advertising can be a very expensive activity, especially if we get it wrong. It can be tempting to sit back and congratulate ourselves on a thorough job analysis that resulted in workable and user-friendly documents, ie the job description and the person specification. We need, however, to be just as systematic and methodical in our approach to advertising the vacancy in terms of the content and design, the timing of the advertisement and our choice of media.

In commencing the advertising process you need first to be aware of the sources of possible recruits:

- existing employees, ie internal recruitment

- job centres

- employment agencies or recruitment consultants

- advertising

  - shop windows or factory gates

  - local and national newspapers

  - the ethnic press, publications and meeting venues

  - professional, specialist or technical journals

  - local radio

  - television

  - the Internet

- the 'milk round'

- word of mouth (personal recommendations)

- networking

- headhunters

- 'waiting lists' or speculative queries

- open days

- liaison with schools and colleges.

Different sources are appropriate depending on the group of potential applicants that you wish to target. For instance, you may decide to use the free facilities of the job centre for semi-skilled positions, especially when you expect to find a wealth of unemployed talent in the immediate locality. However, if you wish to attract managerial, specialist or technical personnel you will probably need to spread the net further and make use of national newspapers, appropriate journals and/or the Internet. This will obviously be more expensive, but there is also a cost attached to not filling a key post, eg in overtime payments and missed opportunities. We do assert that an advertisement is cost-effective only when it is concisely worded, well designed and attracts a sufficient number of suitably qualified candidates.

You should note that in order to comply with equal opportunities legislation vacancies should be advertised as widely as possible. Relying entirely on internal recruitment, 'on file' applications or personal recommendations may leave the organisation open to criticism, and is highly unlikely to move it towards an appropriate gender or race balance in its staff profile.

The *timing* of the advertisement is also of crucial importance, especially when advertising in newspapers and journals. You must ensure that:

- for the local press, you choose the day job-seekers know that jobs will appear

- you avoid advertising just before a holiday or shutdown period, because you may miss potential applicants who are on holiday or disillusion others who cannot contact the organisation for further information

- you check the dates for final copy and meet them in order to avoid unnecessary delays in recruitment (this can be protracted if using monthly publications).

Another important tip is that you need to be very specific regarding the section of the publication in which you wish to place your advertisement. Odd-numbered pages are generally more widely read than even-numbered ones, but also you do not want your advertisement for a new chief executive to be lost among the double-glazing sales pitches or the lonely hearts column!

We shall now concentrate on the *design* and *content* of the advertisements themselves. One of the most popular mnemonics used by personnel practitioners is AIDA. This provides a guide to successful advertising by highlighting the four steps below:

*A*ttention

*I*nterest

*D*esire

*A*ction

To work, an advertisement must catch the *attention* of the target audience and hold the reader's *interest* so that the whole message is read.

## CASE STUDY 12

### Financial controller

This is an exciting opportunity to join one of England's top football clubs. The successful candidate will be a qualified, experienced accountant used to working in a commercial environment who understands the importance of 'bottom line' and has a flair for evaluating systems and ideas for their business potential and cost effectiveness.

Reporting to the Company Secretary, you will be responsible for the financial control of all Club operations.

Age is not important, a dynamic, enthusiastic attitude is. A competitive salary will be offered together with a full executive benefits package. Please send your CV to:

**G Taylor, Neversaydie Football Club, Green Lane, Neverton**

As you can see, the advertisement is poorly located (how many potential financial controllers will be reading this section of the *Daily Telegraph* on a Monday?), is not designed to grab your *attention* or hold your *interest* (the fact that the job would entail working for a football club is not capitalised upon at all), gives vague and limited information about the job and the person sought and so fails to arouse *desire* (further, there is no indication of the salary banding), and it is unclear about the application procedure ie the *action* that should follow, because there is no contact number for further information and no closing date.

Further, it should arouse *desire* for the opportunity offered and stimulate *action* in the form of applications from the target audience.

This may be easier said than done, but studying examples of advertisements is very useful for highlighting good and bad practices. An example of an advertisement that fails to comply with AIDA is provided in Case Study 12 above; it was found in the General Appointments section of the *Daily Telegraph* on a Monday, and is reproduced without reference to the real organisation in order to avoid embarrassment.

So what should we do to avoid making mistakes in advertising? There are no golden rules, but generally an advertisement, drawing on and summarising the job description and the person specification, should be composed as follows:

- job title/location/salary (these are of key interest to job-seekers)
- brief description of the job
- brief description of the nature of the organisation (unless very well known)
- brief description of the 'ideal person' (highlighting, as a minimum, the essential requirements)
- organisational benefits and facilities (if attractive)
- unique features (such as hours of work, need for mobility, accommodation provision)

- application procedure and closing date
- reference number (if used)
- equal opportunities statement
- reference to the organisation's web pages, where applicable.

In essence, you must give enough information about the job (to target the right people) and the person required (to attract suitable candidates only to apply). The *image* portrayed should be inviting but also reflective of the style and culture of the organisation. For instance, an eye-catching headline seeking an 'Action Man or Wonder Woman' would probably not be appropriate for a filing clerk's post in a local authority, but has been successfully used for a security officer's role in a large toy store.

---

**Activity 28**

Consider the example of a poor advertisement above. Redesign the advertisement so that it complies with the AIDA guidelines and make proposals for the timing and placing of the advertisement in the media of your choice. Justify your choice and find out how much it would cost. Discuss the drafting of your advertisement with one or more of your learning sources.

---

We have mentioned Internet recruitment (or e-recruitment) above. Here we are referring to advertising on your own company website or using specialist online recruitment websites. The former can be very useful in that the company retains total control over the process but will be less successful if your organisation is not well known or if insufficient attention is paid to maintaining the website. We will be concentrating on the latter in the activity that follows.

---

**Activity 29**

What factors would you take into account when deciding whether to advertise a technical post:

a)   in a specialist journal

b)   via an established online recruitment website such as www.job-site.co.uk, www.stepstone.co.uk or www.monster.co.uk?

Compare your response with the feedback provided at the end of this chapter.

---

Assuming that your advertisement has attracted a manageable number of suitably qualified and experienced candidates, we shall now move on to the important stage of selecting the right candidate. Please note that, as we indicated earlier, the processes of recruitment and selection are not discrete, so you should by now have made the decision on which selection methods you wish to use (see Figure 1, page 112).

## The selection process

You should make your decision on the successful candidate as a result of:

- candidate data collection
- candidate assessment
- comparison.

You should always avoid making a simple comparison of candidates with each other, as this is likely to be highly subjective and will lead to an offer of the position to the candidate who was deemed to be 'the best on the day'. Instead you should use the person specification and, at each stage, compare the candidates with the essential and desirable requirements listed.

### Candidate data collection

Information is gathered about candidates through:

- application forms
- curricula vitae (CVs)
- interview performances
- tests (ranging from physical, intelligence and aptitude through to personality)
- appraisals (for internal candidates)
- references
- online questionnaires
- assessment centre performances (now being used not only for large-scale recruitment, graduates and senior positions but across a large number of appointments to specialist, technical, customer service and other positions within many organisations).

In order for this process to be directed at achieving your aim, ie to recruit the person who most closely fits your person specification profile, you should ensure that you collect only relevant information about the candidates. For example, an applicant's bizarre taste in music or socks is unlikely to be relevant and can lead, like discussions of which football team he or she supports, to unfounded prejudices.

We are now going to consider three of the above methods in more detail. We will start with interviews and then move on to provide summaries of the latest thinking about tests and assessment centres.

These latter two methods are increasing in popularity and are designed to provide more information about the candidate than can be gained by exclusive use of the much-maligned interview. Tests and assessment centres have also usually been validated to see whether the tests and exercises used adequately measure relevant characteristics and abilities in order to predict job success. There is a wealth of reading and commentary on this area for your further enlightenment. Articles in the CIPD's *People Management* magazine would be a useful starting-place; see also the CIPD publications listed under further reading on page 143 at the end of this chapter.

*The interview*

Unlike tests and assessment centres, the interview, as a selection tool, has been much criticised for its lack of validity (the results of unstructured interviewing have been found to be only slightly higher than random selection at predicting future success in the job!). Nevertheless, any coverage of recruitment and selection would be incomplete without reference to 'the interview'. Though we can see the pitfalls of its use, few appointments are made without the interview playing some role. You should note that the effectiveness of interviews can be improved by thorough preparation and by ensuring that all the questions asked are relevant (and seen to be relevant) to the job. The majority of employing organisations still use interviews as a crucial stage before deciding on new appointments because they see that interviews can be useful for:

- verifying information

- exploring omissions

- checking assumptions

- providing information to the candidate.

In fact, candidates themselves seem equally loath to dispense entirely with interviews. Many feel that the interview provides the only opportunity for them to reveal their personalities and to 'sell' themselves to the employer.

So how do we get the best out of an interview? The structure of the interview should, in simple terms, follow the mnemonic WASP:

*W*elcome

*A*cquire – What information do you have?

– What else do you need?

– What should you check?

*S*upply – What information should you impart?

– What will happen next?

*P*art

**Table 7**  Interviewing checklist

BEFORE
- Familiarise yourself with the job description and personnel specification.
- Read the application form and CV.
- Meet the rest of the interview panel to agree the list of questions and roles to be played eg chair, scribe, timekeeper.
- Arrange the interview at an appropriate time and place.
- Book the venue.
- Inform the applicant well in advance, providing details of location, time, expected duration, need for preparation, travel expense provisions, number of stages in the selection process etc.
- Ask if special arrangements need to be made eg a personal loop system for a candidate hard of hearing.
- Confirm the arrangements with the panel members.
- Notify security and reception of the arrangements.
- Ensure that the venue is private and that interruptions will not occur.
- Allow enough time between interviews for breaks, discussions, and completion of assessment forms and, at the end of all the interviews, for a full review.

DURING
- Start on time.
- Start with a welcome.
- Seek to establish rapport.
- Explain the purpose of the interview and the stage in the selection process.
- Ask relevant questions (see Table 8).
- Allow the applicant to do the majority of the talking.
- Listen actively.
- Do not seek to fill silences (or you may discourage the candidate from providing more information).
- Observe non-oral behaviour (and check anomalies between this and the oral messages).
- Check gaps, omissions, or contradictions.
- Check claims *re* level and type of experience.
- Use a logical sequence of questions and provide links between sections.
- Provide brief information on the job and organisation.
- Allow sufficient time for the applicant's questions.
- Take brief notes.
- Keep control of the content and timing.
- Summarise.
- Close on a positive note – thank the candidate and reiterate the next stage of the process.

AFTERWARDS
- Compare the information gained about the applicant with the personnel specification requirements.
- Complete the assessment form and keep proper records.
- Follow up the interview with the appropriate documentation eg invitation to the next stage, rejection letter.

**Table 8** Types of interview questions

Generally questions should be:

*open*     to encourage full responses
            eg 'Tell me about. . .'

*probing*    to check information provided in the application or interview
            eg What, Why, How, Explain. .

Probing questions include hypothetical or situational or behaviour-based questions to elicit practical experience or judgement; and 'contrary evidence' questions to check an assumption made about the candidate by seeking evidence to the contrary.

*Closed* questions, ie those demanding a yes or no response, should be used only for clarification or control eg bringing a line of questioning to its conclusion.

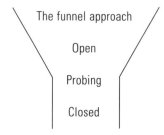

The funnel approach

Open

Probing

Closed

We recommend a *funnelling* approach, as indicated above. You should start with an *open* question, eg 'Tell me about your current responsibilities', followed by progressively narrower *probing* questions, eg 'What experience have you had of formal negotiating situations?' At the end of this section of questioning you should use a *closed* question such as 'So would it be accurate to say that you have had limited experience in formal negotiating situations, and if you are successful in being offered this vacancy, you would welcome specialist training in this area?' The candidate is very likely to say yes, effectively bringing about a 'full-stop' to this section. You should then provide a link to the next section of questioning eg 'Thank you for your responses to those questions; we will now move on to discuss. . .'.

The following types of questions should generally be avoided:

*leading*     eg 'You are fully trained in the use of an XYZ Personnel Information System, aren't you?'
            (The candidate knows exactly what answer you are looking for here!)

*multiple*    eg 'Tell us about your educational background, your career history to date, and your strengths and weaknesses.'
            (By the time the candidate has finished telling you about his or her educational qualifications, you will probably both have forgotten what else you asked. Further, a clever candidate will undoubtedly tell you about his or her strengths but ignore the issue of weaknesses!)

If you do fall into either of the above traps, it is relatively easy to rectify your mistake by asking additional probing questions. Keeping brief notes, both of the candidate's responses and the further questions that you feel it necessary to ask, will help you here.

Thus you should bear WASP in mind when drawing up your list of questions for interviewees. If you are involved in a panel interview, each member of the panel can lead a different section of questions while still maintaining a logical structure overall. A checklist for successful interviewing practice and an examination of the types of questions to be used and avoided are reproduced in Tables 7 and 8. Note, however, that the checklist in Table 7 is likely, with some adaptation, to be applicable to a large number of interviewing situations, not just those designed for staff selection purposes.

The above guidelines apply to a range of approaches to interviews, eg behaviour-based, situational and telephone interviews:

a) **behaviour-based interviewing** has developed in recent times, in line with the use of competency frameworks (see Table 6 on page 118 for an example)]. It is based on the premise that the best way to predict future job performance is to understand a candidate's past behaviour in job-related situations. It allows candidates with limited job experience to compete on equal terms with more experienced candidates. (See further reading on page 143 for more information on this subject.)

Let us take the example of a vacancy for a bar attendant in a hotel. There are three steps to follow:

- developing a behaviour competency profile based on the behaviour necessary to be a successful bar attendant, eg adherence to health and safety, hygiene and quality standards, customer service, knowledge of the hotel's products and services, selling ability and cash handling

- developing appropriate 'benchmark' interview questions against which the interviewers measure each candidate's response to a specific situation: these are open-ended questions which focus on the candidates' describing critical incidents in their current and previous jobs as well as in their life experiences

- scoring the responses by measuring each candidate's answer against each of the respective profile statements.

Advocates of this approach say that their organisations have achieved financial benefits due to reductions in recruitment and training costs, improvements in productivity of newly appointed workers and reductions in staff turnover.

---

**Activity 30**

Draft behavioural questions which seek to determine whether a candidate possesses the following competencies:

- effective leadership skills

- the ability to handle conflict

- problem-solving ability

- project management skills.

Compare your responses with the feedback provided at the end of this chapter.

---

b) **situational interviewing** is similar to behaviour-based interviewing in that it centres on critical incidents but, instead of focusing on past behaviour, it is future-oriented. Thus questions tend to be hypothetical and are related to dilemmas that job-holders might encounter. It is based on the assumption that intentions predict behaviour. Candidates are presented with 'What if . . .' job-related scenarios and asked 'What would you do in this situation?' The responses are then assessed against a pre-prepared scoring guide covering the possible range of responses, indicative of poor, average or good performance.

Proponents of this approach point to its high predictive validity, reliability and freedom from bias, and there is research evidence that backs up this contention. There are, however, many dissenters who have concerns that candidates may not actually behave in the real world in the same way that they say they will in the interview. We would conclude that this approach is useful, especially when applicants do not have experience in your industry or sector, but would suggest that it is used alongside a variety of other questioning approaches.

c) **telephone interviews** are increasingly being used by busy HR specialists for two main reasons:

- As an initial short-listing device it is more cost-effective than a face-to-face interview.

- Many employees now spend a large proportion of their time in communicating with customers by telephone, eg call centre staff.

There are drawbacks to telephone interviews, especially when candidates have not been notified that they may receive a call and that it is a crucial part of the selection process. It is possible, however, to capitalise on their use by following the rules of thumb below:

- Thoroughly prepare your questions beforehand and have at hand an 'easy to complete' interview assessment form.

- Telephone the candidate at the agreed time and explain the nature, purpose and structure of the telephone interview.

- First ask screening questions such that candidates must answer these satisfactorily before progressing on to the remainder of the interview.

- Next ask a range of probing questions, such as behavioural or hypothetical questions, so that you are able to assess as many skills or competencies as possible.

- 'Sell' the job opportunity and provide information on the company, as required.

- Check the candidate's understanding and continuing interest in the post.

- Provide details of the next steps in the selection process and tell the candidate when he or she will be notified about progression (or not) to the next stage.

● Make a preliminary decision on the candidate's suitability and complete the paperwork while the interview is fresh in your mind.

Those in favour of this approach point to the advantages to both parties in that neither has to travel. More importantly, they say that people are less inhibited than in face-to-face interviews and so the quality of information provided can be higher.

We will now move on to consider the use of tests in selection decisions.

### Tests

The use of psychometric tests is certainly on the increase though they tend to be used more extensively by larger organisations with established personnel departments. The main application of such tests in the recruitment and selection field is that they can be used to measure individual differences in personality and ability.

The CIPD's Quick Facts sheet on psychological testing broadly supports the concept of testing but recognises the many concerns about their use. It answers these by setting out six key criteria for their use:

1 Everyone responsible for the application of tests including evaluation, interpretation and feedback should be trained to at least the level of competence recommended by the British Psychological Society.

2 Potential test users should satisfy themselves that it is appropriate to use tests at all before incorporating tests into their decision-making processes.

3 Users should satisfy themselves that any tests they decide to use actually measure factors which are directly relevant to the employment situation.

4 Users must satisfy themselves that all tests they use have been rigorously developed and that claims about their reliability, validity and effectiveness are supported by statistical evidence. (The Data Protection Act 1998 is relevant here. If candidates are selected by an automated process, they have the right to know the logic used in the selection decision.)

5 Care must be taken to ensure equality of opportunity among all those individuals required to take tests.

6 The results of single tests should not be used as the sole basis of decision-making; this is particularly relevant with regard to personality tests.

We next consider assessment centres (ACs).

*Assessment centres*

The use of assessment centres (ACs) (and development centres) is on the increase with, according to the Industrial Relations Services (1997: 14–15), almost 50 per cent of organisations using them. Research by Fletcher and Anderson (1998), however, comes to the worrying conclusion that only half of these employers are adopting good practices.

What are ACs? There is no typical AC but a good AC should include the following:

- a variety of selection methods or assessment techniques: ie a combination of any of the following – interviews, psychometric tests, in-tray exercises, job sampling or simulations, questionnaires, team-building activities, structured discussions, presentations, report writing, role-playing exercises

- assessment of several candidates together

- assessment by several assessors/observers

- assessments against a number of clearly defined competencies.

Thus ACs answer some of the criticisms of the use of sole techniques such as interviews and tests. This is because they enable assessors to observe and assess candidates' behaviour in a number of different situations that provide a more comprehensive and rounded picture of the individuals concerned, as demonstrated by the example AC matrix in Table 9 opposite.

We have seen that we need to gather a range of data about our candidates via various methods such as the application form and the interview. We shall now consider candidate assessment.

## Candidate assessment

In assessing our candidates, we need to evaluate each candidate against the job-relevant criteria detailed in the person specification and reach a considered and objective judgement in each case. Here your skills in defining those criteria in very specific and measurable terms should stand you in good stead. Referring to the example person specification form shown in Table 5 (see page 116), as we have already stated, the requirements should really be defined further. In the absence of a competency framework, it is necessary to define what you mean by terms such as 'good oral communicator'. For instance, should our successful candidate be an articulate, experienced and polished presenter or simply have a reasonably good vocabulary?

At the shortlisting stage you are likely to have only the information contained on the application form. If this has been well designed it should be relatively easy to filter out those candidates who do not meet the minimum (essential) requirements. Curricula vitae (CVs) are often used at this initial short-listing stage, but because they are not standardised and often contain incomplete information, they may be much less useful

**Table 9** Example matrix – Project manager

| | Selection technique | Interview | Group exercise | In-tray exercise | Presentation | Written report |
|---|---|---|---|---|---|---|
| **Competencies** Leadership | | X | X | | | |
| Problem-solving | | X | X | | | X |
| Verbal communication | | X | | | X | |
| Written communication | | | | X | | X |
| Time management | | | | X | X | X |
| Decision-making | | | X | X | | X |
| Negotiating and influencing skills | | X | X | | X | |
| Analytical ability | | | X | X | | X |

here. Actually you can help this process by giving clear instructions to candidates regarding the type of information that you want them to provide in submitting their application forms and CVs.

If you still have a large number of potentially suitable candidates, you may shortlist further by producing a list of candidates who appear to possess a number of the desirable requirements also. Interviews, tests and exercises can then be used to gain more information on your shortlisted candidates. Depending on the number of suitable applicants and the seniority of the post, the selection process may consist of one, two or even three stages (with a different combination of selection methods and personnel involvement at each stage).

### Comparison

Here you are comparing the candidate assessment with the person specification and looking for the 'closest fit'. The candidate who most closely matches the 'ideal person' described in your person specification should be offered the vacancy. You do not select the person who performs 'best' overall, because this is likely to result in an overqualified person (ie in excess of your requirements) or an underqualified person (ie all the candidates fell short of your requirements) being recruited. If you are confident that you have carried out a systematic job analysis, you should realise that those candidates who appear to be overqualified for your needs are equally as 'unsuitable' as those who clearly fall short of your requirements. Thus you are aiming to achieve:

*the right person for the job* and

*the right job for the person.*

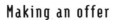

**Activity 31**

Look back at a recent vacancy within your organisation and analyse the process of recruiting and selecting the successful candidate by answering the following questions:

● Was an appropriate choice of advertising media made?

● Was an appropriate choice of selection methods made?

● What lessons have been learned and what suggestions do you have for improvements in the event of similar vacancies arising in the future?

Discuss your recommendations with an appropriate learning source.

## Making an offer

Once you have decided on your preferred candidate, you are in a position to make an offer of employment. It is likely that you will initially make a verbal offer, if you are authorised to do so, but you must be careful to emphasise any 'subject to' conditions. Conditional offers most commonly refer to:

● satisfactory references

● medical suitability

● evidence of eligibility to work in the UK

● confirmation of qualifications.

All these areas are fraught with difficulties and it is not our intention to cover them all here, but you should note the following:

1 It is advisable to make job offers conditional on receipt of references which are 'satisfactory to the company'. If the references you subsequently obtain are unsatisfactory, the offer of employment can then be withdrawn without the employer being in breach of contract.

2 Evidence of health problems should not be used for withdrawing an offer unless it can be justified on material and substantial grounds. For example, a food factory would be justified in not employing someone with a serious nut allergy if they could not make reasonable adjustments for the applicant to avoid contact with nuts. Medical information can help the employer to ensure compliance with the Disability Discrimination Act 1995 (see Chapter 3 for more information).

3    Despite requests by line managers to bring new recruits on board as soon as possible, you would be advised to await references and medical information before confirming start dates. (See Case Study 13 below.)

## CASE STUDY 13

You have probably read over the years a number of stories in the press about employees, particularly in the medical, educational and caring professions, who have lied about their backgrounds and qualifications in order to gain work. Some of these stories have had alarming outcomes; hence the press coverage. It would appear that, due to the competitive nature of today's job market, there is more temptation for some applicants to embellish the contents of their CVs.

One medium-sized organisation found themselves in difficulties recently when they appointed a finance director. His CV indicated that he had an impressive array of qualifications and was experienced in the industry sector. It quickly became apparent, however, that he was not up to the job. The HR manager was notified and was concerned to learn, four weeks after he commenced employment, that a reference request to his former employer had been returned as 'not known at this address'. Further investigations showed that the finance director did not have the qualifications that he claimed and that he had been dismissed by one of his previous employers for alleged fraud, though he had not been prosecuted. The finance director remained unaware of the HR manager's investigation until it had been completed and the decision was taken to dismiss him. This 'damage limitation' strategy was successful in that the company was not financially exposed, but the experience did cost the company time and money and they then had to start the recruitment process all over again.

So do contracts need to be written to be enforceable? The technical differences (and overlaps) between contracts of employment and written particulars of employment have been covered in Chapter 3. In essence, a contract comes into being once a verbal offer has been made and accepted. Good practice suggests that you should ensure that the following occurs:

- Once a successful candidate has been chosen, you make a verbal offer promptly, if your company policy allows this, and state any conditions.

- You follow this up with a written conditional offer accompanied by a written statement of particulars or, as a minimum, the main terms and conditions of employment, eg salary, hours, location, benefits.

- You keep in touch with the chosen candidate during the time he or she takes to make the decision, providing additional information as necessary.

- If he or she does accept, you continue to keep in touch with the successful candidate, notifying him or her when the conditions of the offer have been satisfied and of the arrangements for induction and job training.

- Unsuccessful candidates are treated with respect and notified promptly of your decision.

- If not sent with the offer, a written statement of particulars is provided to the successful candidate as early as possible in the process (but no later than two months after the commencement of employment).

We shall now move on to consider the induction and evaluation processes for our new employee before summing up the role of the personnel practitioner.

# Induction

Successful organisations will ensure that this process is treated as an important activity and has sufficient resources devoted to it. The main reason is that new employees who have undergone an effective induction programme are likely to be competent performers at their jobs more quickly than those whose induction was scanty or non-existent. Also the former group are less likely to leave the organisation at an early stage than the latter group (this phenomenon is commonly known as the 'induction crisis' and signifies a dissatisfaction with the job or the organisation or both).

Different employees have different requirements, but they are all likely to need:

- to learn new tasks and procedures

- initial direction

- to make contacts and begin to develop relationships

- to understand the organisational culture

- to feel accepted.

There are, however, certain groups of employees who may need special consideration, such as:

- school and college leavers

- women returning to work

- disabled employees

- management trainees

- members of minority ethnic groups

- employees who have undergone internal transfer or promotion.

As an example, the first group listed will know very little about the working environment. With more experienced recruits, you can provide basic information and then ask them what else they want to know. You cannot rely on school or college leavers in the same way, because 'They don't know what they don't know'! (The ACAS Advisory Booklet *Recruitment and Induction* provides guidance on these special needs and how they can be accommodated.)

The commencement of the induction process is difficult to pinpoint because, for employees new to the organisation, the imparting of information begins with the job advertisement. We could therefore argue that the process starts at this early stage and plan accordingly. Usually, however, when designing an induction programme, we start with the first day of employment and then timetable activities to be included over the first few weeks.

Induction programmes vary between two extremes: from the simple checklist approach (to cover the essential organisational information that an employee must be told) to comprehensive induction packages (which include, for example, video messages from the chief executive, guest speakers, 'getting to know you' exercises, and group activities). The checklist approach is likely to be brief, take place at the workstation, and involve the new employee and his or her line manager only (possibly with the participation of a representative of the personnel department or the health and safety officer, or both). The second, more sophisticated (and more costly) approach is likely to take place away from the workplace and involve more people at a senior level in the organisation. Also, in accordance with economies of scale, organisations are inclined to provide this programme periodically only, ie when there are sufficient numbers of new employees who can attend. Neither of these extreme approaches is preferable to the other: their worth is gauged by how successful they are in helping the new employee to settle down quickly and become effective in the job.

Finally, let's consider the information that should be provided. As a minimum, employees should be informed about:

- the organisation's background and structure
- the organisation's products, services and markets
- the conditions of employment, eg pay, hours of work, holidays, sick pay and pension scheme
- the organisation's rules and procedures
- the physical layout of the organisation
- health and safety issues (NB it is crucial that these are covered in the very early stages of employment)
- first aid arrangements
- data protection policies and practices
- equal opportunities policies and practices

- employee involvement and communication arrangements

- trade union arrangements (if any)

- welfare and employee benefits and facilities.

Please note that we have concentrated on general induction above. We must not forget that this should be combined with induction that meets the individual's needs as well. During the recruitment and selection process you will have gathered a lot of information about the candidate's skills, abilities and development needs. Instead of filing this information, use it to agree a personal development plan with the individual, which will involve planning on-the-job and specialist skills training as well as other development activities.

---

**Activity 32**

Look back at a recent appointment made within your organisation and analyse the induction programme carried out when the successful candidate took up his or her post (this exercise can still be applicable if the successful candidate was an internal one). What suggestions do you have for improvements in the induction process for the future? Discuss your recommendations with an appropriate learning source.

---

# Evaluation

As with the majority of activities that personnel practitioners become involved with, there is a strong argument for evaluating the success of your recruitment and selection procedures. This is, however, not just a simple matter of concluding that, for instance, an advertisement for a clerical officer's post was successful because 250 applications were received. In fact, it is likely that the reverse is true, because sifting through 250 application forms will have been a time-consuming and costly exercise. Every stage of the recruitment and selection process should be reviewed to see whether mistakes were made and whether a repetition of them can be avoided in the future.

It would be good practice to consider the following questions, but note that some may be more appropriately addressed or re-addressed in three, six or twelve months' time:

1   Did you get the job analysis stage right? That is:

- Did you carry out a thorough field study?

- Is the job description an accurate reflection of the range and type of activities and the level of responsibility involved?

- Are the person specification requirements defined in specific and measurable terms?

- Are there any important omissions or unnecessary inclusions in the person specification?

- Was a new recruit justified or should the work have been organised differently?

- Are the selection criteria too restrictive, eg are age limits stated or is an unnecessarily high level of qualifications called for?

- Have you considered flexible working arrangements to encourage applications from people who are unable to work conventional 'office' hours?

- Is the total employment package sufficiently competitive?

2 Did you get the advertising stage right? That is:

- Is recruitment being targeted too narrowly, eg have you concentrated only on those sources that you have used in the past?

- Did the advert give sufficient information about the job and the person required to encourage suitable applicants only?

- Was the advert eye-catching?

- Did you choose the most appropriate media?

- Did you get the timing right?

- Have you carried out an analysis to see which media produced the most cost-effective results?

3 Did you get the selection stage right? That is:

- Did you choose the most appropriate methods for selection?

- Did you ensure that the information generated by each method was cross-checked for validity?

- Did you ensure that only relevant information was considered in decision-making?

- Have you carried out an analysis to see which of the methods used were the most fruitful and cost-effective?

4 Did you get the induction stage right? That is:

- Did the induction programme run smoothly?

- Was the employee properly assisted to settle in and quickly learn the job?

- How much did the induction process cost?

5 Did you select the right person? That is:

- Did the employee become effective as quickly as expected?

- Did the employee require more assistance, training or support than expected?

- Is the employee still in the post and performing at a satisfactory level?

- Has the employee made satisfactory progress regarding salary reviews or promotion?

6   Did you ensure compliance at all stages with equal opportunities legislation?

7   What would you do differently next time?

Let's return to our example at the beginning of this section of the advertisement for a clerical officer's post. It is tempting to blame the high level of unemployment in the locality for the overwhelming response, but it is quite likely that the job advertisement was too vague in stipulating the essential requirements. Thus potential candidates were not encouraged to deselect themselves from the process and it was necessary to plough through all 250 application forms to see which candidates were really suitable for shortlisting. Thus the person responsible for the poor drafting of the advertisement has not only wasted the time of all those involved in the recruitment and selection process (and organisational money) but has also falsely raised the hopes of a large number of unsuitable candidates.

---

**Activity 33**

Having studied the section above on evaluation, consider which methods are currently employed by your organisation to evaluate the success or otherwise of the recruitment and selection process. Suggest two or three major improvements. Put these down in the form of an action plan with, if possible, timescales and the names of persons responsible. Discuss your recommendations with one of your learning sources.

---

Having considered this important but often forgotten issue of evaluation, we shall now summarise the many roles played by personnel practitioners in carrying out the activities associated with the recruitment and selection of staff.

## The role of personnel practitioners

In considering the activities above we have touched on a number of the roles performed by personnel practitioners at various stages of the recruitment and selection process:

### An advisory role to line managers

It is rare for all of the above activities to be performed solely by personnel practitioners. In any event, it is generally wise to include line managers at the job analysis stage because of their specialist knowledge, and at the selection stage so that they have played a part in selecting their own member of staff and will therefore be more likely to be committed to the new employee's success (and so that you will not get all of the blame for a poor decision!). Following on from this, it is worth noting that an interview panel commonly consists of the line manager and a personnel practitioner. This may involve you in an *influencing* role when, say, the line manager is tempted to offer the post to a candidate for subjective reasons (eg the manager and candidate attended the same school) rather than objective reasons (ie ones linked to the personnel specification).

### An administrative role

This is to ensure that information is sought, chased and checked, that appropriate records are kept, and that all interested parties are kept in touch with the timetable of events.

### A training role

This may cover the design, organisation and delivery of skills training for interviewers/assessors. There will also be an *educational* or possibly a *policing* role to ensure that equal opportunities principles and policies are adhered to at all stages of the process.

### A public relations role

This arises owing to the need to attract suitable candidates and involves conveying information about the job, the person required and the organisation itself. Also, the way in which candidates are dealt with in making enquiries, pursuing applications and attending interviews may confirm or contradict their first impressions of the organisation.

### An assessment role

Personnel practitioners play a role in assessing candidates by interviewing, observing, testing and evaluating them using a range of selection methods.

### An evaluation role

Finally, personnel practitioners are likely to be responsible for ensuring that the process of recruitment and selection is periodically evaluated against its objectives, ie did you employ 'right people in the right jobs at the right time'? (see the section above).

## Summary

You should by now be familiar with the key issues involved in the recruitment and selection of staff. We have looked at why recruitment and selection are important (regardless of the economic climate), the relevant legislation, the various stages involved and the importance of a thorough job analysis. We also considered the keys to effective induction and evaluation processes and the various roles played by personnel practitioners.

You should note that even if your experience of recruitment and selection is limited, it is likely that you will have applied for at least one position for which you were granted an interview or were invited to attend an AC. Thus, if you are unfamiliar with the whole process from the viewpoint of the interviewer or assessor, you will be familiar with it from the candidate's perspective. Nothing can replace the experience of actually conducting your first interview, administering a test or being involved in running an AC but you are likely to have an opinion on the good and bad practices that you observed. Reflect on such experiences to ensure that you do not make the same mistakes that others may have made. Continue this learning process by, if you have not already done so, attempting some of the activities provided above before moving on to the next chapter.

Finally, please note that a list of legislative acts and codes, further reading, and recommended video titles is provided at the end of this chapter.

**Feedback**
**Feedback on Activity 26**

1    The differences between equal opportunities and managing diversity are summed up in Table 10:

Table 10    Equal opportunities v managing diversity

| Equal opportunities | Managing diversity |
|---|---|
| ● entails removing discrimination against specific groups | ● entails maximising employee potential through an appreciation and utilisation of people's differences |
| ● is primarily an issue for personnel specialists | ● involves all managers |
| ● relies on positive action | ● is unlikely to rely on positive action as this will not be inclusive |
| ● has a moral/legislative focus | ● has a business focus |
| ● is driven by domestic and EU discrimination legislation | ● has a global application in that it supports a variety of cultures |
| ● can be adapted to the existing organisation | ● challenges the nature, values and structure of the existing organisation |

**2** The tribunal would have looked areas such as:

- the demographic make-up of the workforce in terms of gender, race, disability, age etc across the various functions and levels and whether this reflected the outside population

- signs of support from top management, eg diversity champions, value statements which incorporate diversity principles, publicity for policies and practices

- attitudes within the workplace as evidenced by witnesses' responses to questions at the tribunal hearing

- recruitment sources, to see whether positive steps were taken to encourage applications from under-represented groups, eg advertising in ethnic minority publications

- selection methods, to ensure that they were not tainted with discrimination and that selection decisions were based on fair and objective criteria

- working arrangements, ie are part-time, term-time, home-working and other flexible working arrangements available?

- training provision, ie have managers received appropriate skills training and has awareness training been provided to all employees?

- the handling of complaints about discriminatory matters, ie are grievances dealt with appropriately and are offenders disciplined?

- the provision of equal access to training and promotion opportunities for all employees, eg are adjustments made to the timing of training events in order to include part-timers?

- an integration of relevant policies with each other, backed up by company practices, eg employee involvement in establishing a dress code that respects differing cultures and needs, a policy on religious observance that is actively promoted rather than tolerated by line managers.

## Feedback on Activity 29

In Table 11 below, there are a number of factors listed and a tick indicates, in general terms, where one avenue has the advantage over the other.

Table 11   Factors

| Factors | a) | b) |
|---|---|---|
| Speed in placing an advertisement | | / |
| Speed in receiving and processing applications | | / |
| Size of target population | | / |
| Ease of access to additional company information | | / |
| Security of information eg CVs | / | |
| Less likely to attract poor quality applicants/time wasters | / | |
| Ability to correct and update information in the advert | | / |
| Less costly | | / |
| Facility to use an online selection questionnaire | | / |
| Established source for this type of vacancy | / | |
| Increasing trend to use this medium | | / |

## Feedback on Activity 30

Your questions should be on similar lines to those listed below. Please note that supplementary questions can then be asked, depending on the responses received.

Table 12   Behavioural questions

| Competencies | Questions |
|---|---|
| Effective leadership skills | Give me an example of a situation in which you were responsible for helping others to complete a task or project . . . what steps did you take to motivate the team members? |
| The ability to handle conflict | Describe a situation where you were faced with views which differed from your own . . . how did you deal with this conflict? |
| Problem-solving ability | Give an example of a problem you had to solve recently . . . what was the outcome and what steps did you take in solving the problem? |
| Customer focus | Tell me about a difficult situation which involved you in dealing with an internal or external customer . . . how did you ensure that you understood the customer's needs and that they were met? |

## References and further reading

The following two booklets are available from the Advisory, Conciliation and Arbitration Service (ACAS), ACAS Reader Ltd, PO Box 16, Earl Shilton, Leicester LE9 8ZZ; tel. 01455 852 225:

*Advisory Booklet on Recruitment and Induction.* (Revised 1998) Leicester, ACAS.

*Advisory Booklet on Employment Policies.* (Revised 1997) Leicester, ACAS.

ATKINSON J. (1984) 'Manpower strategies for the flexible organisation'. *Personnel Management.* August. pp28–31.

COHEN D. (1997) 'Behaviour-based interviewing: improve productivity and reduce turnover by hiring more effectively'. *Human Resources Professional.* (April/May). pp29–31, 33, 36.

COURTIS J. (1994) *Recruitment Advertising: Right first time.* London, Institute of Personnel and Development.

FLETCHER C. *and* ANDERSON N. (1998) 'A superficial assessment'. *People Management.* 14 May. pp44–46.

FOWLER A. (1997) *Writing Job Descriptions.* London, Institute of Personnel and Development.

HACKETT P. (1998) *The Selection Interview.* London, Institute of Personnel and Development.

INCOMES DATA SERVICES (1998) 'Assessment centres'. *IDS Studies 648.* April.

INDUSTRIAL RELATIONS SERVICES (1997) 'The state of selection: an IRS survey'. *Employee Development Bulletin 85.* January.

ROBERTS G. (1997) *Recruitment and Selection: A competency approach.* London, Institute of Personnel and Development

TAYLOR S. (2002) *People Resourcing.* London, Chartered Institute of Personnel and Development.

WHIDDETT S. *and* HOLLYFORDE S. (1999) *The Competencies Handbook.* London, Institute of Personnel and Development.

WOODRUFFE C. (2000) *Development and Assessment Centres.* 3rd edn. London, Chartered Institute of Personnel and Development.

See also the following, available on the website of the Chartered Institute of Personnel and Development (CIPD), www.cipd.co.uk/Infosource:

Age and Employment

Bullying at Work

Disability and Employment

Discriminatory Questions at Selection Interviews

Harassment at Work

Managing Diversity (Position Paper)

Psychological Testing

Recruitment
Recruitment on the Internet
References
Telephone Interviewing

## Acts of Parliament and codes of practice

Disability Discrimination Act 1995
Race Relations Act 1976
Sex Discrimination Acts 1975 and 1986

The following is available from the Commission for Racial Equality, Elliot House, 10–12 Allington Street, London SW1E 5EH; tel. 020 7404 1213:

*Code of Practice: For the elimination of racial discrimination and the promotion of equality of opportunity in employment.* (1984) London, CRE.

The following is available from HMSO Publications Centre (mail, fax and telephone orders only), P.O. Box 276, London SW8 5DT; tel. 020 7404 1213:

*Code of Practice: For the elimination of discrimination in the field of employment against disabled persons or persons who have had a disability.* (1996) London, HMSO.

The following is available from the Equal Opportunities Commission (EOC), Overseas House, Quay Street, Manchester M3 3HN; tel. 0161 833 9244:

*Code of Practice: For the elimination of discrimination on the grounds of sex or marriage and the promotion of equality of opportunity in employment.* (1984) Manchester, EOC.

## Videos

*It's Your Choice.* (1993) Video Arts (selecting candidates).
*More than a Gut Feeling.* (1988) Melrose.
*When Can You Start?* (1988) Video Arts (attracting candidates).

# • Training and Development

**CHAPTER OBJECTIVES**

After reading this chapter you will know how to:

- distinguish between training and development
- identify training needs arising from change, whether internal to or external to the organisation
- plan a training programme incorporating a variety of learning experiences
- implement training activities
- evaluate training and development beyond the level of course questionnaires.

## Introduction

Training is a process through which individuals are helped to learn a skill or technique. The skill may be primarily manual, as in using a keyboard, or essentially intellectual, such as negotiating a house sale. The latter is often referred to as a 'soft skill' since no 'hard' equipment is involved. Instruction is a very typical form of training, but there are many others. There is often an end point, perhaps the achievement of a specific data-entry speed.

Development places emphasis on the growth of the individual. It relates to acquiring a very broad range of soft skills through planned activities and experience. Management of people, handling work relationships and leadership are typical of broad ranges of skills that are *developed*. Success in all these areas requires maturity of judgement. There is no fixed end point to development, because individuals can continually improve, for example, their leadership skills.

The structure of this chapter follows the steps in the 'training cycle', which we shall look at in a moment. First, though, we consider the importance of training and development activities.

## Why are training and development important?

We shall be looking at the unrelenting pace of change in the world and at its implications for training needs. If our organisations respond to change early, they will prosper and gain rewards in terms of security, profit or attainment of their goals. Today commercial products can be imitated, some almost immediately. So technological advantage may give one producer an 'edge' over others, but these other producers can catch up quickly. In a free-market economy all organisations have similar access to capital, to customers and to employees. It is their effectiveness in operating, as organisations of people, that primarily distinguishes one from another. Key factors in operating effectively are the knowledge and skills of people.

In the commercial world, then, if we train our people and continually ensure they have up-to-date knowledge and up-to-date skills, it follows that we shall able to compete effectively, and reasonably expect to prosper. Few, if any, jobs today are protected from commercial realities. Even those not originally seen as being commercial organisations, for example charities, now place considerable importance on obtaining well-trained professional people to run their operations.

As a personnel practitioner you have an important role to play. You should be able to relate to commercial needs and your corporate mission, using them to help identify suitable training. Training and development, like every other operation, needs to be managed. Personnel practitioners need to acquire advanced skills and knowledge to do so effectively.

We shall commence with a look at the training cycle, which helps identify the main principles involved in managing training and development activities.

## The training cycle

Figure 2 describes how training is managed. It is a continuous cycle. We shall look first at how training needs are identified, usually referred to as 'training needs analysis'. Then we shall look at how to plan a training programme, highlighting the ingredients available to satisfy those needs that have been identified. When training is designed and implemented, we need to be aware of the different learning styles that individuals prefer, and we shall look at the four styles. Last, and not least, we shall look at how the effectiveness of training can be evaluated.

Successive British governments have recognised the need for training if Britain is to compete internationally. They have developed and supported initiatives to encourage employers and employees to take responsibility for training. One of these initiatives is the Investors in People (IiP) Award given to organisations that can show they are truly investing in their people, ie increasing their skills and knowledge towards corporate objectives. So it is worth looking at the four IiP principles. Organisations that have demonstrated their ability to satisfy these principles display the prestigious IiP insignia on their letterhead and at their premises. The principles are interesting, because you will see similarities between them and the training cycle.

Figure 2   The training cycle

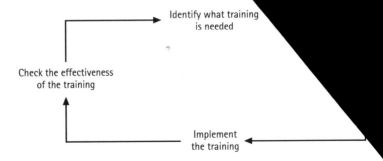

Identify what training
is needed

Check the effectiveness
of the training

Implement
the training

## Investors in People principles

● *Commitment*
An investor in people is fully committed to developing its people in order to achieve its aims and objectives

● *Planning*
An investor in people is clear about its aims and its objectives and what its people need to do to achieve them

● *Action*
An investor in people develops its people effectively in order to improve its performance

● *Evaluation*
An investor in people understands the impact of its investment in people on its performance.

*© Investors in People UK 2001*

The four principles of the Investor in People Standard are reproduced here by permission of Investors in People UK.

---

**Activity 34**

If your organisation is seeking, or being reviewed for, the IiP accolade, you may be asked a number of questions during the process. Try asking some of the typical ones of yourself or of close colleagues:

● Does your organisation make any statements about its policy on training and development of which you aware? Are you able to name any of these?

● What do you think are your organisation's business objectives?

● How are you able to contribute to them?

● Considering the possible contributions, how do you think you might improve your ability to perform?

---

Plan how to meet
the training

...uss your training and development needs with

...scribe any opportunities for training that might
...r organisation?

...o take, or have you taken, any of these oppor-

...uous cycle, we shall look first at how train-

## ...aining needs arise because the world changes

Change is continuous; it affects the environment in which organisations operate and it exists within organisations themselves. Employees are affected by change and they must adapt, learn new skills, cope with different pressures, acquire new knowledge and forge new relationships. Training brings additional resources to individuals to enable them to change and develop. When we looked at the organisational context (Chapter 2) we briefly identified the types of changes that affect the corporate environment. We shall now examine these in more detail and relate them to training and development.

- In recent years *political* change has brought about the need for a wider range of management skills in many parts of the public sector. This change has created new challenges for managers who previously had little control over their finances, employment practices, marketing or ability to exploit opportunities. Examples of these changes are privatisation, public/private partnerships and the move of further education establishments out of local government control and into individual corporate bodies. Politicians also seek to influence the participation of organisations and individuals in training. This has led to initiatives such as IiP Awards, National Vocational Qualifications (NVQs) and National Training Awards (NTAs).

- The *economic* conditions of the 1990s caused many companies to restructure, thus cutting out layers of management, closing operations and losing experienced staff. The wider responsibilities of the remaining staff and the loss of experienced employees create the need for greater skills training, particularly in the managerial and supervisory areas.

- *Social* change creates training needs. For example, as more people travel abroad and experience the high levels of customer service in North America and the Far East they become more demanding in their expectations for customer service at home. As a further example, in society we now acknowledge women's right to occupy jobs at the highest levels in companies and institutions. Both these examples indicate the need for training, the first in customer care skills and the second in management skills for women (to help redress the imbalance at senior levels).

- *Technological* change is relentless. The training needs it creates in computer skills, in advanced technical skills and in new ways of doing things are widespread and substantial. For example, the Internet has far-reaching implications for the availability of information, for education, for retail trade and for many more activities. It is changing the way we work. At the same time, technology and the Internet also provide new techniques for trainers to use in the process of training itself.

- The *law* changes continually as well, and personnel practitioners are only too aware of the training needs it creates for them. Keep in mind that employment is only one area affected by the law. Product liability, labelling of consumer goods and regulation of financial services are just a few examples where the law creates training needs for employers.

- The *environment* changes too. The thinning of the ozone layer creates threats for some companies and opportunities for others. In many industries, environmental pollution can be reduced by better training of operatives. (The list continues.)

These changes lead to new products, services and standards of expected performance that, in turn, demand new skills and abilities. Organisations that can respond to these changes quickly by training their employees appropriately steal an advantage over their competitors.

Listening to and reading suitable media material will raise your awareness of the corporate environment. We recommend:

- *People Management*
- other specialist training publications
- quality daily or Sunday newspapers
- quality magazines covering business or current affairs
- BBC Radio 4
- appropriate websites on the Internet.

Individual training needs also arise internally, directly or indirectly, as a result of external changes. Even without those external changes, training needs will arise for employees who are new to the organisation, gain promotion, relocate, are redeployed, or are due to retire. So, when looking at training needs, we have to consider not only changes in the environment but also changes for individuals.

# Training needs arise because people's jobs and careers change

Induction training addresses the needs of new-starters, and similar training is needed for all employees who transfer or are promoted within the organisation. Some special cases are considered below.

- School leavers have much to learn about the world of work. They need to understand the level of commitment required and to be able to assess others' expectations of them. Working *with* adults will be a novel experience, and new attitudes need to be formed. All this is quite separate from the actual mechanics of doing the job. Comparatively simple everyday tasks, such as answering the telephone, can be a major source of anxiety to those who have never been in employment before. (Perhaps you can remember your first day at work!)

- Young graduates, especially those who have not been in employment before, need similar induction to that for school leavers, although they can be expected to learn faster. Most employers give special consideration to graduates, recognising that they may eventually become senior managers in the organisation. Building relationships with people in many departments of the organisation and having a broad understanding of what each function does is critical for those who seek a progressive career. Graduate training schemes invariably recognise this, and graduates often spend time in different functions before settling into their chosen career path.

- New employees who already have experience elsewhere need to learn about the culture of your organisation, ie 'how things are done'. They need to meet, and begin to build relationships with, those with whom they will be in regular contact. Systems and routines will be different from those of their previous employer. At the same time, new employees usually bring alternative approaches that can benefit their new employer.

- Returners from maternity leave, a career break, or a period of unemployment need time and help to build up their confidence. Often there will be new and unfamiliar technology, and perhaps a new working climate with new or different expectations. For example, call centres and direct selling have radically changed the way in which insurance companies, banks and many others do business and hence the way in which people work in such organisations. Given support to adapt and training in new skills, returners usually regain their confidence rapidly.

- Employees who have moved from other departments, functions and sites also need time to acclimatise to their new situations. The building of new relationships and finding the right contacts can be encouraged by team-building events and by deliberate inclusion in social activities.

*Providing mentors and associates to aid all these transitions is a popular way to assist employees. Mentors, usually more senior than the employee, can provide encouragement and support and pass on their own skills and experience as well as leading by example. Associates may be peers of the employee, such as a graduate who joined with the last intake and who can relate easily to a new graduate entrant.*

- Retirement calls for a new set of life skills, and responsible employers recognise the need for training for this. They provide preparatory courses covering subjects such as health and financial planning, as well as introducing employees to pensioners' groups.

- Current employees who are not performing at the right level require specific diagnosis. The problem may lie in a lack of technical skills or in attitude, but very often other factors not directly related to training needs may be diagnosed.

- Promotion creates training needs. Surprisingly this is often not recognised. It does not follow that the best operative is automatically an effective supervisor, that the best salesman is a natural manager, or that an experienced schoolteacher knows how to be a headteacher. The Peter Principle, which suggests that everyone is promoted to their level of incompetence, possibly reflects the lack of training that most employees receive on promotion.

- Future potential is another reason for training and developing individuals. It particularly relates to those who are progressing to managerial or professional careers, where the responsibility for development of skills rests more heavily with the individual. 'Fast-tracking' is the term used when individuals are identified as having significant future potential. Such individuals are singled out for special development. Activities may include studying for professional qualifications, secondments to other sites, departments or companies, special project responsibilities, and mentoring from one or more senior managers.

## Levels of training needs analysis

When we look at the above issue we shall see that training is needed at three levels. These are the organisation, the job or occupation and the individual employee.

### The organisation
Customer care is typical of a training need that originates at the level of

the organisation. It could arise from a board-level decision to change the organisation's image in this one regard.

### Job or occupation

Training in electronic 'point of sales' equipment (eg the scanners familiar at supermarket checkouts) is an example of training that will apply to everyone in a specific job – in this case, checkout operators.

### Individual employee

Here there may be an opportunity for training where an individual has a particular need or the organisation requires an individual to be trained in a particular area. For the personnel officer, an employment law course or secondment to another organisation might be examples.

## Making training needs analysis comprehensive

Jill Fairbairns (1991) has provided a model that emphasises three matters that need to be addressed in making decisions about appropriate training. We shall use this model to describe our approach to identifying where training should be concentrated. In part, it links the three levels above but it can also be applied to evaluating the suitability of training solutions at each level.

Throughout our working lives we increase our levels of knowledge and skills in order to perform work activities well. The acquisition of relevant knowledge and skills opens up opportunities to individuals for increased job performance, career development and personal development. Organisations continually seek the best return on their limited funds so it is necessary to be selective and to identify those areas that will be important in the particular job in question (Important in my job – see Figure 3).

Most jobs today need a wide range of skills and knowledge: some are critical and others desirable for top performance. Job-holders usually have the majority of those skills and knowledge already but, for the reasons outlined above, there will always be areas that can benefit from additional training (In need of training – see Figure 3). So at this point we would be looking for the overlap between importance in the job and need of training.

The third factor involves the culture of the organisation. We looked at culture in Chapter 2 and observed that businesses are characterised by different attitudes and priorities, ie the corporate culture. Training for knowledge and skills that do not fit comfortably with the *corporate culture* will either put the trained person at odds with that culture or, more probably, lead to the training being rejected on the basis that 'it does not work here'. For example, training in customer care may be misplaced if it is immediate additional sales (rather than repeat business) on which success is judged. Another example of a cultural factor is the

**Figure 3** Factors in the selection of training (Fairbairns' model)

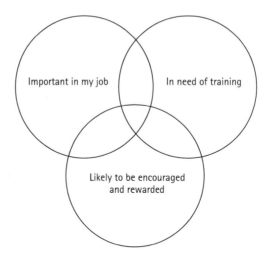

Important in my job

In need of training

Likely to be encouraged
and rewarded

attitude to NVQs or Scottish Vocational Qualifications (SVQs); some organisations are more enthusiastic about these than others. In an enthusiastic organisation an NVQ initiative will receive a better reception and more support from senior managers. Identifying the cultural direction in which your organisation is going will help identify the most relevant training (Likely to be encouraged and rewarded – see Figure 3).

Personnel practitioners will benefit from taking these three factors into account in selecting suitable training activities. It is where such activities address the overlap between all three factors that the most benefits are likely to be realised (again, see Figure 3).

The person being trained is a further factor to be considered. Offering training can imply weakness or that an individual has a problem with some aspect of his or her performance. Unless individuals see training as an opportunity or believe it is important in their jobs and relevant to their organisation, then they are likely to reject it. So individuals should be involved in the plans for their training to encourage their commitment to it.

## Gathering the information

To carry out a training needs analysis for your organisation you will need information that can be evaluated against the factors mentioned above. The information must relate to the level at which you are doing your analysis: organisation, occupation or employee. Suitable source material for the analysis is likely to include some of the following:

- mission and values (formal culture)
- business plans

- succession plans

- competency framework

- views and observations about 'how we do things around here' (this is the informal culture, not necessarily the same as the formal culture)

- appraisal records

- evidence of competence for individuals (eg portfolios)

- opportunities for improvement (eg development opportunities)

- minutes of meetings (eg action points that highlight needs)

- questionnaires

- job descriptions

- performance targets

- observation of employees at work

- relevant NVQs or SVQs

- interviews with:

  - managers

  - staff

  - subordinates

  - internal customers

  - external customers.

Using sources such as these is important because you start with the needs that relate to the business. Once you know what is needed, then you can start to consider the best way to meet those needs.

When you have gathered the source material and feel well informed, it is time to carry out your analysis. This could be at the level of the organisation, job or individual. To illustrate the process we shall consider examples at the job level.

You need to ask what job performance is needed in the particular situation. The answer should be in the form of a level of performance. This could be quantitative (for example, the number of calls handled per hour) or it may be qualitative (for example, all telephone calls are to be answered politely, competently and effectively).

Another way of defining the required performance may be to use an NVQ/SVQ standard or other competency framework that directly defines the competence – for example, to select candidates for jobs within agreed timescales and budgets. Competencies can be invaluable in helping you decide on desired levels of performance. An accepted framework will provide a sound basis on which line managers ers can discuss what is needed.

We shall assume that in these examples training is a suitable rer That may not be the case in all circumstances; for example, if operatio are under-resourced then training is an inappropriate solution.

Next you need to ascertain what performance or competence is being achieved at present. Perhaps callers are kept waiting for a reply with no apology offered when the call is answered. Maybe the person answering does not understand how to handle some of the enquiries, or incomplete messages are taken. In the second example, selection of candidates may regularly overrun both timescales and budgets. The difference between this and the level of performance needed is known as the 'training gap'.

You may have to try to estimate what that 'gap' is *costing* the organisation, or the gain and benefits of closing that gap. We may be able to get information about sales lost owing to poor telephone technique, or estimate the costs of taking an extra day to fill a vacancy. This is important because these costs will provide the justification for the training costs or, perhaps, lead to the conclusion that training is not justified in a particular instance.

## CASE STUDY 14

A manufacturer of plastic pipes found that a market opportunity existed for providing not only pipes but also a variety of equipment associated with customers' use of them. The sale of a 'package of pipe and equipment' enabled higher margins since pipe had often been sold to an intermediary who put then put their own package, and margin, together for industrial customers.

This diversification of its operations was a significant change for the manufacturer.

As a buyer of raw polymers the manufacturer was a major customer of the polymer supplier. Consequently, negotiations were carried out at a very senior level and favourable terms were the norm.

The change in product range meant that as well as processes the manufacturer was also carrying out assembly work. This created a training need that was recognised. However, components had to be purchased from a variety of sources and by junior purchasing staff. Furthermore, the pipe manufacturer was not a significant customer so far as the individual component manufacturers were concerned. Delays began to occur. Deliveries for large orders of pipe were being held up because the equipment to be shipped with them was not ready. The equipment, in turn, was being held up because minor components had not arrived from local suppliers in good time.

Fortunately the company recognised the problem as one of negotiation. It was not sufficient to get the best price for components; reliable delivery had to be part of the deal. Purchasing staff that had been treated well by large polymer manufacturers now had to learn to deal with owners of small engineering works. The process of learning how to work in these circumstances needed to be accelerated and a training programme in negotiation skills was initiated.

next phase is to plan the training and development.

## ‍ing and development plans

a balancing act is required between available resources, which
.‍e influenced by the benefits that have been estimated, and the
identified needs. Achieving such a balance is a matter of skill. As we saw
in the Fairbairns model (Figure 3), you will have to weigh up needs in the
context of the political considerations, style and culture of the organisation.

Let's look at some of the factors that will have to be considered.

### Government initiatives

We have already mentioned Investors in People, National Training
Awards and vocational qualifications. The UK Government is keen to
encourage these achievements and there are invariably financial incentives such as grants and subsidies provided for organisations and individuals seeking these awards, and in some cases, financial rewards and
publicity for achieving them.

In addition there are government schemes on offer to encourage
employment of particular groups such as school leavers (ie Advanced
Modern Apprenticeships) or job seekers (ie New Deal), although what is
available varies from time to time.

Therefore it is wise to investigate the current availability of grants and
subsidies for training. You should approach Learning and Skills Councils
(LSCs) or Local Enterprise Companies in Scotland (LECs), Business
Links, the Small Business Service (SBS) and other sources. Networking
with your learning sources can often reveal useful opportunities. At the
same time you should assess the requirements placed on your organisation by such bodies as a condition of providing grants or subsidies. For
example, you might be expected to train your personnel administrator to
an NVQ/SVQ standard and to train your personnel officer as an assessor. While it may be worthwhile to do such training, it might be time-
consuming. Even if no special conditions apply it is still important to
assess the amount of time you may need to spend on administration and
documentation.

### The internal training and development resources available

You must understand the size of the training budget and how it is structured. Structure can be important; for example, some budgets may
apply only to amounts invoiced; thus the use of a supervisor to train call
centre operators may well not be counted against such budgets. This
does not mean that using the supervisor would be without cost, but it
may save some of the training budget for use elsewhere.

You may have some facilities available internally, such as a training centre well equipped for craft training, management training, computer training or for all of these. On the other hand, there may be very limited facilities. Nonetheless, in most cases there will be equipment available that could be used for training. Production departments, for example, may have idle production lines that could be used for training purposes. Setting up a workstation for call centre training may be straightforward.

Consider the availability and capability of training specialists and trainers within the company. These may be increased by training supervisors in the techniques of instruction, for example. In addition, experienced employees may be available for training-based activities. At more senior levels, experienced managers may be willing to coach or mentor more junior managers or staff. This can be a valuable *development* activity for both the senior and the junior.

Another valuable development activity is secondment to another section, site or associated company. Equally, these locations and jobs themselves may provide project opportunities. A local non-competitor may have a good call centre operation and be willing to share expertise. Some organisations are very innovative and engage in formal partnership arrangements, sometimes including a training provider, to share employee development opportunities.

### The external training and development resources available

Using external resources invariably has an opportunity cost. There will be absence from the workplace and, in consequence, temporary loss of production, sales, service or contribution to the business. Often these costs are 'hidden' in that they do not appear in any financial calculations, but they are there nonetheless. In addition, there will be the cost of course fees, travel and accommodation. Such costs are rarely hidden and are likely to need justification. If there are grants or subsidies available, these may help. As we discussed above, you need to know the conditions laid down by the bodies providing them. Expect questions as to whether the external resources are in fact available internally or could be more economically provided internally. Investigate, also, the availability of grants and subsidies for external training from the bodies we mentioned above.

Finally, you need to evaluate the quality of such training, its relevance and its relationship to the culture of the organisation and to the quality standards demanded in the workplace. For example, a local telephone techniques course might not be sufficient to meet your expectations if you work in an international marketplace. Specified competencies can help you and any external provider identify appropriate learning objectives. A discussion that centres on these can help you and your training provider decide if they can, in fact, meet your expectations. You should also consider the relevance of training to an individual's career. Qualifications, in particular, can be relevant to the needs of both the organisation and the individual; we look at these next.

## Qualifications

In many organisations it is important to have qualified people; in some cases, third parties may impose such requirements. Hospitals are obvious examples, where qualifications are necessary for doctors and nursing staff. In industry, accountants and engineers are examples of professional people who are frequently required to be suitably qualified. Even when not a statutory requirement, qualifications help to show that responsibilities are taken seriously. Health and safety qualifications, for example, indicate a responsible approach to an important issue, one for which a company may be held liable for injuries and occupational ill health.

Qualifications provide external verification of skills, competence or knowledge. This can be helpful, for example, where pay is related to level of qualification.

- *Examination-based qualifications* provide evidence of knowledge and ability to examine issues and solve problems. High performance in examinations may also imply judgement. However, such a guide is not always reliable and, furthermore, examinations rarely assess practical skills.

- *Competence-based qualifications* depend on providing evidence of ability to carry out specific tasks to the standard expected in the workplace. Evidence is assessed by a qualified assessor who judges whether it provides sufficient evidence of competence. Typical evidence might include documents prepared by the 'candidate', reports, copies of correspondence and witness testimony about carrying out activities to a specified standard. Competence can also be assessed by observation.

- *NVQs and SVQs* are nationally recognised competence qualifications. They provide detailed descriptions (standards) of vocational competencies, breaking them down into units of competence, then into elements of competence. Units of competence can be accredited individually, accumulating into a qualification. Elements of competence describe activities (such as leading a meeting) and have performance criteria against which competence in the activity can be judged (eg handling of conflict). The detailed descriptions can be invaluable in preparing training for specific skills and for checking achievement. LSCs, LECs, the SBS and colleges can help employers identify relevant NVQs/SVQs for their employees.

The use of competence-based workplace training can involve the use of internal advisers and assessors. While these would naturally be supervisors and experienced employees, the cost of training advisers and assessors, of administering the system and of providing the training may be substantial. One point of caution on competence-based training and NVQs/SVQs: take care not to allow the collection of evidence to develop into a 'paper-chase', because this may obscure the need to develop skills and impart relevant knowledge, ie to help employees to learn – a point we take up now.

## Choosing appropriate learning experiences

This choice should take into consideration the range of techniques available and individual learning styles.

### Training and development techniques

There is a temptation to associate 'training' with the provision of 'training courses'. In practice the majority of learning takes place outside such courses, and is often left to chance. Learning opportunities abound and the training specialist should seek to manage these as effectively as possible. So 'training and development techniques' include using naturally occurring or deliberately created learning opportunities. The examples of techniques and opportunities that we list here can also help you to address your own training and development needs.

### On the job

- Job instruction
- Coaching and mentoring
- Work diaries and log books
- Records of continuing professional development
- Rotating a person's job with someone else at a similar skill level
- Enlarging the job by providing more tasks or responsibilities at the same level
- Enriching the job by adding tasks at higher level of responsibility
- Group meetings
- Projects and assignments
- NVQ/SVQ programmes
- Computer help facilities, online and offline.

### Off the job

- Seminars and workshops
- Attending talks and presentations
- Guided reading
- Local discussion groups
- Local meetings of professional bodies, such as the CIPD or Institute of Administrative Management (IAM)

- Visits to other organisations

- Business games

- Delivering talks and presentations

- Programmed learning in books, computers, interactive video, CD-ROM and the World Wide Web

- Computer simulation

- Assignments prepared for a course

- Action learning

- Outdoor development training.

---

**Activity 35**

Look at the lists of training techniques above. Are any of those listed unfamiliar to you? Discuss any that you are unclear about with a learning source and undertake further reading, as appropriate.

---

## CASE STUDY 15

An assembly factory found itself continually running into problems meeting its delivery targets. They had a full manufacturing requirements planning system in place, good reliable suppliers and excellent industrial relations. On the face of it the planning system should have enabled the targets to be met comfortably, but this was not happening. The training officer became involved and he went to talk to the supplier of the planning system.

There was, it seemed, a familiar problem. The system worked but senior people circumvented it. If a customer asked for a special delivery, an improvement on an existing delivery date or a change to the order, it would be granted – even if it meant circumventing the system. Any attempt to resist on the part of the planning staff would be referred to the managing director who invariably supported the sales staff. Indeed, he tended to bypass the system himself. If the

system were overridden for special circumstances it clearly could not be blamed if delivery dates went awry.

Because of this problem the computer supplier had developed a computer simulation programme. Rather like a flight simulator this provided the opportunity to experiment with the system and experience the effects of different options. The appropriate senior managers were persuaded to take part in a simulated exercise. Because this wasn't the real factory (any more than a flight simulator is a real plane) they could 'crash' the system again and again until they learned that, if they followed the rules of the system, the planning worked. The process took several days but it convinced the managers that if the system were followed, and everything was put through the system, the delivery targets would be met.

## E-learning

Computer simulation can be viewed as a form of e-learning. This is a wide term covering opportunities that are posed by the electronic age and merits separate mention. It can, of course, take place on the job or off the job. The term includes both PC-based learning and web-based learning. The UK government via the 'University for Industry' and its brand name Learn Direct is encouraging the latter form of learning.

Searching the web can also unearth other online training opportunities. This is a rapidly developing area where reading current literature and networking will help to keep you up to date. Most commentators in this area agree that e-learning that also has tutorial support, perhaps via e-mail, is more successful than other approaches. Some web opportunities that you might find useful for yourself are access to your local university library resources, mailing lists, forums, conferences and chat-rooms, and online courses.

---

**Activity 36**

Explore the learning opportunities available on the Internet. Prepare a short briefing for your organisation on how using these opportunities could best help it achieve its current objectives.

---

## Learning styles

In choosing appropriate experiences we need to acknowledge that individuals are different. In particular they learn in different ways. Honey and Mumford describe four learning styles that enable individuals to be categorised by their preferred approaches to learning. We have summarised these styles as follows:

| | |
|---|---|
| *Activists* | Their approach to learning is very open-minded. They thrive on activity and tend to decide first and learn afterwards. They learn best from short 'here and now' exercises, eg business games, group work. |
| *Reflectors* | They gather and reflect on all available information before making a decision. They take account of the wider picture. They prefer to stand back, listen, observe and record information, eg diaries, time logs. |
| *Theorists* | They think problems through in a logical, step-by-step way. Their decisions tend to be 'black and white', ie categorical. They use models, systems, concepts and theories, eg conventional science teaching. |
| *Pragmatists* | They are keen on practical approaches and on solving problems. They are down to earth – 'If it works, it works.' |

They seek to establish a close link between the subject matter and its practical application, eg projects, work-place training.

For individuals, it is valuable to play to strong learning styles, although it is also useful to seek to develop the other learning styles. Groups of individuals may benefit from emphasis on a particular style, too: a group of supervisors is more likely to respond to a pragmatic approach, whereas a group of young science graduates would probably respond better to a theoretical approach. In choosing appropriate learning techniques and opportunities you should consider the preferences of the individuals. Training that centres on a number of individuals will have to accommodate a variety of activities to cover the different styles of the participants.

---

**Activity 37**

Look back at the learning style descriptions. From these you should be able to decide who will benefit most from each of the following activities:

- 'having a go'

- taking a back seat in a meeting

- applying a new technique to a current problem

- an intellectual debate

- keeping a daily log

- being coached by an expert

- exciting experiences

- being cross-examined on a decision he or she has made.

---

Compare your views with those at the end of the chapter.

## Implementing training and development activities

The key to successful training activities is planning and preparation. In planning, it is helpful if you can regard people at events as *participants* in a learning process. Use of terms such as 'attenders', 'trainees' or even 'students' implies they are passive rather than actively involved in a process for which they have responsibility. Carefully consider each of the following:

- the learning objectives of the event (these can be broad or very specific but the accuracy with which they have been determined will be a major factor in the success of the event)

- how many will be trained at any one time

- the length of your learning sessions and how much will be learnt each session

- how much time is available and how you will divide it up

- the likely preferred learning styles of participants

- the range of training techniques available and their suitability

- how to involve participants in the learning process

- the pace of learning.

If you plan to run a workshop, seminar or training course you will also have to consider:

- the practical arrangements – room, layout etc

- the use of support material – handouts, videos, computer-prepared slides, other visual aids

- the training resources – flipchart, video tape recorder, overhead projector, data projection equipment etc. Make sure you know how to use any technology!

## CASE STUDY 16

The authors run workshops. Having identified the needs either generally or in conjunction with a client, their starting point is a series of behavioural objectives. These are similar to those in the chapters of this book but typically also include specific objectives for skill development.

We set a limit of 12 delegates at a time. Sometimes the more delegates you have the fewer questions are asked, and we encourage questions, so 12 works well. Most of our workshops run for six hours and we aim for blocks of about an hour and a half. These are not 'solid' blocks, but contain a mixture of approaches to cater for different learning styles.

We are keen also to provide *pragmatic* solutions, thus we provide frameworks for 'having a word' with an employee or for a 'return to work' interview. These give delegates techniques that they can take away and use.

Invariably there is some *activity*. Typically we seek to reinforce knowledge and techniques with practical exercises, perhaps a role-play, or a brief presentation.

Because many of our subjects have a legal underpin there has to be some *theory* behind the techniques we advocate. So as to involve the delegates, the flip chart is a useful visual aid. As we said, we love questions as these help delegates to test out theories and models.

We usually ask questions as well as answer them, because pertinent questions can encourage *reflection*. Finally, we ask delegates to plan some actions that they will take subsequently, as a result of the workshop. This provides further opportunity for reflection.

Neither training nor development activities need to take place in a work-shop or course environment, as we have already seen with the examples given in an earlier section. They should nevertheless have clear objec-tives, planned activities and appropriate support. Performance improvements should reviewed against those objectives regularly, until the desired performance is achieved.

Development will be a longer-term process with a cyclical pattern of broad objectives, actions, review and further objectives. There should be a senior trainer, coach or mentor to oversee the programme, help with review and to ensure that individuals have access to developmental opportunities.

---

**Activity 38**

Take training or development needs at your place of work. Write some learning objectives for addressing a specific need. These may include behavioural objectives, for example: 'to be confident about "having a word" with a subordinate'. Decide the activities that might be available as options for the training or development and select suitable ones. Write out a plan that addresses the issues discussed in this section. Then discuss your plan with a learning source.

---

Tip: If you want to develop your ability to plan programmes further, read some of the books in the further reading section on pages 170 and 171. We find that the content of Siddons (1997) and also of O'Connor and Seymour (1994) is very relevant to planning training activities.

When we have implemented our training there is one more task. It is not really the last task, because it is only one step in the training cycle. It is appropriate for it to lead to identification of further needs.

## Why should we evaluate our training and development?

It is important to remember that training and development activities are not ends in themselves. The nineteenth-century biologist T. H. Huxley said: 'The great end in life is not knowledge but action.' Unless our activi-ties result in some positive changes in the performance of our organis-ation, they have no relevant value. Therefore we should evaluate the action that results from our training, if we are to know whether it was worthwhile.

You will have noticed the emphasis placed on evaluation when we con-sidered the IiP principles earlier in this chapter. It is good practice to evaluate any business investment to learn lessons for the future. When we look at training, some particular reasons to consider are:

* justifying the expense

- providing feedback to the trainer

- providing feedback on techniques

- establishing whether the needs and objectives of the training have been met

- improving future programmes

- identifying further needs

- providing data for justifying further expenditure

- helping top management understand the broad costs and benefits of developing people.

We might be prompted to ask the question posed in the next heading.

### Why is training and development so frequently not evaluated?

Looking at the answers to this question helps to identify the practical problems.

- The benefits of training and development are often intangible: effectiveness may improve, but in ways that are not immediately obvious. Development activities help people to grow, to improve their judgement and to increase their value to an employer. Such skill develops gradually and may not become suddenly apparent on completion of the activities.

- Sometimes the objectives of the training and development have not been defined or, when they have, it may be difficult to measure whether they have been achieved.

- Even where measurable change exists, it is not always easy to establish a direct link between the training or development and the results, because there are many other factors that may impinge on the same changes.

The result is that evaluation is often confined to questionnaires completed by trainees at the end of a training course. Notwithstanding that courses are only one form of training activity, there are some reasons to be cautious in attaching too much importance to such questionnaires. Easterby-Smith and Tanton (1985) point out three drawbacks:

*Evaluations can be conservative*
This is because of:

- the personal investment made by trainers and their understandable anxiety about criticism

- the mutual interests of trainers and trainees in perpetuating a course

- the danger of adverse criticism reflecting on a trainee.

*Evaluations can be counter-productive*

This is because:

- they focus on what trainees want rather than what they need

- they encourage tutors to adopt styles that meet approval rather than being geared to meeting objectives.

**Table 13** Hamblin's levels of evaluation

| | **The levels** | **Methods of evaluation** | |
|---|---|---|---|
| ***Level 1*** | Reactions of the trainees – to the content and methods of training, to the trainer, and to any other factors perceived as relevant. What the trainee thought about the training. | Discussion<br>Interviews<br>Questionnaires<br>Recommendations of trainees<br>Desire for further training | |
| ***Level 2*** | Learning attained during the learning period.<br>Did the trainees learn what was intended? | *Behaviour*<br>*Knowledge and*<br>*understanding*<br>*Skills*<br><br><br><br>*Attitude* | Objectives attained<br>Examinations and other tests<br>Analysis by observation of demonstrated skill<br>Evidence of skills applied<br>Projects or assignments<br>Questionnaires |
| ***Level 3*** | Job behaviour in the work environment at the end of the training period.<br>Did the learning get transferred to the job? | Production rate<br>Customer complaints<br>Discuss with manager/subordinates/peers<br>Activity-sampling<br>Self-recording of specific incidents<br>Evidence of competence<br>Appraisal | |
| ***Level 4*** | Effect on the department.<br>Has the training helped the department's performance? | Minutes of meetings<br>Deadlines met<br>Stress indicators<br>Quality indicators<br>Interview other managers and superiors | |
| ***Level 5*** | 'The Ultimate Level'. Has the training affected the ultimate well-being of the organisation in terms of business objectives? | Standing of the training officer<br>Growth<br>Quality indicators<br>Stress indicators<br>Achievement of business goals and targets | |

*Inaccuracies may arise*

This is because:

- questionnaires are designed to look fair
- participants who feel aggrieved in one way respond in another.

It is worth noting that the fourth IiP principle states that an Investor in People understands the impact of its investment in people on its performance. This implies that we have to evaluate training beyond the level of course questionnaires and discover measures of performance within the organisation.

What we find particularly helpful in evaluating the effectiveness of training is a model proposed by Hamblin and described by Reid and Barrington (1999: 257) – see Table 13 – in which there are examples of measures for assessing the true value of training at each of five levels.

If, on evaluation, a particular piece of training has achieved its objectives and made a significant contribution to the success of your organisation, then you might consider applying for an NTA for your organisation (the awards are competitive). If successful, this accolade would provide substantial publicity: it would publicly recognise your success in following the training cycle.

---

**Activity 39**

Evaluation of a training programme, course, or exercise should be measured *against its objectives*. The result of the evaluation may legitimately lead to improved objectives, but the training event itself should be reviewed against the original objectives.

Take a learning activity in which you have been involved recently, perhaps a group exercise on a Certificate in Personnel Practice (CPP) programme if you are currently a participant. Investigate the objectives of the activity. Then discuss with others who have followed a similar activity the effectiveness of that activity. Try to decide how that effectiveness might be measured *at your place of work*. Concentrate on Level 3 of Hamblin's model (see Table 13) and, if you feel it appropriate, Level 4 or even 5. Look for some tangible measures, remembering that it is *actions* that really count in the workplace. Relate these back to the objectives in order to make your decision.

---

## The role of personnel practitioners

Your role in training and development activities will be largely determined by the structure and culture of your organisation. As a personnel practitioner you may be expected to take responsibility for training and development activities. If so, then the content of this chapter will be especially relevant to you.

### An influencing role

If you want to influence line managers towards better training decisions, you will benefit by learning to understand their needs. That means talking to them about what they are trying to achieve. You will then be in a position to make positive and helpful suggestions.

By becoming familiar with Government initiatives and sources of grant support you will increase your own value and credibility and, hence, your ability to influence.

Remember that many organisations still give training and development low priority. According to Sir John Harvey-Jones (1995), British businesses rarely spend more than 2 per cent of their total payroll budget on training and development, and yet compete with businesses who regard 10–20 per cent as a more appropriate figure. In the new millennium, has that percentage really changed? Your most valuable contribution could be to research the value of training and development for your employer and make clear cost-justified cases for improvement.

### An administrative role

You take this on when you concentrate on making the arrangements for training and for keeping the records. Significant costs from the previous training budget can be saved by effective arrangements and diligent negotiation. Well-organised records on objectives and outcomes can provide valuable information for evaluating the true benefits of training activities. However, if you want to break out of the administrative mould you should use your learning in this chapter and your unique access to training records to move towards an influencing role.

### A training role

This comes into play when you are appointed as a personnel *and* training practitioner. If you are so appointed, you will have clear training responsibilities. If this also involves *delivering* training on a regular basis, then you may consider trying to specialise in training or personnel rather than spreading your skills and responsibilities too thinly.

Delivery of training requires planning and thorough preparation. Personnel responsibilities often require you to respond to demands that arise suddenly and unexpectedly. Therefore the two responsibilities do not always sit very comfortably alongside each other.

### A decision-making role

Here you have the opportunity to make decisions about training needs, about the response to those needs and about the effectiveness of the response. This chapter should have given you the basic understanding you require to start making decisions. If you are new to the task, then commence slowly and build up your experience as you go round the training cycle.

### An overseeing role

This role requires you to keep in touch with all the training activities in your sphere of responsibility, which will help you to influence others, as we discussed above. You may be able to pick out many ways of improving the relevance and effectiveness of training.

## Summary

We have looked at the steps of the training cycle and used those to examine the management of training and development. It is the changes in the environment in which a business operates, and people's job and career changes, that create the need for training.

Training needs can be identified at the level of the organisation, job or occupation, and at the individual employee level. We have to consider not just what may require training but whether that is both important in the job and likely to be recognised or rewarded within the culture of the organisation.

Training needs are established by examining the gap between the performance that is sought and the performance currently being achieved. A wide variety of sources is available to help determine both the desired performance and current performance. Competency frameworks can be particularly useful.

In formulating plans for training and development it is important to examine the internal resources available, the external resources and the relevance of qualifications. We can select from a wide variety of techniques and opportunities and should never restrict our concept of training and development to training courses alone. Individuals have preferences for the ways in which they learn – their learning styles. The choice of training activities should take this into account.

To complete the learning cycle, we emphasised the value of evaluating training, considered some of the practical obstacles and identified a model that can help structure our evaluation.

If you have the opportunity to be involved in training and development activities, then we suggest you involve yourself with enthusiasm. There is much to be gained.

**Feedback on Activity 37**

Activists like to 'have a go' and are unlikely to shrink from exciting experiences.

Reflectors are more likely to take a back seat in a meeting so as to absorb what is happening. Keeping a daily log is consistent with a tendency to learn from reflection.

Pragmatists like techniques that solve problems and should respond well to coaching (from those who know how to get tasks done, that is to say, not from a counsellor who may reflect the problem back on them)

Theorists will welcome an intellectual debate and are likely to be tolerant should their reasons for a decision be cross-examined.

## References and further reading

ARKIN A. (1997) 'Call centre stress'. *Personnel Management*. 6 February. pp22–25.

EASTERBY-SMITH M. *and* TANTON M. (1985) 'Turning course evaluation from an end to a means'. *Personnel Management*. April. pp25–27.

FAIRBAIRNS J. (1991) 'Plugging the gap in training needs analysis'. *Personnel Management*. February. pp43–45.

HARRISON R. (2002) *Learning and Development*. London, Chartered Institute of Personnel and Development.

HARVEY-JONES SIR J. (1995) *All Together Now*. London, Mandarin.

HONEY P. *and* MUMFORD A. (1992a) *The Manual of Learning Styles*. Maidenhead, Honey.

HONEY P. *and* MUMFORD A. (1992b) *Using Your Learning Styles*. Maidenhead, Honey.

O'CONNOR J. *and* SEYMOUR J. (1994) *Training with NLP*. London, HarperCollins.

REID M. A. *and* BARRINGTON H. A. (1999) *Training Interventions: Managing employee development*. 6th edn. London, Institute of Personnel and Development.

WHIDDETT S. *and* HOLLYFORDE S. (1999) *The Competencies Handbook*. London, Institute of Personnel and Development.

Investors in People UK provide a number of publications, in particular:

*The Investors in People Standard* (IiP80a).

*How to Become an Investor in People* (IiP82a).

There is a variety of information available from your local LSC, LEC or SBS on NVQs/SVQs. See also the Chartered Institute of Personnel and Development's *Management Shapers* and *Training Essentials* series, which covers all aspects of the training cycle. In particular see:

BOYDELL T. *and* LEARY M. (1996) *Identifying Training Needs*. London, Institute of Personnel and Development.

BRAMLEY P. (1996) *Evaluating Training*. London, Institute of Personnel and Development.

SIDDONS S. (1997) *Delivering Training*. London, Institute of Personnel and Development.

National Training Awards publish a brochure giving interesting case studies from award winners. For more information, contact National Training Awards Office, W8, Moorfoot, Sheffield S1 4PQ; tel. 0114 259 3419.

### Websites

| | |
|---|---|
| BBC Education | www.bbc.co.uk/education/home/ |
| Chartered Institute of Personnel and Development | www.cipd.co.uk |
| Investors in People UK | www.investorsinpeople.co.uk |
| Qualifications and Curriculum Authority | www.open.gov.uk/qca/ |
| National Training Awards | www.open.gov.uk/dfee/nta |
| National Vocational Qualifications | www.dfee.gov.uk/nvq.htm |
| *People Management* | www.peoplemanagement.co.uk |
| Fenman Ltd | www.fenman.co.uk |
| Malcolm Martin Associates | www.personnel-practice.co.uk |

• Performance Management

## CHAPTER OBJECTIVES

After reading this chapter you will:

● understand that performance management is a broader concept than performance appraisal and involves a number of people management interventions

● appreciate the wide variety of performance appraisal schemes within organisations and be able to take steps to ensure your own scheme is working effectively

● be able to identify the key components of your organisation's payment system and the part that they play in motivating employees.

## Introduction

Recent research shows that many organisations claim to adopt performance management techniques, of which there are several, though the mix of these activities varies greatly from one organisation to the next. According to Armstrong and Baron (1998: 391), the attitudes of managers and workers towards performance management are positive ones and both parties feel that they gain from the process. Research by the Industrial Society suggests that performance management schemes boost staff retention. As with most personnel and development activities, experiences will vary greatly and among the success stories there will be accounts of poorly designed and implemented performance management systems.

In the next section, we shall consider why performance management is important for personnel practitioners and the organisations they work for, before looking at the differences between performance appraisal and performance management. We shall then go on to look at performance appraisal in more detail: its purposes, history and trends; the move towards competence-based performance review; the various components of schemes, including the issue of objective-setting; and best-practice considerations. We shall then provide sections on good practice in giving and receiving feedback, payment systems, particularly performance-related pay (PRP), and the legal considerations. Finally, we shall examine the differing roles played by the personnel practitioner and the skills necessary for effective appraisal interviewing.

Before doing this we would draw your attention to another distinction in terms: performance management *v* managing performance. The first term tends to be used in reference to activities designed to motivate and encourage employees to work towards objectives that are in line with organisational goals. The second term includes managing good and poor performance, and therefore encompasses activities such as disciplinary procedures and absence control. We shall be concentrating here on performance management, not managing performance, and would refer you to the chapter on Employee Relations (Chapter 8) for reference to managing poor performers via disciplinary or capability routes. Please note that the two processes of disciplinary procedures and performance appraisal should complement each other in these circumstances.

## Why is performance management important?

Suffice it to say here that without performance management, work will not be organised to achieve the optimum results. For instance:

- Salespeople may be achieving their sales targets, but the discounts and special incentives that they offer customers in order to do so have a detrimental effect on the profit margins – profit being the driving force of the company they are working for.

- A university lecturer whose brief is to recruit a certain number of students to a full-time course of study may find that in the current economic climate there is less money available for grants and other means of finance. Thus there is a smaller pool of potential candidates with the requisite qualifications than in previous years. The college tutor decides that, rather than failing to reach the target, he or she will have to lower the entry requirements to the course. This will satisfy the immediate 'input' need but is likely to lead to problems at the 'output' stage, because a larger percentage of students may fail to get the qualification under study. The university's finances (and business goals) will be dependent on the overall input *and* output targets being reached.

- Computer helpline staff may point to the numbers of users they have helped over a period of time as an indication of their hard work and efficiency. However, this figure does not take account of those users who failed to get through the busy switchboard system and had to seek assistance elsewhere. If the main aims of the computer company are to increase market share and maintain customer loyalty, then this aspect of 'after sales' service would need to be re-evaluated. The dissatisfied group of customers will be less inclined to buy from the same supplier again and will also not recommend friends and colleagues to do so.

Thus we can see, in the above examples, that the employees concerned were all seeking to do what they had been told to do, ie they were probably being efficient, but were they being effective?

**Efficient** – doing things right
**Effective** – doing the right things

The answer is no: in each case, insufficient thought had been giving to ensuring that employees' individual targets were geared towards the overall business goals. The key is to ensure that there is a clear link between the tasks and activities that employees are involved in and the achievement of organisational goals. It is also crucial that evaluation methods are set up to judge whether this is the case. We shall return to this question in the following section.

## Performance appraisal v performance management

In very simple terms, performance appraisal is the 'tail that wags the dog' in its relationship with performance management. The exercise of appraising performance is necessarily retrospective, because it concerns making a judgement about the past performance of employees. Appraisals can be used to improve current performance by providing feedback on strengths and weaknesses. (NB 'weaknesses' are probably better labelled 'areas for improvement' or 'developmental needs' if we wish to emphasise the positive and constructive nature of this feedback.) Appraisals can, therefore, be effective in increasing employee motivation and, ultimately, organisational performance. Performance appraisal can, and should, be linked to a performance-improvement process, and can then also be used to identify training needs and potential, agree future objectives, focus on career development and solve problems. One such performance improvement process would be a performance management system (PMS).

Performance management is a vehicle for the continuous improvement of business performance via a co-ordinated programme of people management *interventions* (or systems). Mike Walters (1995: x) lists these interventions as follows:

- strategic planning
- the definition of organisational goals, priorities and values
- the identification and application of appropriate performance goals and measures for the organisation, for key processes, for functions and for individual employees
- appraisal
- personal development planning
- learning and development activities
- various forms of PRP.

The last of these, PRP, demonstrates the need to ensure a link between the PMS and your organisation's payment system and administration.

## CASE STUDY 17

The company sells and hires cars as well as running a garage to sell petrol and other goods. Several staff are employed, each specialising in one of the above areas or in accounting or clerical positions. The majority of staff enjoy their jobs and feel that they are reasonably well rewarded in terms of financial and other benefits. There is no formal means of appraising staff, but the owner-manager does see all staff on a regular basis to inform them of their progress and to discuss any problems. He adopts a well-used 'open-door' policy. In the main, the employees are highly motivated and industrious, and achieve high efficiencies in the work that they do.

With such a favourable environment, you might assume that the overall business performance of the company would be optimised. But you would be wrong, because the owner-manager recently discovered that the profits for the last tax year were not as high as he had expected. To cut a long story short, he employed a placement student studying a personnel management qualification to investigate the reasons for this enigma. The answer, when it was discovered, was a simple one: the employees were hard-working but, because there was no link between their personal objectives and the organisational goal (in this case, profit), the result was that though they could be deemed to be efficient, they were not effective.

After a period of research, which consisted mostly of interviews with staff, the student produced a comprehensive report for the owner-manager. This covered her research findings as well as providing a lot of information on performance management in general. The owner-manager saw that there were some systems already in place but that there was a lack of co-ordination between them all. For instance, the car sales staff were expected to provide relief cover when the person employed on the hire car counter was at lunch. The sales staff resented this because they felt that they might miss sales opportunities owing to being 'tied up' at the car hire desk. Their individual and team per-

formance sales targets were naturally seen as a much higher priority than the need to provide a quality service to potential car hire customers. Further, the former activities were rewarded by the payment of commissions, whereas the latter 'customer care' activities were not formally assessed by their manager and did not attract any sort of reward, financial or otherwise. The hiring of cars, however, did contribute substantially to the overall profit level of the company and, unlike car sales, provided a steadier flow of income, because car hire is less subject to seasonal trends. To the owner-manager, who set the business goals, it was equally important to maintain a good reputation for selling quality cars as it was to provide a reliable and competitive car hire service.

With the help of the student, the owner-manager decided to clarify the business strategy, review the existing interventions and to scrap, modify or replace them (as appropriate) in line with the company's goals. However, he also learnt that a balance needs to be struck between reward-driven and development-driven approaches. This is because performance management systems can fail when their implementation becomes dominated by the link to reward. Thus schemes designed to improve employee performance, eg incentive, bonus, profit-sharing and commission approaches, can have the opposite effect when employee expectations are not realised. In fact, the owner-manager had experienced this in the past when there was an unexpected rise in the price of petrol. In order to preserve his profits, he was forced to reduce the pot of money available for a discretionary bonus paid to the shop staff. They therefore received much less than had been anticipated based on their past experiences. Although the reasons were fully explained at the time, it took quite a while for the shop staff to regain their normal levels of motivation: they felt that though they had been working hard, they had been punished for something that was outside their control.

**Figure 4**   The two-way links model

As we point out in Chapter 4, good computer links between the payroll and other personnel systems are often difficult to make. If, for instance, poor communications (or links) lead to late or incorrect payment of PRP, this will be detrimental to the motivational effects of a good PMS. Each and every intervention needs to be clearly linked together in order that their overall impact on business performance can be carefully co-ordinated. We discuss payment systems and PRP in particular in more detail in a later section.

As we have already stated, there is no universally accepted definition of performance management, but we can safely say that it is a much broader concept than performance appraisal. To demonstrate this, consider the example of a small owner-managed garage in Case Study 17.

The main lesson that the owner-manager learnt in the above case study was that there should be clear and co-ordinated two-way links in all the stages between the strategic plan and individual objectives (see Figure 4).

This model does not mean that individuals cannot seek to satisfy their own personal objectives, but it does help to focus them on their own roles and contribution to the overall business performance. The result will hopefully be a motivational one as their efforts are directed at those activities which best serve organisational goals. (Further consideration of this motivational aspect is provided in the following text.)

The issues are the same regardless of the size of organisation; the key is to ensure that there are feedback mechanisms in place, as demonstrated in Figure 4. To return to our case study, the owner-manager was able, with the help of the student, to begin the process of ensuring that the new and revamped PMS was fully co-ordinated and geared towards the achievement of business objectives. This was not a trouble-free process, but the result was an encouraging improvement in the level of profits in the following year. One example of a new intervention was the one set up to reward the achievement of a monthly car hire target, based on maximising the use of the hire cars. The car hire employee was sent on a selling course in order to improve her skills at getting new business (she had previously viewed her job as simply an administrative one). The system involved accumulating points towards the team target and included all those staff who provided cover on the car hire desk. This may not have been a perfect solution but did ensure that all the staff involved were 'rowing in the same direction'.

We shall now consider one aspect within the wider framework of performance management: performance appraisal. There have been major developments in the field of performance appraisal in recent years and, after explaining its purposes, we shall briefly cover its history and trends.

## Performance appraisal

### Purposes

There are three main groups of purposes for performance appraisal (and most schemes incorporate at least two of these):

- *performance reviews* – managers discuss with employees progress in their current posts, their strengths and the areas requiring further development, in order to improve *current performance*

- *potential reviews* – managers discuss with employees the opportunities for progression, and the type of work they will be fitted for in the future and how this can be achieved, by identifying their *developmental needs* and career aspirations

- *reward reviews* – these are usually separate from the appraisal system but the decisions on *rewards* such as pay, benefits, promotion and self-fulfilment are fed by the information provided by performance appraisal.

Properly conducted performance appraisal interviews will usually involve a manager and employee in a constructive discussion concerning the employee's recent performance (say, over the previous 12 months), plans for improved performance, which will probably involve agreeing future objectives or targets (see below), and plans for meeting the developmental needs of the employee. At a later stage, a reward review interview will be arranged so that the manager and employee can openly discuss, for instance, the level of PRP that has been awarded.

As personnel practitioners, you are likely to know already that such events do not always go according to plan. For instance:

- Not all employees are good performers, and managers may not be as constructive as they should in their delivery of feedback.

Table 14   Performance appraisal and employee motivation

| Peters and Waterman factors | How performance appraisal can satisfy these needs |
|---|---|
| Need for meaning | Clear linking of individual jobs with the objectives of the organisation |
| Need for control | Joint discussion between subordinate and manager regarding future job priorities and targets |
| Need for positive reinforcement | Provision of effective feedback from manager to subordinate |
| Actions shape attitudes and beliefs | Performance appraisal as the starting-point for deciding future action, which entails senior-level commitment to help the individual develop |

- In an organisation in which there are few promotion opportunities, employees (and their managers) may view learning and development activities as somewhat pointless.

- If a high-performing individual's expectation of PRP is not realised (often through factors outside his or her own control) then he or she may decide not to try so hard to achieve targets or objectives in the future.

Thus the motivational effect of performance appraisal is often debatable. On a positive note, Hale and Whitlam (1995: 2) provide an interesting model – see Table 14 – of how performance appraisal can be used to satisfy employees' basic motivational needs (based on the now famous research of Peters and Waterman (1982) into successful organisations).

We shall discuss the skills of performance appraisal interviewing, applicable in both good and poor performer situations, in a later section.

## History and trends

As we have already said, with the emergence of performance management the main change in performance appraisal schemes has been the establishment of clearer links between individual objectives and organisational goals. In recent years there have been other changes, many of which have complemented this principle. Hale and Whitlam (1995: 19–22) provide the following breakdown of recent trends.

*From traits to results-based assessment*
In the 1960s a Management by Objectives (MbO) approach evolved,

based on a more scientific approach and on more forward-focused performance appraisal. Thus there was a move from schemes that made judgements on employees' traits and behaviours such as leadership, teamwork and diligence to those where the emphasis was placed on the achievement of results and outputs linked to targets. MbO schemes are still in existence today, but many have foundered because they failed to establish the link between individual and organisational objectives.

### From effort to results focus
In line with the MbO approach, the method of assessment has shifted away from effort measures such as concentration, enthusiasm and self-organisation to results measures such as quality of work, sound decision-making and financial performance.

### From judgemental to joint problem-solving
The closed type of appraisal scheme in which the manager told the employee what judgement had been made on his or her performance has given way to a more open, joint identification of strengths and weaknesses, as well as joint planning for improved future performance. (In line with this we have seen self-appraisal play a much more important role in the whole process – indeed it may form the basis for the appraisal interview in some schemes.)

### From managerial to all jobs
Whereas many organisations still operate separate schemes for appraising managerial and non-managerial posts, there has been a move towards incorporating employees at all levels within the performance appraisal system.

We can add two further trends to this list:

### From top-down to 360-degree appraisals
Appraisals have moved on from a fairly simple manager–subordinate (or top-down) relationship (possibly including self-appraisal) to 360-degree appraisals, involving stakeholders who provide feedback on an individual's performance.

Figure 5 shows an example of the stakeholders that might be involved in an individual's appraisal. There is a great variety in the way in which 360-degree appraisal is implemented in organisations. On the one hand, the appraisal interview may include all the stakeholders giving face-to-face feedback to the appraisee (who may well feel that the term 'victim' is more appropriate here!). On the other hand, some organisations operate systems whereby the collection of feedback from the chosen stakeholders is done via formally constructed questionnaires. This information is then collated and fed back to the individual by a neutral third party (possibly a personnel practitioner). Larger organisations have even invested in computer packages to cut down on the administrative burden attached to collecting and collating this information on a large scale.

**Figure 5**  Stakeholders in 360-degree appraisal

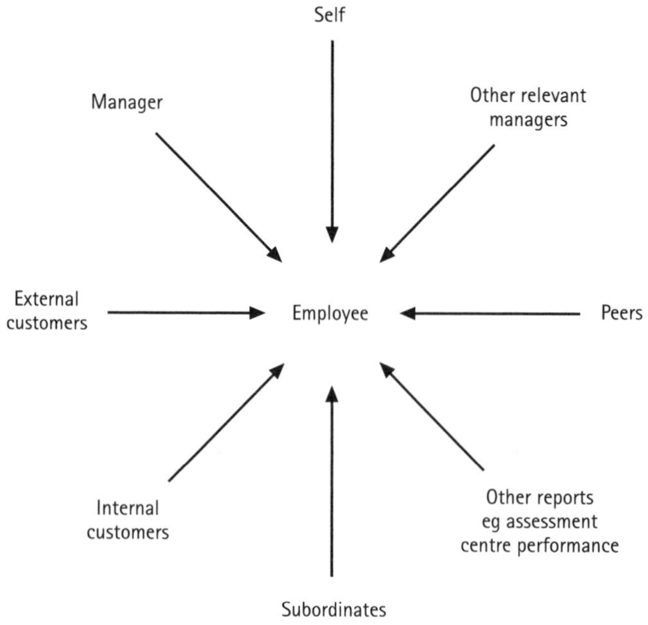

*From achievements to competencies*

Following on from the shift in focus from 'effort' to 'results' above, we have seen a move from just concentrating on 'what' a job-holder achieves to also assessing 'how' the job is carried out. Thus many organisations now review the achievement of objectives and targets as well as the behaviour exhibited by the job-holder. This competency-based approach can be applied across the full range of personnel and development processes, but is particularly relevant to job evaluation, recruitment and selection, training and development, performance review and reward.

## Performance review

As a result of the above trends, most performance appraisal schemes nowadays follow the stages of the performance review cycle as set out in Figure 6.

According to Whiddett and Hollyforde (1999: 94), competencies can make significant contributions to all stages of the performance review process, ie by:

● identifying factors relevant to performance in the job

● collecting information on performance

● organising the information

Figure 6   The performance review cycle

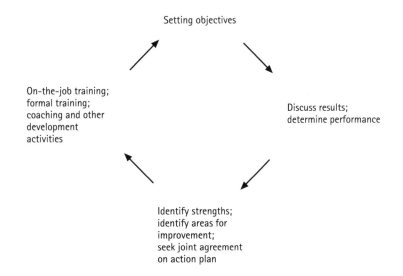

- discussing or reviewing the information (eg for solo reviews)
- agreeing outcomes.

We shall discuss the much-debated issue of objective-setting shortly, but first let's look at the various components of performance appraisal schemes.

### Components of performance appraisal schemes

If you are designing a performance appraisal scheme, you need first to determine its purpose (or purposes) and seek to integrate the new scheme into your PMS, if one exists. Against this backdrop you then need to make the following decisions, depending on the organisational circumstances:

1   Who is to be appraised? That is, you must decide what levels or functions of employees are to be involved.

2   Who appraises? This could be the employee; the manager only; the manager and subordinates; or other stakeholders (see the previous section regarding 360-degree appraisal).

3   What is to be appraised, and what criteria will be used? The options include traits v results v competency-based assessment, and achievement of objectives.

4   What assessment methods will you employ? You could opt for a descriptive or narrative report; a checklist; ratings or gradings; comparison with objectives; comparison with others (ranking individuals in order of performance); critical incidents (recorded incidents of positive and negative behaviours); or

**Figure 7** Meeting customer needs

Anticipates, responds to and seeks to exceed the expectations of existing and potential customers

| Competent | Needs developing |
|---|---|
| Strives to provide the best customer service | Unhelpful to customers, not taking time to understand what they need and then jumping in with any solution |
| Adopts a positive and professional approach to meet the needs of customers | Sees customers as 'not part of my job' – focuses instead on internal or administative requirements |
| Provides advice that is beneficial to both customers and the Bank | Does not combine products to meet customer needs |
| Always ready to help by anticipating and responding to customers' needs in the most appropriate way | Is target-driven, ignoring customers' real requirements |

Self-control

Performs effectively by keeping emotions under control, particularly in stressful and difficult situations

| Competent | Needs developing |
|---|---|
| Patient and even-tempered | Flustered – runs around panicking |
| Remains calm, does not appear to become irritable or anxious | Takes the reactions of other people very personally |
| Does not panic under pressure | Appears childish, petulant |
| Does not react to provocation – maintains poise and professionalism when challenged | Loses cool, becomes aggressive or defensive |
| Accepts refusals and rebuffs, does not take things personally | Bottles up stress and explodes – takes out frustrations on others |

Extracted from the Barclays Bank plc *Performance Attributes Directory* and reproduced with their kind permission.

competence-based (assessment against the achievement of set standards). An example of this last method is provided in Figure 7 above.

Please note that you may need to define different standards for each competency, according to the level and responsibilities of the job under consideration.

5 Will you incorporate assessment of promotion potential; a link to reward or a salary review; a means of appeal against a (perceived) unfair assessment?

6 How often is the formal appraisal interview to be carried out – once every three, six or twelve months? Will you include interim reviews to accommodate the pace of change?

7   How will you ensure that the action points are implemented (eg the meeting of training needs)?

8   How will you evaluate success (ie the achievement of the purpose(s) of the scheme)?

---

**Activity 40**

Find out as much as you can about the appraisal scheme(s) used by your organisation (or another organisation with which you are familiar). Investigate the paperwork, talk to your manager and other line managers, talk to other employees, and use other learning sources to compare your practices with those of outside organisations. Then answer the eight questions above.

---

The ACAS advisory booklet *Employee Appraisal* (1998: 14) lists the following key points for successful appraisal schemes:

- Make sure that senior managers are fully committed to the idea of appraisals.

- Consult with managers, employees and trade union representatives about the design and implementation of appraisals before they are introduced.

- Monitor schemes regularly.

- Give appraisers adequate training to enable them to make fair and objective assessments and to carry out effective appraisal interviews.

- Keep the scheme as simple and straightforward as possible.

We could add the following suggestions:

- Before implementing the scheme across the whole organisation, carry out a pilot run in, say, one department in order to gain invaluable feedback on possible teething problems that can then be solved before the main launch. Start with the most senior people in your pilot area, so that you gain their commitment and encourage them to lead by example and to cascade their learning downwards.

- Ensure that appraisers and appraisees jointly identify strengths and areas for improvement, and that appraisers provide constructive feedback on performance and support the appraisee in meeting their development needs in line with business goals.

**Activity 41**

Following on from Activity 40, suggest some improvements that could be made to the scheme(s) you have chosen for your analysis. Present them in the form of a written report to senior management, making sure that you justify your proposals.

We have mentioned the place of objective-setting several times within the context of performance appraisal and performance management. We shall now seek to examine this concept further.

## Objective-setting

The recent trend from a focus on traits or behaviours to a results-oriented approach has seen the emergence of objective-setting as a key issue. Objectives are about improvement and there are a number of levels:

- business objectives
- team/division/departmental objectives linking with the above
- individual objectives linking with all of the above

as well as

- individual objectives resulting from developmental needs
- project objectives
- training and development objectives.

However, rather than seeking to *set* objectives, managers would be better advised to attempt to *agree* objectives with their staff. Thus, during the course of the appraisal process the manager and employee should seek to agree objectives for the forthcoming period which comply with the mnemonic SMARTS:

*S*pecific

*M*easurable

*A*greed

*R*ealistic

*T*imebound

*S*tretching

Which of the following two objectives is SMARTS?

1   To improve supervisory skills by taking responsibility for the training and development of a new trainee over the coming year.

2   To research, design and implement a new sickness absence monitoring system that differentiates between certified and uncertified absences and that records frequency, duration and reasons for absence. (This new system would be linked into a company-wide initiative to reduce costs by appropriate absence management techniques.) The budget for this exercise is $x$, the ongoing maintenance costs should be limited to two clerical labour hours a month, and the time-scale for implementation is $y$ months.

The first example is not SMARTS because it is not specific and its outcomes would be difficult to measure. However, the second example provides a *specific* task with several *measurable* outcomes for the evaluation of success. The objective is presumably (barring disasters) *realistic* for the employee working with available resources, and is clearly *timebound*. It would also be *stretching* if it involved the employee in areas of work that he or she would not normally encounter in day-to-day activities. Thus he or she would be able to build on new experiences and develop new skills and would be more likely to *agree* it. This individual objective is also clearly linked to an organisational goal: cutting costs.

Obviously, not all objectives can be defined in this way because many lean more to qualitative rather than quantitative measurement, which is necessarily more subjective. Nevertheless, the mnemonic SMARTS provides an ideal to which you should aspire as far as possible.

---

**Activity 42**

Think about your own job role and what you would like to achieve over the next 12 months. Write down three to six key objectives for this period. Make sure that the majority of them tie in with business goals and that they all comply with the SMARTS guidelines. Discuss them with one of your learning sources.

---

We shall now return to considering performance appraisal in general terms by looking at the benefits of a well-designed and implemented scheme before we summarise best-practice issues.

### Benefits of performance appraisal

Employees are often suspicious of new or revised appraisal schemes, particularly during times of rapid change or rationalisation. If you are faced with the task of introducing a new or updated scheme, you should pick your timing carefully, because many employees (sometimes rightly) view such innovations as a cynical way of selecting candidates for redundancy. As a consequence, many employers (particularly in the educational field) have sought to shift the emphasis from an appraisal approach (current performance) to a developmental approach (future needs).

Table 15   Benefits of performance appraisal

| For the organisation | For the individual |
| --- | --- |
| Improved communication of business goals | Increased understanding of strategic aims and own role in organisational success |
| Improvements in work performance and therefore overall business performance via, for example, increased productivity or customer service | Increased motivation

Increased job satisfaction |
| Identification of potential to aid succession planning | Development of potential

Better informed career planning |
| Training provision or development activities targeted at identified needs rather than provided on an ad hoc or 'first come, first served' basis | Increased ability to meet own individual objectives as well as wider department or business objectives |
| Evaluation of effectiveness of selection criteria for new or newly promoted employees | Opportunity to publicise ambition |
| More objective distribution of rewards | Better understanding of the link between effort, performance and reward |
| Improved retention of employees | Employability security |

In any event, if the design incorporates the list of key points provided in the section above on the components of performance appraisal schemes, the benefits for both the organisation and the individual should include the items listed in Table 15.

The above benefits demonstrate why organisations should seriously consider the value of introducing performance appraisal, but they should also bear in mind the many potential pitfalls. A half-hearted attempt to introduce formal performance appraisal may be more damaging in the long run than no attempt at all.

The training videos in this field usually present excellent 'good' and 'bad' practice scenarios for comparison (see the end of this chapter for recommended titles). The examples of bad practice may be considered extreme, used for their entertainment value only, but there are indeed many genuine horror stories to relate regarding employees' experiences of performance appraisal.

In order to help you to avoid the pitfalls suffered by some performance appraisal schemes, we have summarised a list of best-practice features.

## Best practice in performance appraisal

Performance appraisal should incorporate the following:

- support from top management
- systems that are open and participative
- agreement at all levels about the purpose(s) of the scheme
- separation of reward reviews from the appraisal interviews
- clear, specific and well-communicated (SMARTS) objectives that are jointly agreed
- line managers' recognition of their role in this process, ie it is not seen as a personnel function
- clear link to the disciplinary procedure when handling poor performance so that the messages to the employee are the same
- training for appraisers *and* appraisees, including giving and receiving feedback
- a 'maintenance' programme to ensure that follow-up action is taken, eg training or development programmes are arranged as agreed
- a flexible culture to cater for individual and organisational needs
- simple administrative procedures
- consistency in managers' reporting standards
- formal regular appraisals and interim informal reviews between managers and their staff regarding performance and progress.

Finally you should ensure that there is vertical and horizontal integration of the performance appraisal scheme within the business. Vertical integration means that there needs to be a link between the purposes of performance appraisal and the business strategy. Horizontal integration means there has to be a 'fit' between performance appraisal and other personnel and development activities.

In the list above, we pointed out that appraisal training should include instruction in giving and receiving feedback. We will now consider this important issue.

## Giving and receiving feedback

Here we are not referring only to the giving and receiving of feedback in formal performance reviews, but also to the regular and informal

**Table 16** The dos and don'ts of giving constructive feedback

Do ensure that your comments are:
- objective and based on facts or observations
- specific
- focused on behaviour, not personality (what people do, not what they are)
- based on behaviour that can be controlled by the recipient of the feedback
- timely
- given in an adult-to-adult, respectful, non-judgemental way
- regular and informal, not only given as part of the appraisal process
- an appropriate balance of positive and negative
- non-prescriptive, leaving the recipient with the choice of whether or not to change
- in amounts from which people can learn
- two-way.

Don't:
- start by asking questions – for example, 'Guess what's in my mind?'
- make a statement, and then soften it by going round the houses with ifs, buts and maybes
- go straight to suggestions of how things might be put right
- talk down to people, tell them off or adopt an 'I know best' attitude.

*Source*: SWINBURNE P. (2001). 'How to use feedback to improve performance'. *People Management*. 31 May. p46.

feedback that employees should be able to expect throughout the year. Obviously not all feedback will be positive and anecdotal evidence unfortunately suggests that managers are reluctant to give negative feedback and employees are poor at receiving it. But poorly handled feedback can have a detrimental effect on future performance and working relationships so we must work hard to try and get it right.

In Table 16 above we seek to identify how feedback, whether negative or positive, can be given in a constructive way.

Following this advice can be very powerful in terms of getting your message across in the right way and in helping the recipient to understand and accept what you are saying. This is demonstrated in the case study below.

## CASE STUDY 18

The manager of the soft furnishings department of a large store in Oxford Street, central London, was not known for his tact and diplomacy. He was regarded as a workaholic and expected his staff to meet his own high standards of commitment and loyalty. He particularly detested poor timekeeping and any behaviours which he considered amounted to less than 100 per cent attention to customer service. Last week he bawled out one of his retail assistants when she returned late from her lunch break. He called her 'a lazy, idle, good-for-nothing' in front of two of her colleagues. The assistant was very upset about this incident and is thinking of handing in her resignation rather than carry on working for this man.

---

**Activity 43**

In case study 18

1    What 'sins' did the manager commit?

2    How should he have tackled this situation?

Compare your responses with the feedback provided at the end of this chapter.

---

In the case study above we saw how destructive feedback can be and, in such a situation, it would be difficult for the recipient to react in a constructive way. In any event, employees often lack the skills to receive feedback effectively, even positive feedback. For instance, when someone unexpectedly praises or thanks you, you may be inclined to reply with statements such as 'it was nothing' or 'it's just part of my job'. What's the result? That person may be less inclined to praise or thank you next time!

So how should we receive feedback?

**Table 17**    Tips for receiving feedback

- Listen to the message
- Do not defend or argue
- Clarify if you are unsure
- Accept praise; don't write it off
- Focus on what is being said; don't feel that you have to agree or disagree
- Ensure that you understand what is being said; show that you understand
- Consider asking what they would like to see done differently
- Thank the giver – they have just taken a risk for you.

*Source*: SWINBURNE P. (2001). 'How to use feedback to improve performance'. *People Management*. 31 May. p47.

Throughout the discussion of performance appraisal above we have been touching on the related issue of reward and, more particularly, payment systems. We shall now examine this topic further.

## Payment systems

### Performance-related pay

UK organisations have in recent years tended to move away from the incremental salary systems established in the 1970s, and performance-related pay (PRP) is nowadays the dominant force. PRP is, however, another of those terms that mean different things to different people. The Institute of Personnel Management (now the CIPD) provided a useful definition on this subject (IPM 1990: 1):

> *Performance-related pay is the explicit link of financial reward to individual, group or company performance (or any combination of the three)... The principal types of performance-related pay are merit pay, individual incentives, group/company perform-ance bonuses and other variable payments which employees may earn which are related to team performance improve-ments.*

Thus, payment systems such as salaries, fixed hourly rates and, if we concentrate only on cash rewards, profit-related pay and profit-sharing, are not included.

We stated earlier in this chapter that if a PMS is to be successful, then each and every aspect of it (or each 'intervention', to use Mike Walters's term) must be clearly linked and work towards the overall aim of con-tinually improving business performance. This can be achieved only through your employees, who will expect to be rewarded for their loyalty, hard work and contribution both *extrinsically* (factors generated by others) via promotions, salary, fringe benefits, bonuses, stock options etc and *intrinsically* (self-generated factors) via feelings of achievement, responsibility, personal growth, competence etc. The satisfactory inte-gration of reward into the PMS is undoubtedly a difficult thing to achieve – not least because the factors that motivate employees vary from indi-vidual to individual. Further, for each individual, motivating factors fluc-tuate in their importance according to the changing circumstances of their lives. There is even disagreement about whether some extrinsic rewards have any motivational impact at all, but here we shall proceed on the assumption that they do have a short-term effect in increasing effort and, therefore, productivity.

---

### Activity 44

We do not intend to cover motivation theories as this text focuses on practice rather than theory and they are well documented elsewhere, for example in *Employee Reward* in this People and Organisations series (see further reading, page 199) Find out what you can about the established theories such as those provided by Maslow, Herzberg and Vroom and decide which one you relate to most and why. How do you think your chosen theory could increase productivity or efficiency in your organisation? Discuss your conclusions with one of your learning sources.

---

In the context of performance management, we are concerned with the types of payment system available to organisations to encourage their employees to make worthwhile contributions towards the achievement of business goals. Armstrong and Murlis (1991: 282) state that for payment systems to act as real incentives to employees they must satisfy three basic requirements:

- that the reward should bear a direct relation to the effort

- that the payment should follow immediately or soon after the effort

- that the method of calculation should be simple and easily understood.

Thus payment systems such as salaries, fixed hourly rates and profit-sharing do not satisfy all of the above requirements. However, many PRP schemes are designed to succeed on all three counts. For instance, merit pay schemes may provide salary or wage increases in recognition of excellent job performances during the review period, and incentive or bonus schemes may provide payments in addition to base salary or wages related to the satisfactory completion of a project or the achievement of an individual or group target.

But PRP is not without its problems, mainly because of the difficulties encountered in trying to measure individual or team performance objectively and in establishing the most appropriate pay-out levels. For instance, working hard all year to be eligible for a maximum merit award of 4 per cent would probably be less motivating than seeking to achieve, say, three specific targets and a bonus payment of 10 to 20 per cent. Further, as stated in the IPM Factsheet (IPM 1990: 4):

*Consideration needs to be given to the balance of variable and non-variable pay; rewards for individual, team and organisation contributions; discretionary rewards and rewards triggered automatically; cash rewards and non-cash rewards; and current and deferred pay.*

The main lesson to be learnt here is that inclusion of a payment system such as PRP is not essential to the success of a PMS. However, where PRP is badly conceived or designed, it is unlikely to deliver the results expected and may threaten the whole standing of the PMS. With careful thought PRP can be introduced as an effective strategic tool linked to business needs, but it should not be relied upon as the sole motivator for employees: a PMS requires the right combination of financial and non-financial motivators.

It is worth noting that there was a backlash against PRP during the 1990s by many organisations, when the expected improvements in business performance did not materialise. As Armstrong (2002: 225–226) states:

> A number of major research studies failed to demonstrate any causal link between PRP and performance or productivity. Some organisations are introducing second-generation schemes which aim to avoid earlier mistakes. Others are questioning the validity of PRP in its original form and are trying competence-related and career development pay.

Let us now consider the contribution of other financial and non-financial rewards.

### Financial and non-financial rewards

In the previous section we concentrated almost exclusively on PRP but this is not the only motivator and, as we have seen, it is debatable whether it is a motivator at all in some instances. There is a wide range of other financial and non-financial rewards at the disposal of employers when they are seeking to motivate staff and, generally, a mix of both is to be recommended.

---

**Activity 45**

Think about the key components of your organisation's payment system, eg hourly rates of pay, incremental rises, shift premiums, competence-related pay, recognition schemes. List three financial and three non-financial rewards you feel help to motivate individuals to improve their performance.

Compare your response with the feedback provided at the end of this chapter.

---

Before progressing any further we must now pay careful attention to the legal considerations in this area.

## Legal considerations

The two main pieces of legislation relevant to the area of employee reward are the Equal Pay Act 1970 and the National Minimum Wage Act 1998. Both have been mentioned in Chapter 3 of this book.

With regard to performance appraisal, it would appear at first sight that there is no specific legislation. Yet Appendix 1 of the ACAS advisory booklet *Employee Appraisal*, summarised (and updated) opposite, leaves little room for doubt concerning the relevance of certain legal considerations.

### Appraisal – the legal considerations

1   Employers who recognise trade unions are required (if requested by the union) to disclose information for the purposes of collective bargaining. In these circumstances, particularly where merit pay schemes are in operation, they may be requested to explain how appraisal systems operate and to describe the criteria against which employees are rated. (Since publication of this handbook, the Employment Relations Act 1999 has extended rights of recognised trade unions. They now have a statutory right to be informed and consulted on training policies and plans).

2   The Data Protection Act 1998 gives individual employees a legal right of access to personal data (such as appraisal details). 'Personal data' includes not just factual information but also opinions expressed about employees. Therefore employees could have access to opinions recorded about their performance or attitude at an appraisal. However, any indication of intentions, such as an intention to promote, is outside the scope of the Act.

3   Under the Race Relations and Sex Discrimination Acts, employees who feel that they have been refused promotion or access to training on grounds of their race or sex have the right to make a complaint to an employment tribunal. The Disability Discrimination Act 1995 introduced a similar right for disabled people treated less favourably because of a reason related to their disability, without a justifiable reason.

In discrimination cases appraisal forms and procedures may be used by employees to support their complaints. It is important for employers regularly to monitor their appraisal systems and promotion policies to ensure that criteria used to assess performance are non-discriminatory in terms of race, sex and disability.

4   Employees dismissed on grounds of inadequate performance and who subsequently complain of unfair dismissal sometimes indicate in their applications that they have received little or no indication of alleged poor performance while in employment. Appraisal schemes should not be used as a disciplinary mechanism to deal with poor performers but it is important to establish a procedure for informing employees in writing of unsatisfactory markings. The consequences of failure to meet the required standards should be explained to the employee and confirmed in writing. The appraisal form however is not the place to record details of verbal or written disciplinary procedure. There should be space on the appraisal form to record unsatisfactory performance together with the notes of action to be taken, both by the individual and by management, to remedy these deficiencies.

Clearly the legislative background to performance appraisal is fairly complicated. Further, you should be aware that when dealing with poor performers there is an important link between the disciplinary procedure and the appraisal system. Large organisations may in fact have a separate capability procedure to cover this eventuality (see Chapter 8 for more guidance on this).

We have already said that managers are often loath to tackle poor performance as part of the appraisal process. There may be a temptation to duck the issue entirely and, for example, rate the employee concerned as 'satisfactory'. It is not difficult to imagine the reaction of all concerned when, shortly afterwards, formal action is taken to warn the employee of the consequences if a significant improvement in performance is not seen within the following three months.

This area is a complex one, but the ACAS advisory handbook *Discipline at Work* provides excellent guidance on how to handle problems concerning poor performance; it is essential reading in this area.

We shall next consider the role of personnel practitioners in designing, administering, maintaining and evaluating performance appraisal within their organisations.

## The role of personnel practitioners

Personnel practitioners adopt a multifaceted role in the area of performance appraisal and within the wider remit of performance management within their organisations. Those of you in generalist roles are likely to get involved, with varying degrees of support from outside consultants, in a number of the following stages:

- identifying the need for a new or revised scheme
- designing the scheme
- implementing and communicating the scheme
- designing and organising training for appraisers and appraisees
- administering the scheme
- monitoring the scheme
- maintaining the scheme (ie is it working efficiently?)
- evaluating the scheme (ie is it working effectively and does it meet its objectives?).

You will thus carry out all or some of the following roles (or possibly assist outside consultants in undertaking their roles):

### A research role

This covers finding out about the various types of scheme in other organisations, their purposes and links to the achievement of business objectives etc. (See the previous section on the components of performance appraisal schemes.)

### A creative role

The aim here is to design a scheme that is tailored to your organisational circumstances and the needs of your employees.

### An influencing role

The purpose of this role is to 'sell' the benefits of the scheme to senior managers, to the line managers who will be operating it, and to each and every employee who will be appraised.

### A training role

This may cover the design, organisation and delivery of training for both appraisers and appraisees in relation to their familiarisation with the scheme and the skills of appraisal interviewing.

### An administrative role

This involves implementing the scheme, communicating with all those affected at each stage and ensuring that all the paperwork flows through the system according to the requisite timescales, and that action points are followed up.

### An advisory role

Advice has to be given to managers regarding, for example, developmental opportunities for their staff.

### A monitoring role

You need to oversee consistency in applying standards, allocating rewards and ensuring that appeals are handled fairly and constructively.

### Maintenance and evaluation roles

These ensure that the scheme continues to enjoy a high priority and that feedback on the success of the scheme (in reaching its objectives) is acted upon in amending, updating and enhancing it.

### An appraisal role

This is both as an *appraiser* for your own staff and as an *appraisee* in your own right. Further, if your organisation operates a 360-degree appraisal scheme, you may be involved as the neutral third party to

**Table 18** Appraisal interviewing – the appraiser

| | **Do** | **Don't** |
|---|---|---|
| Before | • give the appraisee notice of the meeting and any preparation necessary<br>• book a suitable venue (checking whether any special arrangements need to be made for disabled appraisees)<br>• allow sufficient time<br>• read the job description<br>• identify suitable competencies if you intend to use these as the basis for discussion, and provide details of the competencies to the appraisee<br>• review past appraisals and achivement of objectives<br>• review performance over the whole period<br>• check on development opportunities<br>• collect facts and examples, perhaps using any chosen competencies as a framework<br>• reflect on what you are trying to achieve<br>• consider future objectives<br>• plan the agenda | • wait for the formal appraisal interview to tackle performance issues (good or bad)<br>• be swayed by the 'halo or horns' effect (ie when one feature exhibited by the appraisee governs your perception of his or her overall abilities. An example of the 'halo' effect would be a belief that because an employee has a business studies degree she is highly numerate. On the other hand, the 'horns' effect would apply when you assume that an employee who is persistently untidy lacks commitment and is unproductive. The beliefs may be correct but need to be verified by more objective methods)<br>• be overly influenced in your assessment by recent events |
| During | • seek to establish rapport<br>• state the purpose and structure of the interview<br>• check whether the appraisee wishes to add any other relevant items to the agenda<br>• invite the appraisee's views on his or her own performance<br>• keep notes<br>• praise strengths and discuss areas for improvement<br>• listen actively and maintain eye contact<br>• ask open and probing questions<br>• jointly seek solutions<br>• invite the appraisee to summarise first<br>• agree an action plan and future objectives<br>• end on a positive note | • be afraid to tackle difficult issues<br>• be bullied<br>• be afraid to use silence<br>• concentrate on weaknesses at the expense of strengths<br>• concentrate on personality issues at the expense of results<br>• make assumptions eg about ambitions<br>• argue<br>• give vague responses to questions<br>• make false promises<br>• impose future objectives |
| Afterwards | • complete and return paperwork<br>• ensure that the appraisee and other authorised parties receive copies of the form<br>• ensure follow-up to action points<br>• carry out regular reviews<br>• hold frequent discussions *re* progress. | • file the papers and give the matter no more thought until the next review! |

provide feedback to a number of employees on the collated information provided by all the stakeholders involved in the process. (See Figure 5, page 180).

# Interviewing skills

Chapter 5 provides general guidance on interviewing techniques and skills. The majority of these are also applicable in an appraisal situation, although the purposes of appraisal interviews are of course different from those of selection interviews. Here we are concentrating on the skills necessary to be an effective appraiser.

We shall tackle appraiser skills by referring to the 'Dos and Don'ts' of appraisal interviewing: see Table 18.

---

**Activity 46**

If you are inexperienced in appraisal interviewing – either as an appraiser or as an appraisee – set up a role-play with a like-minded individual so that you can both practise and receive feedback on your skills in appraisal interview situations. (See Table 18 and the video titles on page 200, which give guidance on appraiser and appraisee skills.)

---

# Summary

In order to achieve the learning objectives of this chapter, we have sought to distinguish between the broad concept of performance management and the part played by performance appraisal within this framework. We have also explored the importance of the link between individual objectives and business goals, and have concluded that a lack of integration is the major stumbling block towards a truly effective PMS for many organisations.

Performance appraisal has been examined in detail – its purposes, motivational effect, history and trends. The differing components of performance appraisal schemes have been highlighted, including those involving the setting of objectives, and the major benefits and best-practice issues, including those concerning feedback, have been detailed.

Payment systems, including financial and non-financial rewards, have been considered in general terms and, in the concluding sections, the legal considerations, the role of personnel practitioners and the skills necessary to be an effective appraiser have been identified.

You will by now be familiar with the terms used and will be able to relate your learning to the scheme or schemes with which you are familiar. References, further reading and recommended video titles are provided at the end of this chapter for your information, and Activities have been suggested throughout. You are encouraged to complete some, if not all, of these activities in order to reinforce and apply your learning.

---

**Feedback on Activity 43**

1    What 'sins' did the manager commit?

It's difficult to find anything that this manager did get right so you will probably have highlighted the facts below:

- he was not objective

- the feedback was not two-way as he did not check the reasons for the lateness

- he focused on personality traits not behaviours

- the feedback was not timely and was made in public

- he was not respectful and adopted a parent-to-child role rather than adult-to-adult.

2    How should he have tackled this situation?

He should have:

- held the discussion at an appropriate time and in an appropriate venue

- remained unemotional

- related what he observed, ie that the assistant returned late from her lunch break

- stated how that made him feel, eg that it had been inconvenient as the department was short-staffed during a busy period

- asked for an explanation

- sought clarification, if necessary

- discussed with the assistant how to avoid a recurrence

- jointly agreed with her a plan of action.

---

**Feedback on Activity 45**

You are unlikely to have listed financial rewards such as hourly rates of pay, service-related benefits, profit-sharing and other team or company-based rewards where the links between individual effort and the reward are difficult to establish. Table 19 indicates some of the rewards that would be more likely to have a motivational impact.

Table 19

| Financial | Non-financial |
|---|---|
| individual PRP | praise |
| bonuses | feedback |
| incentives | prizes/awards |
| commission | training and development opportunities |
| accelerated service-related pay | responsibility |
| skill-based pay | autonomy |
| competence-related pay | self-development |

### References and further reading

The following are available from the Advisory, Conciliation and Arbitration Service (ACAS), ACAS Reader Ltd, PO Box 16, Earl Shilton, Leicester LE9 8ZZ; tel. 01455 852 225:
*Advisory Booklet on Appraisal-Related Pay.* (Revised 1997) Leicester, ACAS.
*Advisory Handbook on Discipline at Work.* (2000) Leicester, ACAS.
*Advisory Booklet on Employee Appraisal.* (Revised 1998) Leicester, ACAS.

ARMSTRONG M. (2002) *Employee Reward.* 3rd edn. London, Chartered Institute of Personnel and Development.
ARMSTRONG M. and BARON A. (1998) *Performance Management: The new realities.* London, Institute of Personnel and Development.
ARMSTRONG M. and MURLIS H. (1991) *Reward Management: A handbook of remuneration strategy and practice.* 2nd edn. London, IPM and Kogan Page.
EGAN G. (1995) 'A clear path to peak performance'. *People Management.* 18 May. pp34–37.
GILLEN T. (1998) *The Appraisal Discussion.* London, Institute of Personnel and Development.
HALE R. and WHITLAM P. (1995) *Target Setting and Goal Achievement.* London, Kogan Page.
INSTITUTE of PERSONNEL and DEVELOPMENT. (1997) *Key Facts: Team Reward.* London, Institute of Personnel and Development. (No longer available.)
INSTITUTE of PERSONNEL MANAGEMENT. (1990) *IPM Factsheet No. 30: Performance-Related Pay.* London, Institute of Personnel Management. (No longer available.)

MARCHINGTON M. *and* WILKINSON A. (2002) *People Management and Development.* 2nd edn. London, Chartered Institute of Personnel and Development.

PETERS T. J. *and* WATERMAN R. H. (1982) *In Search of Excellence.* London, Harper & Row.

SWINBURNE P. (2001). 'How to use feedback to improve performance'. *People Management,* 31 May. pp46–47.

WALTERS M. [ed.]. (1995) *The Performance Management Handbook.* London, Institute of Personnel and Development.

WHIDDETT S. *and* HOLLYFORDE S. (1999) *The Competencies Handbook.* London, Institute of Personnel and Development.

The following competency frameworks, at commercial prices, are available as shown below:

STANDARDS in PERSONNEL SUPPORT, from Cambertown Ltd, Rotherham S63 9BL; tel. 01709 881276; website www.empnto.co.uk

MCI STANDARDS, from MCI, London WC1B 5BZ; tel. 020 7872 9000; website www.meto.org.uk

## Acts of Parliament and codes of practice

See page 144 for reference to relevant legislative Acts and codes of practice.

## Videos

*The Appraisal Interview.* (1994) Melrose (showing both sides of the appraisal interview).

*The Dreaded Appraisal.* (1994) Video Arts (showing both sides of the appraisal interview).

# 8 • Employee Relations

---

## CHAPTER OBJECTIVES

After reading this chapter you will:

- be able to define the differences in the purposes, content and operation of disciplinary, capability and grievance procedures

- understand the good practice steps that are necessary to ensure the effective handling of conduct or capability cases

- be able to assess the suitability of a range of tools for managing long- and short-term absences

- realise the importance of responding appropriately to employee grievances concerning individual and collective matters

- appreciate the part played by employee involvement initiatives, including employee communications and consultation, in unionised and non-unionised environments, in seeking to introduce change and maintain harmonious employee relations

- be able to analyse which employee involvement approaches are likely to be suitable for your own organisation.

---

## Introduction

In this chapter we will be considering employee relations within organisations. David Farnham (2000: xxiii) defines employee relations as:

> *that part of managing people that enables competent managers to balance, within acceptable limits, the interests of employers as buyers of labour services and those of employees as suppliers of labour services in the labour market and workplace. Within this framework, the main task of those responsible for managing the employment relationship is to develop appropriate institutions, policies and rules to promote 'good' working relationships with those whom they employ. This means preventing unnecessary conflict between management and employees over those matters in which both parties have mutual, though sometimes, diverging, interests.*

Thus employee relations involves managing conflict situations and seeking to gain the commitment of employees to organisational goals. Conflict, potential or actual, may be of an individual or collective nature. In this chapter our emphasis will be on individual conflict situations, ie discipline, capability and grievance-handling, as these are the ones most likely to be faced by the majority of the readers of this book. We will, however, later in the chapter, be referring to strategies aimed at averting collective conflict, ie situations that involve groups of individuals or the whole workforce. Our contention is that collective conflict is often triggered by organisational changes such as restructuring, changes in ownership or working arrangements and relocation. Managers must take care to ensure that they comply with their legal obligations in their communications, consultations and other means of involving employees as well as adopting good practices.

In the opening sections of this chapter, we set out to explain what we mean by disciplinary rules and disciplinary, capability and grievance procedures. We highlight the effects of the revised ACAS Code of Practice in this area and consider good practices in disciplinary and grievance-handling as well as exploring a number of absence management tools. We then move on to consider effective strategies for employee involvement, including those involving trade unions. All of the above is set against the backdrop of relevant legislation, much of which has been covered in Chapter 3.

Finally, we look at the complex nature of the role of personnel practitioners in employee relations. Suggested activities, to develop your knowledge and skills in this important area, can be found throughout the chapter. More information on the associated skills can be found in Chapter 9.

First, we shall consider why it is so important that potential individual conflicts, such as disciplinary incidents and employee grievances, and potential collective conflicts, such as plans to introduce new technology, are handled with skill and according to laid-down procedures.

## Why is it important to manage employee relations?

Concentrating on discipline first, rules and procedures exist to help employees to improve their performance. They should not be regarded as just a means by which managers can dismiss employees legally. There are several outcomes of poor practice:

- A lax approach to potential disciplinary incidents will lead to an ill-disciplined workforce who do not respect management's authority and are likely to 'play the system' to their own advantage, eg by making their own decisions about working methods and break times. When managers do want to assert their authority by, say, enforcing break times, employees will rightly point to the fact that established custom and practice have overridden written policy and procedure.

- An overenthusiastic use of the disciplinary rules and procedures (often applied in a haphazard and inconsistent way) will lead to employee discontent and is unlikely to be beneficial in realising employee potential and thus maximising productivity.

- Ultimately, management may be faced with a decision to dismiss an employee. If their reason is insufficient (eg they have over-reacted to the incident) or if they act unreasonably in dismissing that employee (eg by failing to follow the procedure correctly) then the chance of the employee making a successful claim of unfair dismissal to an employment tribunal is increased. Fighting such a claim will be costly and time-consuming and, regardless of the out-come, does little to enhance the reputation of the organisation in the eyes of its employees and outside parties.

Turning now to grievance-handling, procedures exist to enable employees to have a formal means of complaint about their terms and conditions, working environment and related issues. Failure to encour-age use of this system or to respond appropriately to grievances will result in:

- discontent among the workforce because they feel that manage-ment are not interested in and do not value their views. This may lead to poor motivation and low productivity.

- missed opportunities to tackle problems at an early stage to ensure that they do not continue, thus creating difficulties for other employees. For example, claims of harassment, discrimi-nation and bullying should be handled carefully and be fully investi-gated to avoid accusations of unreasonable delay or indecision. Failure to do this could lead to constructive dismissal claims.

- the threat of industrial action when complaints about issues which affect several employees, such as health and safety matters, are perceived by the workforce to have been handled badly.

Similarly, with regard to collective conflict situations, failure actively to involve employees, listen to their requests or concerns and/or seek their buy-in to proposals can result in a range of responses from apathy and lack of commitment to employment tribunal claims, strikes and other forms of industrial action.

We will turn first to discipline-handling.

## Discipline

The legislation relevant to the handling of disciplinary matters (and grievances) is referred to and commented on throughout this chapter. The major piece of relevant legislation is the Employment Rights Act 1996 (ERA). This Act contains most of the legislation applicable to the individual rights of employees, including the right not to be unfairly dismissed for employees who have one year's continuous service, regardless of the number of hours worked.

Obviously, not every disciplinary situation will result in a dismissal, fair or unfair, but personnel practitioners and line managers would be well advised to bear in mind the provisions of ERA and the guidelines provided by ACAS (see below). This is because the manner in which previous disciplinary situations have been handled will be taken into account by employment tribunals when considering unfair dismissal applications. Let's consider two examples of this:

- A manager who claims that a dismissed employee was previously warned about the consequences of continued poor timekeeping will have to be able to produce the requisite records, the notes of disciplinary interviews and letters of confirmation to the employee concerned.

- In a case of poor performance, the manager will need to produce evidence that he or she reviewed the situation with the employee at regular intervals, communicated the standards of performance required, set realistic targets for improvement, provided the necessary support mechanisms to help the individual to improve, monitored the situation and kept records of subsequent performance before any decision to dismiss. Further, the manager would have to show that the messages given out to the employee at formal appraisal interviews did not contradict those issued in the disciplinary context.

All organisations should have in place written disciplinary and grievance procedures and, we would recommend, a separate capability procedure to deal with poor performance and ill-health cases. These form part of the conditions of employment within the organisation. The Advisory, Conciliation and Arbitration Service (ACAS) Code of Practice *Disciplinary and Grievance Procedures* 2000 gives guidance to employers on the content and operation of disciplinary rules and procedures and is complemented by the ACAS advisory handbook *Discipline at Work*, which gives further practical advice. Although it is generally accepted that smaller organisations, ie those with fewer than 20 employees, are unlikely to have sophisticated procedures in place, written rules and procedures are strongly recommended (and in a unionised environment have to have been agreed with the trade union(s)). (Current proposals, if implemented, will mean that all employers will need to show they have complied with new statutory disciplinary, dismissal and/or grievance procedures when defending unfair dismissal claims.)

### Disciplinary rules

We shall deal first with disciplinary rules. These set the standards of behaviour and conduct expected in the workplace. The contents of the rules vary greatly depending on the size of the organisation, the industry, management style, history of employee relations etc. It is likely, however, that they will refer to the following:

- general conduct
- health and safety
- security
- time-keeping and attendance.

Examples of disciplinary rules under each of the above might include:

- Disorderly conduct, threatening behaviour, skylarking, horseplay or loitering are strictly forbidden in any part of the works.

- Any defects in personal protective equipment must be reported immediately by the employee to his or her supervisor.

- Employees are strictly forbidden to take from the works any materials, tools, equipment, or other company property unless written permission is first obtained from their departmental manager.

- Under no circumstances is an employee permitted to deface his or her clock card, clock any card other than his or her own or to tamper with the clocks.

The type of organisation to which these rules might be applicable is not difficult to guess. What do you think – a small retailing outfit, a high-street bank or a heavy engineering concern?

Disciplinary rules help to ensure a consistent and fair approach to the treatment of employees. Managers obviously wish to have a disciplined workforce, but the majority of employees are likely to be just as keen to have a set of rules in operation so that their working lives can be reasonably orderly. Also, employees want to know what the rules are in order to determine what they should be doing (or not be doing) in order to be successful within the organisation. In fact, in unionised environments it is often forgotten that trade unions also have a common interest with management in promoting standards of conduct. They have two major roles to play:

- to enable members to gain increased *control* over their working lives

- to *represent* members in promoting and protecting their rights.

(See Chapter 3 for more information on the roles played by trade unions in the workplace and see page 222 for discussion of the new statutory right to accompaniment in disciplinary and grievance hearings.)

Breaches of disciplinary rules vary in their seriousness. The types of action you should consider are as follows:

- Minor infringements might merit an oral warning (recorded or unrecorded) – eg an occasional late arrival at work.

- More serious infringements might result in a written warning – eg failure to complete quality checks properly.

- Gross misconduct will probably result in summary dismissal (dismissal without notice or pay in lieu of notice) – eg theft, fighting, negligence, fraud or a serious breach of the organisation's policy on, say, smoking or drugs and alcohol in the workplace.

You should always point out to an employee that failure to heed warnings by engaging in repeated breaches of the rules, eg continued poor attendance, may ultimately result in dismissal.

It has been mentioned that management must seek to be fair and consistent in applying the disciplinary rules. However, no two disciplinary incidents are ever identical. Thus managers must always ensure that they take into account the circumstances of the case before them. For instance, they are likely to deal less severely with a previously satisfactory employee whose poor attendance is due to temporary domestic commitments than with a short-term employee whose loyalty and commitment are already in some doubt.

It may be that because of a manager's sympathy with the circumstances of an employee's case, he or she decides that disciplinary action is inappropriate and arranges for counselling to take place (see Figure 8 on page 212). Some may see this as a soft option (putting off the inevitable), but this approach is entirely consistent with the aim of disciplinary rules and procedures, ie to assist employees to improve their performance rather than providing the means for managers to dismiss employees legally.

We shall now consider disciplinary procedures. For more information on disciplinary and capability procedures and practices, refer to the book by Tricia Jackson on *Handling Discipline* (details at the end of this chapter).

### Disciplinary procedures

We have seen that where standards of conduct are not met then management may decide to take some form of disciplinary action against the employee(s) concerned. Disciplinary procedures provide guidelines for adherence to the rules and a fair method of dealing with infringements.

The ACAS Code lists the following essential features of disciplinary procedures (the bracketed comments in italics are explanatory ones). Disciplinary procedures should:

(i) be in writing *(if they are not, it will be assumed in employment tribunal cases that they encompass the ACAS guidelines)*

(ii) specify to whom they apply *(as there may be different procedures for different groups of employees, eg salaried staff v hourly-paid employees)*

(iii) be non-discriminatory

(iv)  provide for matters to be dealt with without undue delay

(v)   provide for proceedings, witness statements and records to be kept confidential

(vi)  indicate the disciplinary actions which may be taken *(eg oral warning, written warning, final written warning, dismissal and reference to management's discretionary right to suspend an employee with pay in order to carry out a full investigation)*

(vii) specify the levels of management which have the authority to take the various forms of disciplinary action *(eg first line supervisors may have the authority only to issue oral and written warnings; middle management may be authorised to issue final written warnings; and potential dismissal cases may be within the remit of senior managers only)*

(viii) provide for workers to be informed of the complaints against them and where possible all relevant evidence before any hearing

(ix)  provide workers with an opportunity to state their case before decisions are reached *(thus even employees apparently 'caught in the act' should never be instantly dismissed without a proper disciplinary hearing)*

(x)   provide workers with the right to be accompanied *(see page 222)*

(xi)  ensure that, except for gross misconduct, no worker is dismissed for a first breach of discipline *(organisations usually provide a list of examples of gross misconduct in their disciplinary procedures)*

(xii) ensure that disciplinary action is not taken until the case has been carefully investigated *(in potential gross misconduct cases it is generally advisable to suspend the employee concerned on full pay during such investigations; it should be made clear that this is not a punishment in itself – one is innocent until proven guilty)*

(xiii) ensure that workers are given an explanation for any penalty imposed *(ie the reason for the decision, the timescale for which the disciplinary action will remain on the employee's personal record and the consequences of future breaches of the disciplinary rules)*

(xiv) provide a right of appeal – normally to a more senior manager – and specify the procedure to be followed *(for example, employees might be required to state that they wish to appeal against a disciplinary decision in writing and submit this to the personnel department within four working days of the disciplinary hearing decision. The appeal would ideally be heard by a manager senior to the one who took the original decision and must be one who has not been involved in the case previously, ie an independent third party. Depending on the size of the organisation, it is possible that only the managing director or chief executive can hear appeals against dismissal decisions. See the section on the three stages of disciplinary procedures on page 209).*

The Code also advises that, except for oral warnings, disciplinary actions should be confirmed in writing to the employee concerned. Further, when deciding on the level of disciplinary action (if any), managers should take account of the employee's record and any other relevant factors (often referred to as 'extenuating circumstances').

ACAS is empowered by the Secretary of State for Employment to issue codes of practice such as the one referred to above. Failure to observe the provisions of a code of practice will not of itself render a person liable to any proceedings. However, a code of practice is admissible in evidence in any tribunal proceedings and, if any provision is relevant to any questions arising in the proceedings, it shall be taken into account in determining that question. Furthermore, if the statutory right to accompaniment is infringed, the employer may be liable to pay up to two weeks' pay in compensation.

The message here is very clear: regardless of the size of your organisation, you should ensure that you incorporate the 'essential features' listed above in your disciplinary procedure. Further, once disciplinary rules and procedures have been formulated in conjunction with interested parties, managers must ensure that the written procedure matches up with the actual practice within the organisation (or employees will have a 'head start' in pursuing their claims to an employment tribunal).

Failure to follow the correct procedure is one of the commonest arguments put forward (often successfully) by representatives of unfair dismissal applicants. Examples of such failures include:

- not distinguishing between misconduct and poor performance – eg a failure to achieve performance targets may be the result of inadequate training or poor supervision, rendering a disciplinary sanction inappropriate. Alternatively the shortfall in performance may be due to a medical problem in which case a capability procedure should be followed. (See the section on capability procedures on page 213.)

- an incomplete or prejudiced investigation – eg managers ignoring the evidence of a key witness or failing to keep an open mind about the possible outcome of the enquiry

- the improper constitution of a disciplinary hearing – eg a supervisor on night-shift making a decision to issue a final written warning when he or she is not authorised to do so

- the absence of a person suitably independent to hear an appeal against a disciplinary decision – eg because the manager who should hear the appeal has been involved in either the investigations or the discussions leading up to the disciplinary decision

- an employee not being accompanied – eg because the manager assumed that the employee was familiar with this right and would make his or her own arrangements

- an employee not being reminded of the right to appeal and the procedure for so doing (this is an illustration of the importance of keeping accurate notes of all disciplinary hearings so that the validity of such an allegation can be checked).

ERA also states that employers must give new employees written particulars of employment within two months of their starting date. The written statement must include details of the disciplinary rules and procedure and the grievance procedure (see the section on grievance-handling on page 217 for further details).

Managers should not, however, assume that 'offending' employees are fully conversant with the contents and operation of the organisation's employment policies. It is often the case that our working lives are so busy that we are forced to adopt a 'need to know' approach regarding the information that we take in. Thus previously exemplary employees would have had no need to know intimately the workings of the disciplinary procedure.

So what can the employer do to bring the disciplinary rules and procedures to the attention of the workforce? There are several options – incorporate this subject into the induction programme, make copies readily available to all employees, provide training for newly appointed line managers and refresher training for existing ones (organisations often wait for disasters to occur before doing this, eg a finding of unfair dismissal at a tribunal hearing!). Further, if management decide to 'clamp down' on certain activities, eg timekeeping, 'casual' sickness absence or private work during company time, they should publicise this by, say, including it on the agenda of team meetings, by issuing memoranda and by compiling reports highlighting statistical trends.

Before moving on to look at capability procedures, we will first summarise the three stages of disciplinary procedures.

### Three stages

Alan Fowler (1996: 2) stresses that all disciplinary procedures should have three main stages:

- a disciplinary enquiry or investigation to determine the facts and decide whether disciplinary action is necessary

- if indicated by the investigation, a disciplinary interview or hearing

- an appeal procedure

and that, wherever possible, each stage should be handled by a different person. This avoids the possible criticism that a manager has prejudged the situation and is not, therefore, of an independent mind.

It is worth pointing out that, in disciplinary situations, including dismissal, managers are not expected to prove that an employee is guilty of an offence (as in a court of law) but to establish, after a full investigation, a 'reasonable belief' that the employee committed the offence.

With regard to the first stage, that of investigation, you will need to collect relevant facts and accompanying documentation. As well as the disciplinary procedure itself, you will need copies of relevant rules and company policies, eg health and safety, equal opportunities, and the employee's contract of employment and employment records on, say, attendance, training, appraisal and previous disciplinary incidents. Factual data such as production figures, cost or quality information may also be needed along with physical evidence such as 'stolen property' and video recordings.

If you need to interview the employee during this stage, ensure that he or she is aware that it is an investigatory hearing and not a disciplinary hearing. Further, make sure that, in practice, this distinction is a clear one.

We have already mentioned the second stage, the disciplinary hearing, above and we return to summarise the key elements in Figure 9 on page 224. Let us now consider the third and equally important stage of conducting the disciplinary appeal.

The ACAS advisory handbook *Discipline at Work* (2000: S.7) recommends that an internal appeals procedure should:

- specify any time limit within which the appeal should be lodged – five working days is usually appropriate

- provide for appeals to be dealt with speedily, particularly those involving suspension without pay or dismissal

- wherever possible, provide for the appeal to be heard by an authority higher than the one responsible for the disciplinary action

- spell out the action that may be taken by those hearing the appeal

- provide that the employee, or a representative if the employee so wishes, has an opportunity to comment on any new evidence arising during the appeal before any decision is taken.

The ACAS handbook also provides guidance to employers on how to conduct an appeal hearing and this is reinforced by case law. The rules of natural justice applicable to appeals hearings are summarised below:

- Allow the employee to challenge evidence obtained in the course of the appeal.

- Make sure that the person conducting the appeal is not 'judge and jury in his or her own cause', which could arise if he or she has been personally involved in the initial disciplinary hearing.

- Ensure that the appeal procedure is conducted in a fair and open manner overall, and the final decision is reached on the evidence in front of the appeal body and not on any preconceived opinions.

## CASE STUDY 19

Is it possible to get it right? One organisation, a charity, did. The organisation found that porno-graphic images were stored on an IT employee's computer and there was evidence to suggest that such material had been passed between the members of the department. There was a concern among the managers that if they were not seen to take decisive action, they would be viewed as condoning similar behaviour in the future as well as running the risk of receiving harassment claims. After an investigation, the IT manager was unable to identify the guilty party or parties so reluctantly decided to dismiss all four employees in the department. One employee appealed but the appeal was turned down and subsequently the same employee submitted an unfair dismissal claim.

In summarising the reasons for the finding of fair dismissal, the tribunal chair pointed out that:

- the organisation did have an established Internet and e-mail policy that clearly speci-fied what was 'acceptable use' and which actions were prohibited

- infringement of this policy was listed as an example of gross misconduct in the organis-ation's disciplinary procedure

- a thorough investigation had taken place, but the employer had not been able to discover which employee/s were to blame so had dis-missed all four employees on the grounds of a reasonable suspicion

- it was noted that the employees had been unhelpful during the investigations and there were no mitigating factors to be taken account of.

---

**Activity 47**

If you are inexperienced in handling disciplinary situations, ask if you could sit in on a disciplinary interview as an observer only. Try to ident-ify good and bad practices (diplomatically, of course). Did you agree with the decision reached? If not, seek to discuss the reasons for the decision with the manager concerned.

---

We have now looked at the content and operation of disciplinary rules and procedures as well as the effect of relevant employment legislation. Before moving on to the issue of capability procedures, we need to con-sider when disciplinary action is necessary. The flow chart in Figure 8 should help.

Here we can see that though conduct is unsatisfactory in some manner, there may be extenuating circumstances that merit consideration and

**Figure 8**  Disciplinary action checklist

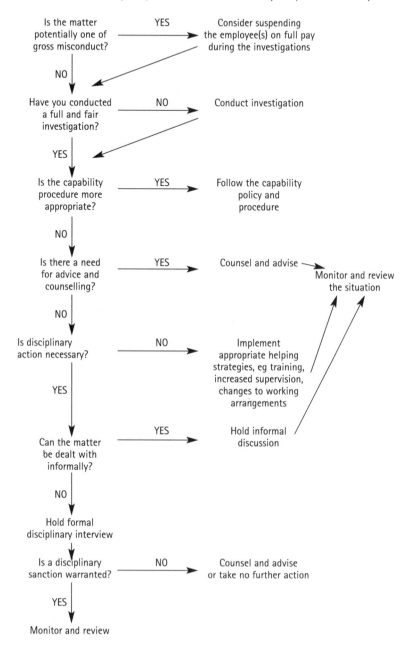

A breach of disciplinary rules has occurred – is disciplinary action necessary?

Is the matter potentially one of gross misconduct? — YES → Consider suspending the employee(s) on full pay during the investigations

NO

Have you conducted a full and fair investigation? — NO → Conduct investigation

YES

Is the capability procedure more appropriate? — YES → Follow the capability policy and procedure

NO

Is there a need for advice and counselling? — YES → Counsel and advise → Monitor and review the situation

NO

Is disciplinary action necessary? — NO → Implement appropriate helping strategies, eg training, increased supervision, changes to working arrangements

YES

Can the matter be dealt with informally? — YES → Hold informal discussion

NO

Hold formal disciplinary interview

Is a disciplinary sanction warranted? — NO → Counsel and advise or take no further action

YES

Monitor and review

render disciplinary action unwise or unjustifiable. The manager may decide that counselling is a more appropriate option and will either personally undertake this role or arrange for a 'specialist' to do so (see Chapter 9 for more information on counselling). In this process the manager is likely to have asked whether the unsatisfactory conduct is within the control of the employee or not. If not, then disciplinary action is rarely appropriate as there is an underlying assumption that the employee has the ability to change.

## Capability procedures

These may be designed to cover poor performance and ill health. We will deal first with poor performance cases.

### Poor performance

Employers are entitled to expect their employees to produce work of good quality and in accordance with sensible deadlines. Where an employee fails to meet the required standards, the manager concerned may decide to invoke disciplinary action. This would be appropriate if the employee is simply not trying and has the ability to change his or her behaviour. Our suggestion, however, is that poor performance is generally not a conduct issue and therefore a separate capability procedure would be more appropriate.

The ACAS advisory handbook *Discipline at Work* (S.10) stresses the need to carry out a full investigation in seeking to identify the cause of the problem. It suggests that:

- the employee is asked for an explanation and the explanation checked, or

- where the reason is a lack of the required skills, the employee should, wherever practicable, be assisted through training and given reasonable time to reach the required standard of performance, *ie by setting realistic targets for improvement*

- where despite encouragement and assistance the employee is unable to reach the required standard of performance, consideration should be given to finding suitable alternative work

- where alternative work is not available, the position should be explained to the employee before dismissal action is taken

- an employee should not normally be dismissed because of poor performance unless warnings and a chance to improve have been given *(exceptions might include a case of negligence which had serious consequences)*

- if the main cause of poor performance is the changing nature of the job, employers should consider whether the situation might properly be treated as a redundancy matter rather than a capability or conduct issue.

Further, where poor performance may arise from a disability (and learning difficulties can be a disability), consideration must be given to any reasonable adjustment that could enable the employee to reach a reasonable standard of performance. In an assembly environment, for

## CASE STUDY 20

A company selling electrical goods had employed one sales executive for three years. He reported to one of four regional sales managers (RSMs) who, in turn, reported to the sales director. In the last six months, the RSM had issued the sales executive with two written warnings for minor incidents. One concerned the late submission of a report and statistics and the other his failure to follow the notification of sickness absence procedure. More recently she issued him with a final written warning (FWW) because she couldn't contact him during working hours. The sales executive felt that he had been badly treated and lodged an appeal.

At the appeals hearing, which was conducted by the sales director, the sales executive said that his problems with his job had several causes. He hadn't told the RSM anything about them as he didn't get on with her and felt that she would be unsympathetic. The causes were:

- he had a number of personal problems, not least trying to gain access to see his children since his marriage break-up

- there had been a change in the computer package used for his work and he was really struggling to adapt to it

- he was feeling very stressed and insecure and, at the suggestion of his GP, had been visiting a counsellor when the RSM had tried to contact him. He had a letter confirming his state of health from his GP and pointed out that he had made up the time the following day.

The sales director concluded that this case had been inappropriately dealt with under the disciplinary procedure to date, though there were understandable reasons for this. She upheld the appeal and withdrew the FWW. Nevertheless she informed the sales executive that his performance still needed to improve. In future, this would be handled in accordance with the company's capability procedure and the company would do its best to help him with regard to IT training and his personal and health problems.

example, a reasonable adjustment could mean providing special seating for an employee with back problems.

It is essential that the performance is monitored at all stages and that full records including notes of meetings are kept.

These good practice steps are demonstrated in Case Study 20.

Next we consider cases of ill health.

*Ill health (long-term and short-term)*
Case law suggests that disciplinary procedures are inappropriate in most circumstances relating to sickness absence whether it is long-term or short-term. Ill-health capability procedures follow a rather different route from disciplinary procedures (though both may have the same conclusion, ie dismissal of the employee). The key elements of an ill-health capability procedure are:

- consultation with the employee, ie maintaining regular contacts throughout the period of absence and fully involving the employee in the decision-making process. Remember that, if such consultations could lead to demotion, dismissal or some other action against the employee, the employee has a statutory right to be accompanied (see page 222).

- medical investigation, ie gathering medical evidence on the likelihood of an early return to work and the suitability of the current position

- consideration, where appropriate, of alternative employment (and/or reasonable adjustments in the case of disabled employees) before any decision to dismiss (or retire) the employee.

In tribunal proceedings, the panel, in reaching their decision on whether a dismissal was fair or unfair, will consider whether these three elements were provided by employers.

Unfortunately, there are other pitfalls in store for you in ill-health dismissals. You may have followed the above good practice guidelines, but what if the dismissal occurred during the employee's contractual entitlement to sick pay? In such a case the employee may have a claim for breach of contract if there is no express term to permit this. You should note the following three-stage approach to dismissing an employee on the grounds of sickness:

1   Check the contract of employment for relevant clauses and seek legal advice if there are ambiguities.

2   Ensure that you follow a correct procedure (see the key elements listed above).

3   Ensure that the provisions of the DDA 1995 are taken into account before making your final decision.

We have mainly concentrated above on long-term sickness absences. What about short-term absences? Sometimes we tend to forget that employees may genuinely be sick, and if these are infrequent occurrences where proper notification and certification procedures have been followed, then no further action is likely to be necessary. If the absences are genuine but frequent, you should follow the capability procedure as set out above.

On the other hand, if investigations show that absences are not genuine (for instance, an employee returning from a period of absence with a deep sun tan might lead you to investigate more fully!), you should follow the normal disciplinary procedure as this is a conduct issue. However, it is often the case that suspected 'casual' absences cannot be proven, so you should be wary of treating absences as misconduct. Do not despair, though, as unacceptable levels of attendance can be dealt with by ensuring a fair review of the attendance record, allowing the employee to make representations, gathering medical evidence (which could reveal genuine underlying causes), seeking to help the employee to improve his or her attendance record and warning him or her of the consequences should that not occur. If there is no adequate improvement, dismissal should be a justifiable option.

## Sickness absence management tools

Whatever the cause, duration or validity of sickness absences, it is undisputed that the cost to industry is very high. A survey of 1,466 UK employers conducted by the CIPD in 2001 revealed that UK employees are taking an average of 8.7 sick days off every year, at an average cost of £487 per employee per year.

**Table 20**  Most effective tool for managing short-term absence (cited by over 10% of respondents)

| Most effective part of short-term absence management approach | % of organisations specifying this as most effective tool (n = 1322) |
|---|---|
| Return-to-work interviews for all absences | 43 |
| Line management involvement in absence management | 27 |
| Disciplinary procedures for unacceptable absence | 20 |
| Providing sickness absence information to line managers | 19 |
| Restricting sick pay | 15 |

**Table 21**  Most effective tool for managing long-term absence (cited by over 10% of respondents)

| Most effective part of long-term absence management approach | % of organisations specifying this as most effective tool (n = 1277) |
|---|---|
| Occupational health involvement in absence management | 43 |
| Line management involvement in absence management | 21 |
| Return-to-work interviews for all absences | 12 |
| Return-to-work interviews for longer-term absences | 10 |
| Restricting sick pay | 10 |

*Source*: CIPD. (2001) *Employee Absence: a survey of management policy and practice. Survey Report*. June. p21.

According to the survey, managers felt that a third of sickness absence was not genuine and that attempts to tackle the problem were hampered by:

- legislation on unfair dismissal and disability discrimination
- occupational sick pay schemes, ie the more generous the provisions, the more likely employees were to take casual sickness absence.

So what can you do to reduce sickness absence? You would be advised to adopt the good practice steps outlined above alongside a combination of absence management tools. You may wish to make your choice based on the conclusions of the CIPD survey which looked at a range of absence management tools and drew conclusions on their effectiveness as shown in Tables 20 and 21 opposite.

Other less widely used approaches were also seen as the most effective by their users, with 39 per cent advocating rehabilitation programmes, 36 per cent pointing to nominated case managers and 22 per cent extolling the virtues of attendance incentives. Finally, 48 per cent of respondents used flexible working arrangements as part of their approach and, though the results were not conclusive, there was some evidence that they were successful in reducing absence.

---

**Activity 48**

Consider your own organisation. Which absence management tools are currently used? How successful do you think they are? If you were to adopt a different approach, which tools would you recommend and why? Discuss your thoughts with one of your learning sources.

---

Now we turn to grievance-handling.

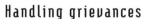

## Handling grievances

There is little detailed guidance regarding good practice in handling grievances in the workplace. The revised ACAS Code of Practice does, however, give more guidance than previously, including the new statutory right of accompaniment (see page 222), and you would be advised to read this fully. For more information on this subject, refer to *Handling Grievances* by Tricia Jackson (2001).

Employers are not currently specifically required by law to have grievance procedures. Nevertheless, there are a number of strong legal arguments to support the case for formal grievance procedures within all employing organisations and it is generally accepted that employees must be provided with a means by which they can officially raise complaints and seek redress. In your role as personnel practitioner, you should encourage this process so that problems can be dealt with at an early stage before they start to affect other employees. Otherwise they may escalate into more serious issues and can even result in industrial action. This is more likely if the grievance raised affects a large number of employees rather than just a handful. Nevertheless, it is difficult to predict which unresolved grievances could provide the trigger for industrial unrest, eg a poorly handled redundancy selection programme affecting only one or two employees could have a disruptive effect on the motivation and productivity of the rest of the workforce. In theory, then, managers should welcome grievances, but the experience of many employees is that management view those who raise them as nuisances or troublemakers. What is your view?

As has already been noted, ERA declares that details of the grievance procedure must be contained in the written statement of employment. The statement must include details of 'the name or description of the person with whom the employee can raise a grievance, how such applications can be made' and an explanation of any additional steps in the grievance procedure. This requirement is applicable to all organisations, regardless of their size.

Thus you should ensure that employees are aware of the existence of the grievance procedure by publicising it through the induction programme for new employees, making copies readily available to all employees, making known the results of successfully resolved grievances and providing specialist training for all levels of management likely to be involved in handling grievances. It cannot be stressed enough how important it is for grievances to be dealt with in an appropriate manner. If an employee has decided to make a complaint formal, it usually means that he or she feels strongly about the issue and will not, therefore, appreciate a manager attempting to trivialise the complaint. Further, if employees perceive that managers never seem to respond to formal complaints, then the incidence of grievances may fall; this does not then mean that there are no problems but that employees are too demotivated to raise them. This is unlikely to result in an energised and productive working situation.

Examples of issues likely to be raised under the grievance procedure within most organisations, large or small, are as follows:

- working conditions, eg light, heat

- use of equipment, eg poorly maintained

- personality clashes

- refused requests, eg annual leave, shift changes

- shortfalls in pay, eg late bonus payments, adjustments to overtime pay

- allocation of 'perks', eg Sunday overtime working

- the imposition of new company policies or practices.

The type of issues included within the scope of grievance procedures vary from one workplace to the next. Unlike more sophisticated or larger organisations, small establishments may have a written grievance procedure but will not have in place other consultation arrangements or appeals mechanisms to deal with complaints about:

- disciplinary action

- safety issues

- job evaluation results

- sickness absence dismissals

- catering matters

- discrimination, harassment or bullying claims

- the operation of workplace policies, such as smoking or drugs and alcohol policies

- negotiated pay deals

- terms and conditions.

You should be prepared to advise employees as to the most suitable procedure to use when they wish to raise a grievance (see page 222 for discussion of the provisions of the Public Interest Disclosure Act 1998).

The last two examples on the list above are collective rather than individual issues and are likely to be dealt with, in a unionised environment, under the organisation's disputes procedure (see the next section). In non-unionised environments, individuals may be invited to 'negotiate' their pay and terms and conditions on an individual basis, but in reality the balance of power is very much on the side of the employer, so individuals may have a limited influence only.

We shall now look more specifically at the content of grievance procedures.

### Grievance procedures

Grievance procedures are the means by which employees can formally raise complaints with management. The aim is to resolve these issues as near as possible to the location of the original complaint. Grievance procedures should be:

- equitable in the way in which employees are treated

- simple to understand

- rapid in their application.

Further, in the interests of natural justice, the investigation of a grievance should be conducted by an unbiased individual.

A successful outcome of a grievance would be a solution that satisfies all the parties. For example, an employee with a justifiable complaint about the unequal distribution of overtime would probably be satisfied if a new written procedure was drawn up to avoid this in the future. Management are also likely to be happy, because this should minimise the likelihood of similar complaints in the future. Sometimes, though, there is no satisfactory solution available, so management's job becomes one not of problem-solving but of explanation and persuasion. Employees will often initially view the effect of a decision as unfair but will be more likely to accept it if they know why it was made. (See Chapter 9 for more information on the important skills of negotiating, persuading and influencing.)

There are no absolute rules regarding the content of grievance procedures, but generally they follow the stages set out below:

*Informal stage*   The employee should first raise the matter with his or her immediate manager or a manager from another department if that is more appropriate.

*Stage 1*   If the matter remains unresolved, the employee can raise the matter formally, via a representative if he or she wishes, with the immediate manager or a manager from another department if that is more appropriate.

*Stage 2*   If the matter remains unresolved, a meeting will be arranged with the employee, the representative (if applicable) and the relevant senior manager.

*Stage 3*   If the matter remains unresolved, a meeting will be arranged to include the functional director and the union regional officer (if applicable).

NB Each stage will be timebound so that a speedy resolution can be sought.

If there is a failure to agree at Stage 3, the arrangements outlined in the organisation's disputes procedure come into play, eg independent conciliation or arbitration or, possibly, a ballot for industrial action. Thus the grievance procedure and the disputes procedure dovetail at the final stage. Any form of industrial action is precluded until all the stages have been completed and a failure to agree recorded, ie the procedure has been exhausted.

## CASE STUDY 21

A company was faced with a grievance submitted by a female employee who had been nominated to attend a weekend training event. The employee did not want to go and approached her immediate manager to complain that she was only given two weeks' notice and would find it difficult to arrange for childcare. The line manager followed the procedure, met with the employee to clarify the problem and sought expert advice on a range of possible options. He realised that the training was necessary and would be expensive to cancel. He found it difficult to reach a decision that was satisfactory to all parties. In this instance, the employee was not satisfied by the response she received at this informal stage, but did agree to the compromise solution proposed at Stage 2.

---

**Activity 49**

In carrying out his investigations, what questions did the supervisor need to find the answers to before reaching a decision?

Compare your response with the feedback given at the end of this chapter.

---

Personnel practitioners often feel that they are in a difficult position in handling grievances. Generally, their only formalised role is to take receipt of grievances at Stage 1 and onwards. A good record-keeping system should assist them in determining whether any previous decisions have established precedents for handling similar grievances. More proactive personnel practitioners will initiate the investigations and discussions necessary in order to address grievances and may also attend grievance hearings. These actions will help them to keep a tight rein on such matters so that line managers do not seek resolutions to grievances without thinking through the consequences for the rest of the organisation. For instance, in our previous example regarding the unequal distribution of overtime, it is unlikely that changes to overtime allocation arrangements within one department could be taken in isolation of all other departments. Dependent on the organisational position of the personnel department (and personal standing of its members), personnel practitioners will have varying degrees of success in seeking to influence such decisions.

Before moving on to examine the statutory right to be accompanied at disciplinary and grievance hearings, we must add a final note of caution regarding whistleblowing. Whistleblowing is the term used to describe a situation in which an employee perceives a wrongdoing at work and reports it to an outsider. The Public Interest Disclosure Act 1998 contains employment guarantees for employees who have made a protected disclosure so that they may not be dismissed or suffer detriment for so doing. The types of disclosure covered by the Act concern criminal offences, failure to comply with legal obligations, miscarriages of justice, health and safety risks and environmental damage.

Employers must, of course, comply with the terms of the Act but could be more proactive by reviewing the arrangements that would be necessary to allow employees to raise these types of concern. It may be that the existing grievance procedure can simply be revised or that a separate procedure should be implemented to reflect the greater sensitivity and seriousness attached to such matters.

### The right to be accompanied at hearings

As we have already stated, the revised ACAS code of practice on disciplinary and grievance procedures provides guidance on the statutory right for workers to be accompanied when they face certain disciplinary or grievance hearings by either a fellow worker or a trade union official.

This right applies to any hearing at which action may be contemplated against an employee. Thus it may be that it would not apply to the investigation, especially if that is solely concerned with obtaining facts. It would apply to a consultation on ill-health absence, if continuation of employment could be an issue – even though this is not a disciplinary matter.

Your disciplinary and grievance procedures and practices should already reflect this new right. Why don't you check to ensure that this is the case?

---

**Activity 50**

Familiarise yourself with the written particulars of employment issued to new employees (and to existing employees on request) within your organisation. Does the statement include the following details?

- any disciplinary rules applicable

- the name or description of the person to whom an employee can apply if dissatisfied with a disciplinary decision, and the manner in which such applications should be made

- the name or description of the person with whom the employee can raise a grievance and the manner in which such applications should be made

- an explanation of any additional steps in the disciplinary or grievance procedures.

If there are any omissions, bring them to the attention of the person(s) responsible for issuing written particulars of employment.

---

Before moving on to consider the case for employee involvement, we will deal with the skills necessary for successful disciplinary and grievance interviews.

## Interviewing skills

We have seen that personnel practitioners (and line managers) need to acquire a great deal of knowledge in order to be competent in handling disciplinary and grievance situations. They also need certain skills – written and oral communications, investigatory skills, persuasion, judgement, decision-making and analytical reasoning, to name but a few. At no time is the need for this knowledge and these skills more evident than when carrying out the disciplinary or grievance interview, and we shall now examine accepted good practice.

Thorough preparation will help to ensure that interviewers are as professional as possible, regardless of their level of experience. It can safely be said that few managers actually relish the idea of conducting a disciplinary interview and, as has already been suggested, are more likely to view grievance-handling as an unpleasant chore than as a rewarding experience (a visit to the dentist might engender only slightly less enthusiasm!).

Many of the skills required to carry out satisfactory selection interviews (see Chapter 5) are equally applicable to disciplinary and grievance interviewing, eg:

- preparing for the interview
- preparing the environment
- using open and probing questions
- active listening
- maintaining good eye contact
- using appropriate body language
- using silence
- keeping control of the subject matter and timing
- taking notes
- remaining unemotional
- providing clarification
- summarising.

There are obviously differences in the purposes of the three types of interviews: selection, disciplinary and grievance. Thus it is good practice, in selection interviews, to establish a rapport with the interviewee; this generally involves a warm welcome and friendly exchange in an attempt to relax the interviewee so that he or she can perform at his or her optimum during the interview. This behaviour is obviously not entirely appropriate in a disciplinary interview and also, to some extent, a grievance interview. If you are too familiar or too personal there is a danger

**Figure 9** The disciplinary interview

### Before

Inform the employee in advance of the nature of the allegations and where possible all relevant evidence

Suspend the employee on full pay if this is a case of suspected gross misconduct

Carry out a thorough investigation and gather facts. Record all the information that you have acquired, ensuring compliance with the Data Protection Act (DPA) 1998

Consider any relevant precedents and the employee's disciplinary record

Inform the employee, preferably in writing, of the subject matter, time, date, location and nature of the hearing and his or her right to be accompanied

If the employee is disabled or English is not their first language, check whether any special arrangements will be needed at any time during the procedure, eg access facilities, a reader or interpreter

Check whether a companion and any witnesses (for either party) will be present and arrange for their release from duties, if applicable. Be prepared to agree a postponement to the interview should key individuals be unavailable

Arrange a suitable venue for the interview, ie a quiet place free from interruptions, and allow sufficient time in your diary

Ensure that the meeting will be properly constituted according to the procedure, eg in a potential dismissal case, a senior manager must take the decision

### During

Convene the disciplinary hearing

Explain the allegations and the evidence (have this to hand)

Request that supporting witnesses give their statements and are prepared to answer questions from both parties

Listen to the employee or the employee's companion when they give their side of the story and allow them to call supporting witnesses

Ask questions of the employee and the employee's witnesses (and allow your management colleagues to do the same)

Take comprehensive notes (or arrange for someone else to do this)

Seek clarification of the key issues

Give the employee (or companion) the opportunity to reiterate any aspects that he or she wishes to emphasise

Adjourn the interview to allow consideration of the points raised and any extenuating circumstances

Consider the appropriate action to be taken

Reconvene and inform the employee of the decision, and, if appropriate, the change in behaviour needed, and the consequences of a failure to improve in the future

Specify a review date, if there is to be one

Inform the employee of the appeals procedure

Afterwards

Write up the notes of the interview and arrange for confirmation of the decision to be sent to the employee and to be placed on the personal file

Monitor and review

NB Halt the proceedings at any point where it is apparent that the use of the disciplinary procedure is inappropriate and, say, counselling or a capability procedure should be used.

**Figure 10** The grievance interview

Before

Ensure you are familiar with the grievance procedure and what happens should you fail to resolve the grievance at this stage

Request that the employee provide full details of the grievance, preferably in writing

Carry out a full investigation. Seek to establish the facts eg dates, times, places, witnesses

Request details of the nature of any prior discussions from appropriate line managers

Question other parties relevant to the grievance

Consider any information pertinent to the issue raised eg policy and procedures, statistical information, custom and practice, notes of interviews, written statements, personal records, employment legislation, codes of practice

Record all the information that you have acquired, ensuring compliance with the Data Protection Act (DPA) 1998

Inform the employee, preferably in writing, of the subject matter, time, date, location and nature of the interview and the right to be accompanied

If the employee is disabled or English is not their first language, check whether any special arrangements will be needed at any time during the procedure, eg access facilities, a reader or interpreter

Check whether a companion and any witnesses (for either party) will be present and arrange for their release from duties, if applicable. Be prepared to agree a postponement to the interview should key individuals be unavailable

Arrange a suitable venue for the interview, ie a quiet place free from interruptions, and allow sufficient time in your diary

Ensure that the meeting will be properly constituted, according to the procedure

**During**

Convene the grievance interview

Listen objectively to the employee's complaint

Regardless of the eventual outcome of the grievance, thank the employee for bringing the matter to your attention

Hear witness evidence and allow for examination and cross examination, as appropriate, by both sides. Consider any documentation provided by the employee

Be prepared to answer questions/explain current practices etc

Seek clarification of the key issues, including any solutions sought. Summarise your understanding throughout the interview

Arrange for comprehensive notes to be taken

Allow time for the employee to confer in private with his or her companion at any point in the proceedings

Adjourn the interview to allow consideration of the points raised and the circumstances. If the case is particularly complex or further investigations are necessary, request and agree an extension to the time allowed before a response is expected

Consider the appropriate action to be taken, if any, bearing in mind any relevant policies and procedures and possible repercussions

Reconvene and inform the employee of your decision, giving your reasons and seeking agreement, if possible. If an immediate decision cannot be given, ensure that it is communicated to both parties within the appropriate timescale, and confirmed in writing

If a mutually acceptable agreement has not been/is not likely to be reached, inform the employee of his or her right to progress to the next stage and the procedure for so doing

**Afterwards**

Record the results and write up the notes of the interview. Arrange for confirmation of the decision to be sent to the employee and a copy to be placed on the personal file. In the interests of good employee relations and, bearing in mind data protection provisions, you may wish to publicise the resultant changes to all workers

Monitor the situation by, for example, maintaining informal contact with the employee or arranging a formal review meeting (whichever is most appropriate)

Evaluate the success or otherwise of any actions that have been taken as a result of the grievance being raised of not being taken seriously, or of possibly being drawn into arguments and straying into personality issues. A lack of perceived seriousness could invalidate a disciplinary warning or lead employees with a grievance to the conclusion that their views are unimportant. Conversely, an overly formal and impersonal style may seem to compromise reasonableness. Implementation of procedures in ways that are devoid of humanity is likely to lead to dissatisfaction and, in the case of dismissals, successful employment tribunal claims. You need to strike a balance between the two approaches.

In summary, the key points applicable to both disciplinary and grievance interviews are to:

- stay calm and in control

- be reasonable and objective

- be factual and unemotional.

There is no one correct and precise way to conduct a disciplinary or grievance hearing but you should find the charts (Figures 9 and 10 on pages 224–226) provide useful 'step-by-step' approaches.

We now turn to the role of employee involvement in containing or averting collective conflict situations.

## Employee involvement

In this chapter we will be using the term 'employee involvement' in its generic sense. This concept has a broad application and covers all communication, consultation and participation schemes, ie written and verbal, as well as those that are one-way or two-way and are directed top-down, bottom-up and laterally. The purposes of different approaches to employee involvement vary and can be represented on a continuum with 'receiving information' at one extreme and 'having a real say in strategic decision-making' at the other.

There are three main types of employee involvement scheme: direct, indirect and financial. Direct involvement means that workers are directly involved in matters that affect them, ie they are communicated with or consulted with in their own right. On the other hand, indirect involvement means that workers are involved in decision-making via representatives. Sometimes, indirect involvement is split into representative and union-based involvement. Finally, financial participation offers workers a financial stake in the economic success of their employing organisation.

---

**Activity 51**

Decide whether the approaches to employee involvement listed below are examples of direct, indirect or financial schemes:

1   Team meetings

2   Newsletters and intranet bulletin boards

3   Collective bargaining

4   Profit-related pay

5   Employee share ownership

6   Quality circles

7   Worker representatives on the Board of Directors

8   Works councils

9   Cascade networks

10  Joint consultative committees

If you are unfamiliar with any of these terms then look them up in appropriate reference sources before tackling this activity. Compare your responses with the feedback given at the end of this chapter.

---

Other examples of employee involvement are as follows:

- direct – briefing or discussion groups, letters or e-mails to employees, attitude surveys, conferences and seminars, suggestion schemes and training

- indirect – health and safety committees, staff associations and problem-solving or focus groups

- financial – profit-sharing, target-related pay and gainsharing.

With so many choices at their disposal, there is a temptation for organisations to try a 'little bit of everything' in the hope that healthy employee relations or the ability to introduce change with the minimum of disruption will result. The implementation of any new approaches will, however, cost money so it would be foolish to introduce them without first analysing whether they are suited to the organisational circumstances.

There are a number of factors that you should take into account before selecting your choice of approach. These include:

- the presence of trade unions and management attitudes towards them

- management attitudes towards consultation, participation and involvement generally

- trade union attitudes, if applicable, towards these concepts

- the aims and objectives of involving employees

- organisational characteristics, including its size and structure, activities, history, industry sector, relationships between employees and their managers

- past experience of employee involvement initiatives

- the number and levels of employees to be included

- costs of implementation and maintenance of the processes of involvement

- the need for education and training to support the implementation

- legal restrictions and requirements, eg the Trade Union & Labour Relations (Consolidation) Act 1992 on rights of consultation, the European Works Council Directive 1994.

---

**Activity 52**

For the purposes of this activity, consider a small, recently established but rapidly expanding e-recruitment organisation, which is not unionised. The owner-manager is keen to increase the involvement of employees across all activities but wishes to retain full responsibility for all business decisions.

Select six approaches that are likely to be suitable for this company and identify which type of approach they represent as well as their pros and cons. You can assume that the owner-manager has already complied with any legal requirements such as establishing a health and safety committee.

Consider whether the chosen approaches would be suitable for your own organisation. If not, why not?

Compare your response with the feedback provided at the end of this chapter.

---

## Trade union involvement

The role played by trade unions, recognition arrangements, collective agreements and industrial action has already been covered in Chapter 3. Here we will be concentrating on the specific roles played by trade unions in the context of employee involvement in the workplace. Trade unions share in the decision-making within unionised organisations in five main ways:

1  Collective bargaining – this constitutes negotiations between employers (or employers' organisations) and trade unions.

Traditionally, collective bargaining in the UK has centred on substantive terms and conditions of employment, eg pay, hours and holidays. In many cases there has also been bargaining over the allocation of work and job duties and the physical working environment.

2    Statutory consultation – this covers areas where employers are obliged to consult with a trade union, where one is recognised. We mentioned these in Chapter 3. In addition, recognised unions can require the appointment of a safety representative or representatives who have wide powers to access the workplace and to table questions to which management has to respond.

3    Joint consultation – this complements the collective bargaining arrangements in unionised environments and involves managers and trade union/employee representatives meeting regularly to discuss items of mutual concern, eg health and safety, welfare, training, efficiency and quality. From time to time there may be negotiation over procedural matters, eg the criteria to be used for redundancy selection.

4    Dispute resolution – as we have discussed, trade union representatives frequently accompany employees at disciplinary and grievance hearings and may also raise collective grievances.

5    Partnership arrangements – these are based on agreements between management and trade unions and are symbolic of a desire to move away from the old adversarial approach to employee relations (or industrial relations). Gennard and Judge (2001: 311) summarise six key principles on which partnership arrangements are based. These are paraphrased below.

- Both management and trade union are committed to the success of the enterprise and have a shared understanding of its goals.

- Each side has legitimate and separate interests.

- There is a joint responsibility to maximise employment security and improve the employability of employees via training and development.

- The quality of working life will be improved by creating opportunities for personal growth.

- There needs to be a real sharing of 'hard' information.

- Tapping into new sources of motivation, commitment and resources will 'add value' to the business.

We will now examine the role of personnel practitioners in seeking to maintain harmonious employee relations in the workplace.

# The role of personnel practitioners

In the above text we have tended to concentrate on the role of line managers in implementing the rules and procedures applicable to discipline and grievance-handling and in managing employee relations. As personnel practitioners, you will obviously adopt the same role when dealing with your own staff but are also likely to carry out the following roles, depending on the detail of your organisation's rules and procedures:

### An advisory role to line managers

In this capacity your advice is sought when employee relations incidents occur or before disciplinary action is taken or grievances are addressed. This will help to ensure a consistency of approach across the organisation as, in this role, you need to be familiar with relevant employment legislation, case law and accepted good practice. You should also have an appreciation of how such situations have been dealt with in the past and the likely repercussions of decisions taken for the future, as well as being the 'authority' regarding the operation and interpretation of your own rules and procedures. (It has already been stressed that industrial action could result from poorly managed disciplinary and grievance situations – most managers would agree that troubleshooting is generally preferable to firefighting!)

### An overseeing role

In this you bring possible disciplinary infringements to the attention of line managers for their action, eg following a periodic check on attendance records and/or sickness notification and certification records. This again serves to ensure a standardised approach to organisation-wide problems, but difficulties may arise when line managers use this as an opportunity to abdicate responsibility back to the personnel department.

### A secretarial role

You often carry out this role in communication and consultation meetings as well as disciplinary and grievance hearings to ensure that detailed and accurate records are kept. This is especially necessary in the event of appeals against disciplinary action or unresolved grievances that are progressing to the next stage and (every personnel practitioner's nightmare) employment tribunal hearings. See the appendix to this chapter for a checklist on taking notes of disciplinary interviews (this checklist could also, with some slight adaptation, be used for grievance interviews).

### A decision-making role

This concerns the action that should be taken in addressing an employee relations concern, a disciplinary situation or the means (hopefully) to conclude a grievance application satisfactorily. The authority for this role must be stated in the appropriate procedures (except where, as a personnel practitioner, you are acting as the line manager for your own staff). This role is more likely to be adopted in a smaller organisation where, for instance, the personnel manager has the authority to dismiss, and the managing director reserves the independence of a third party of higher status in order to be able to hear any appeals.

### A training or educational role

This is to ensure that managers follow the procedures correctly and are trained to carry out interviews and to gain other requisite skills such as counselling and negotiating. Training may be formal or informal, as appropriate. Most managers, unlike personnel practitioners, do not have a wide experience of handling conflict situations; they may have undergone formal training some time previously but need some coaching to give them the confidence to lead an interview or meeting.

### A persuading, influencing or negotiating role

Depending on the job role, you may find that you need to:

- persuade managers that they need to pay heed to your advice on employee relations incidents

- 'sell' the benefits of organisational changes or the results of disciplinary or grievance proceedings to appropriate personnel

- consult or negotiate directly either with individual employees or union/employee representatives over a range of issues affecting the employment relationship.

See Chapter 9 for more information on the requisite skills. It is essential that the personnel practitioner identifies which 'hat' (or 'hats') he or she is wearing in disciplinary matters and grievance-handling. Employment tribunal cases regarding unfair dismissal claims have been lost by employers when it became apparent that the decision to dismiss was taken by someone other than the person named in the procedure as having sufficient authority.

## Summary

You should now be familiar with the theory and practice of discipline and grievance-handling. We have looked at the content and operation of disciplinary rules and disciplinary, capability and grievance procedures, as well as their importance, relevant legislation and accepted good practice. We have also highlighted a range of absence management tools that organisations have found to be effective in reducing absenteeism and its associated costs. We have considered the purposes, types and factors that would determine the suitability of employee involvement initiatives in unionised and non-unionised environments. The knowledge and skills necessary for dealing with employee relations issues have also been examined, specifically with regard to the role(s) played by personnel practitioners.

Finally, a list of references, legislative Acts, suggested further reading and recommended video titles is provided at the end of this chapter. Activities have been suggested throughout this chapter and you are encouraged to complete some, if not all, of these activities in order to reinforce and apply your learning.

# Feedback

### Feedback on Activity 49

Before reaching a decision, the supervisor would need to answer the following questions:

- Does the contract of employment contain a clause referring to out-of-hours training?

- Which legislative acts are relevant, eg the Sex Discrimination Act 1975 (regarding indirect sex discrimination)?

- What has happened in the past in similar circumstances (ie custom and practice)?

- Has the employee been willing to attend previous training events?

- What is known about the employee's domestic circumstances?

- Can the company provide any help and assistance regarding childcare?

- Can alternative arrangements be made to accommodate this training, eg rescheduling the event to weekdays, changing the attendance requirements?

- What are the likely repercussions of all the possible solutions?

**Feedback on Activity 51**

Table 22   Approaches to employee involvement

| Example | Type |
|---------|------|
| Team meetings | direct |
| Newsletters and intranet bulletin boards | direct |
| Collective bargaining | indirect |
| Employee share ownership | financial |
| Profit-related pay | financial |
| Quality circles | direct (but could be indirect depending on the profile of the group) |
| Worker representatives on the Board of Directors | indirect |
| Works councils | indirect |
| Cascade networks | direct |
| Joint consultative committees | indirect |

## Feedback on Activity 52

There is no right or wrong answer to this question but your response should resemble the following suggestion.

**Table 23** Selecting suitable approaches to employee involvement

| Approaches | Type | Pros | Cons |
|---|---|---|---|
| E-mails | direct | Speedy means of imparting information. | One-way in the main. Employees may suffer from information-overload. |
| Whole-company meetings | direct | Allows for probing, clarification, suggestions and comments. | Time-consuming and will be more difficult to arrange as the company expands. |
| Problem-solving groups (including reps from various functions) | indirect | Able to gain views from different levels and functions. Encourages an integrated approach. Synergistic benefits. | Ideas may not get implemented. Attendance may be viewed as time away from the job. |
| Staff council | indirect | Means of cascading information to all levels of staff while seeking their 'buy in'. | Loss of control of the message, ie the 'Chinese whispers' effect. Reps may view this as paying lip service to employee involvement if they feel they are being told of decisions rather than being involved. |
| Employee share ownership | financial | The time lags attached to the tax benefits of these schemes can encourage employees to stay with the company. | Shares may increase or decrease in value. Employees will find it difficult to assess their individual contribution to company performance and share price. |
| Attitude survey | direct | Confidential means for employees honestly to express their views and make suggestions. | Increases employee expectations so inaction following an attitude survey can lead to employee resentment. |

# Appendix to Chapter 8

### Checklist for taking notes of disciplinary interviews

The following checklist should assist you in ensuring that your written notes fully meet the need to:

- provide sufficient information to whoever is responsible for issuing the confirmation letter to the employee (if this is necessary)

- provide a useful justification and record of the action taken at this stage should the situation deteriorate further (possibly resulting in an unfair dismissal claim being heard at an employment tribunal).

Do the notes include:

YES/NO

1   the date, venue, and start time of the interview?

2   an account of those attending the interview and their roles?

3   details of the allegations stated to the employee and of the supporting evidence?

4   details of the employee's response and of the supporting evidence?

5   a record of any adjournments and approximate timings?

6   consideration of the employee's previous record?

7   the decision on whether disciplinary action was appropriate or not and the type of action taken with the appropriate timescale?

8   the review date and a clear statement of intent if improvement does not occur?

9   reference to the right to appeal and the finish time of the interview?

10   reference to the note-taker's name plus a date and signature?

### References and further reading

The following are available from the Advisory, Conciliation and Arbitration Service (ACAS), ACAS Reader Ltd, PO Box 16, Earl Shilton, Leicester LE9 8ZZ; tel. 01455 852 225:
*Advisory Booklet on Absence and Labour Turnover.* (1998) Leicester, ACAS.

*Advisory Handbook on Discipline at Work.* (2000) Leicester, ACAS.
*Advisory Booklet on Employment Policies.* (1998) Leicester, ACAS.
*Advisory Booklet on Employee Communications and Consultation.* (1997) Leicester, ACAS.

The following are available from the Chartered Institute of Personnel and Development (CIPD), CIPD House, Camp Road, London SW19 4UX; tel. 020 8263 3387:

CIPD (2001) *Employee Absence: a survey of management policy and practice.* Survey Report. June. Chartered Institute of Personnel and Development.

EVANS A. *and* PALMER S. updated by Walters M. (2002) *From Absence to Attendance.* 2nd edn. London, Chartered Institute of Personnel and Development

FARNHAM D. (2000) *Employee Relations in Context.* London, Institute of Personnel and Development.

FOWLER A. (1996) *The Disciplinary Interview.* London, Institute of Personnel and Development.

GENNARD J. *and* JUDGE G. (2002) *Employee Relations.* 3rd edn. London, Chartered Institute of Personnel and Development.

IPD (1995) *Occupational Health and Organisational Effectiveness, an IPD Guide.* Chartered Institute of Personnel and Development.

JACKSON T. (2000) *Handling Grievances.* London, Chartered Institute of Personnel and Development.

JACKSON T. (2001) *Handling Discipline.* London, Chartered Institute of Personnel and Development.

(Or telephone the CIPD's distributors, Plymbridge, on 01752 202 301.)

McCULLOCH B. (1999) *Positive Attendance Management, Great Britain.* PPP Healthcare.

## Acts of Parliament and codes of practice

Disability Discrimination Act 1995
Employment Rights Act 1996
Public Interest Disclosure Act 1998
*Code of Practice 1: Disciplinary and grievance procedures.* (Revised 2000) Leicester, ACAS (reproduced in full in the ACAS *Advisory Handbook on Discipline at Work* above)

## Videos

*Disciplinary Matters.* (1999) Executive Business Channel Ltd (EBC).
*I'd Like a Word with You.* (1996) Video Arts (on disciplinary handling).
*No Smoke without Fire.* (1986) Melrose (on disciplinary and grievance-handling).
*Improving Attendance* (2001) Fenman Ltd (On return-to-work interviews).

CHAPTER OBJECTIVES

After reading this chapter you will:

● understand the concept of self-development and the need to take some risks in seeking to improve your own personal effectiveness

● appreciate the main concepts behind a range of skill areas, ie those under the broad headings of communication, negotiating, counselling, time management and assertiveness

● be willing to identify your existing strengths and development needs in these skill areas and plan to address the latter by proactively seeking out appropriate learning experiences

● be able to select and take appropriate actions to develop your skills.

● plan to employ measures to improve your knowledge and skills continually, in compliance with the CIPD's continuing professional development requirements

## Introduction

The majority of previous chapters contain sections on the role of the personnel practitioner in, for example, recruitment and selection and in handling disciplinary matters or grievances. You may have been daunted by the multiplicity of roles performed by personnel practitioners. This is not the end of the story, though, because in order to perform these roles, effective personnel practitioners have to develop some broad skills that have wide-ranging applications. One prime example is interviewing skills. We have seen that personnel practitioners need to possess well-developed interviewing skills for a variety of purposes: selection, discipline and grievance-handling, appraisals and a whole host of less formal situations.

Interviewing skills having been dealt with in the earlier chapters, in this one we shall be concentrating on the following broad skills areas:

● *communication* – report writing, making presentations and making a business case for introducing change

● *negotiating, influencing and persuading* – in formal and informal situations

- *counselling* – in handling redundancies, early retirements, sickness absence and personal problems

- *time management* – inside and outside the workplace

- *assertiveness* – in work-related and personal situations.

This is not intended to be an exhaustive list, as we are sure that you can think of other useful skills that you utilise in your jobs as personnel practitioners on a regular basis. Nor are the contents of this chapter intended to provide you with comprehensive reading in these areas. We do hope, however, that you will find this introductory guide a useful starting point on the road to personal effectiveness in your role as a personnel practitioner, and in life in general. The important topics of self-development and continuing professional development (CPD) are also covered in this chapter (see pages 240–242, 264–265).

Undoubtedly you will have already acquired some of the skills listed above owing to your past experiences and innate abilities. Others you will need to work hard at developing by gaining as broad a range of experience as possible. Please note that we are not suggesting that you will ever reach the stage when your skills are honed to such a degree that everything runs smoothly. Life is not like that. In the context of your working life, the organisational environment is in a constant state of change (and, if you think about it, without some changes occurring life would be rather dull). Further, you may find some situations more difficult than others and feel that you will never develop the full range of skills necessary. For instance, your job might entail notifying workers whose jobs have been made redundant, dealing with members of staff who appear to doubt your credibility and authority or visiting the spouses of employees who have died in service to discuss pension details. The first time that you are confronted with these circumstances you may feel very inadequate. You will, however, through experience, learn how to effect tasks such as these in a sensitive and professional manner.

## Why is personal effectiveness important?

We saw in Chapter 7 that effectiveness means 'doing the right things' (whereas efficiency means 'doing things right'). In the organisational context it has long been recognised that choosing the 'right things to do' at the individual level means performing those activities or attaining those targets that are in line with business or organisational goals. Thus as personnel practitioners you should seek to determine which activities are the 'right' ones and then acquire the requisite knowledge and skills to perform them to a level that ensures the optimum result. Success then breeds success: a positive result will enhance your status and your credibility in the eyes of your co-workers. That is personal effectiveness.

If you are a member of the CIPD, you will find it useful to consult the

CIPD *Code of Professional Conduct and Disciplinary Procedures.* The Code defines the standards expected of members aligned to achieving the objects of the Institute, ie:

1 to promote and develop the science and practice of the management and development of people (including the promotion of research and the publication of the useful results of such research) for the public benefit

2 to establish, promote and monitor standards of competence, good practice, conduct and ethics for those engaged (or about to engage) in the practice of the management and the development of people, for the public benefit.

Personnel practitioners have a dual role in acquiring the knowledge and skills necessary to perform their tasks and activities effectively at work and to meet the exacting standards laid down by their profession.

Before moving on to look at the skills areas listed above and their importance to you, we shall briefly consider first the much-discussed topic of self-development.

## Self-development

Pedler, Bourgoyne and Boydell (2001) define self-development as:

> *personal development, with the manager* (or employee) *taking primary responsibility for her or his own learning and for choosing the means to achieve this.*

They state that other commonly held views on the meaning and purposes of self-development include career development and advancement, improving performance in an existing job, developing certain specific qualities and skills and achieving total potential, ie self-actualisation.

So, in aiming to improve your personal effectiveness, you will inevitably have to get involved in some self-development exercises. These should include an initial analysis of your strengths and weaknesses in order to highlight areas that require further development. A plan to concentrate on these development needs can then be put into effect through:

● self-assessment questionnaires

● role-playing 'difficult' situations in a safe environment and carrying out a review of performance, possibly using one or other of the last two points below

● setting up real experiences such as secondments, projects and work shadowing (see also the section on page 242 on increasing your personal profile)

**Figure 11**  Kolb's learning cycle

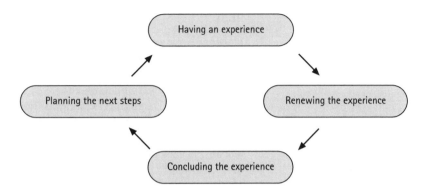

- project work requiring the production of written reports and verbal presentations

- observation and feedback from a trusted third party

- self-analysis of experiences through techniques ranging from diary entries to observation of closed-circuit television recordings of real or simulated situations.

In general terms, you will need to experiment with new behaviours and would be advised to follow the simple stages of Kolb's learning cycle in order to gain maximum benefit from the learning experience (see Figure 11 above).

A general point to note is that attempting to improve skills will usually involve a change in behaviour and will often require you to take a risk (of failure). For instance, if you wish to influence the outcome of a particular management decision that is on the agenda of a meeting you are attending, you will not succeed by sitting quietly and taking no part in the discussions. You will, however, have an improved chance of success if, after carrying out some research, you are able to present your findings logically and put forward proposals that are backed up by sound reasoning. This could be done by way of a written report or an oral presentation. Regardless of the outcome, you should then seek honest feedback on your performance from people whose judgement you trust. (We shall see later in the section on page 250 on Influencing that, at a more advanced level, you may first decide to canvass support from other parties at the meeting to ensure that your ideas get a fair hearing.)

There are two further tips for self-development worthy of comment that will assist you in travelling down the road to enhanced personal effectiveness:

- *Carry out an analysis of how you learn* and make use of this information to plan your learning in the future (Honey and Mumford's 'learning styles questionnaire' is probably the best known in this field – see Chapter 6 and the further reading section on page 269).

- *Increase your personal profile* inside and outside your employing organisation by being proactive. At work 'walking the floor' helps you to get to know a large number of employees and, probably more importantly, to become known by them. Also volunteering to take part in activities that extend your normal range of duties, such as taking notes at meetings, involvement in working parties, project work and making presentations will have the same effect of increasing your profile. If you do not take up such opportunities you may well still be respected for your work, but you will have less chance of really impressing 'onlookers'. Further, a 'backstage worker' approach may mean that someone else gets all the credit for your hard work, for example the person whose name ends up on your report, or your boss when he or she presents your proposals to a senior management meeting. Outside work you should set time aside for networking through, for example, getting involved in your local CIPD branch activities, and attending seminars, meetings and other events designed to facilitate networking. You never know: at the next event you could end up sitting alongside your future boss!

Before moving on to enlarge our understanding of the specific skills areas listed above, it is worth bringing to your attention *A Manager's Guide to Self-Development* by Pedler *et al* (2001). This excellent book covers a vast number of areas and provides several exercises and questionnaires aimed at an initial self-assessment. Another invaluable book is *The Manager's Handbook* put together by Ernst & Young (1994).

## Communication

This is a vast subject, so here we shall be concentrating on two main topic areas: one in the field of written communications (ie report writing) and the other (a classic example) in the field of oral communications (ie making presentations). These activities are both important and may often occur together, especially when, as a personnel practitioner, you are engaged in project work. In fact, we should rarely rely on written reports alone if we wish to influence management decisions: the written word may be powerful but oral communications are much more effective in, say, persuading others to agree to a particular course of action.

The value of good written reports is that they often gain you access to more senior managers in the organisation and hence provide the initial route to influencing them. Writing a report also forces you to think through your ideas in a logical and structured fashion, which is invaluable if you then get the opportunity to present your ideas in a formal presentation.

Let's take an example: you are involved in issuing an attitude survey to all staff prior to your organisation's being involved in a friendly merger with a former rival. The aim is to gauge the feelings of staff about the merger with a view to gradually bringing about a culture change that ensures as smooth a transition as possible. You present your analysis of the attitude survey results, other research evidence and your proposals for the future in a written report. Regardless of how well written and presented the report is, it is unlikely to 'sell' itself (after all, you would be dependent on senior managers reading it thoroughly, which not all managers have the time to do). Thus it would be advantageous for you to make an oral presentation. This would afford you the opportunity personally to 'sell' your ideas and influence decisions, and will have more impact than the written report on its own. A presentation also lends itself to two-way communication, especially if you incorporate a question-and-answer session to address concerns. Brief guidelines on successful report writing and making presentations are provided below.

### Report writing

Reports are written for a variety of reasons. Generally they are based on research into a particular subject and are intended to convey information and ideas. Reports may lead to action because they help managers to take decisions. There are no rigid rules governing the art of report writing, but there are well-accepted guidelines, summarised below:

A *Terms of reference*. Before you commence any analysis, you must be very clear about your terms of reference:

- *what* is the subject matter of your report (eg sickness absenteeism in Company XYZ)?

- *why* is the report necessary (ie what is its purpose – eg to decrease the level of sickness absence)?

- *who* will read the report and what prior knowledge do they have (eg XYZ's senior management team and a college tutor)?

B *Aim*. You must then determine your overall aim in undertaking this project (eg to decrease the level of sickness absence by 3 to 5 per cent within the next 18 months).

*Objectives*. The overall aim should then be broken down into specific project objectives, eg:

- to distinguish between the categories of sickness absence (short-term *v* long-term, casual *v* genuine) in order to calculate the 'size' of the problem

- to compare the levels of each category of sickness absence with those existing within similar organisations or industries

- to analyse the most common reasons for sickness absence and whether these are work-related

- to make proposals to improve the monitoring of sickness absence

- to make proposals to minimise the risk of work-related absences

- to set up a system of sickness absence counselling

- to provide guidelines for managers on the operation of the short-term and long-term sickness absence procedures.

C *Methodology*. Once you know what it is that you are trying to achieve, you can then choose a number of research methods appropriate to the usual constraints of time, money and accessibility. In our example of sickness absence, suitable methods might include analysis of existing company records, discussions with line managers, questionnaires, comparison with other organisations or industries and reference to relevant employment legislation and academic texts.

D *Title*. The title page should contain the title, the name of the author, the organisation's name (if appropriate) and the date. Simple as it may sound, the title should be concisely stated and self-explanatory eg 'A review of sickness absence in Company XYZ' is not as informative as 'A proposal to decrease the levels of sickness absence within Company XYZ within the next 18 months'.

E *Layout*. Informed opinion is generally in agreement on the following sequence:

- Title page

- Summary (abstract or synopsis)

- Acknowledgements

- Contents page

- Introduction

- Main body

- Conclusions, ie research findings

- Options

- Recommendations, including a costed implementation plan

- Appendices

- References and bibliography.

(NB Not all these features need appear in every report. You should select such sections as are appropriate for the length and complexity of your material.)

F *Checklists*. Two checklists are provided in Appendices I and II (see page 266, 267) to give further assistance on the process up to and including the writing up of your report. Like most things, practice makes perfect!

---

**Activity 53**

Approach one of your internal learning sources and ask for help in choosing a personnel issue that is topical within your organisation but which has not yet been tackled. Carry out some research by studying information available internally, eg statistical data, minutes of meetings and externally, eg legislation and journal articles. Write a short report to your learning source and other appropriate members of management. In your report, examine the issue and put forward proposals as to how the organisation should respond. Follow the guidelines provided in this chapter on effective report writing.

---

## Making presentations

The more inexperienced you are in this area, the more likely you are to be filled with dread at the thought of standing up in front of a group of people to make a formal presentation. There are two main ways of attempting to control your nerves:

- Never do it.

- Take a *risk* and have a go!

If you take the former route, you will never conquer your fear and may impede your career as, more and more, managers and professionals are expected to be able to make effective presentations. If you follow the latter route, you will find that your nervousness will create adrenaline that will help you to perform and that, with good preparation, the use of relaxation techniques and more experience you will find the fear diminishes. Never expect to become completely laid back at the thought of making a presentation: even very experienced presenters may find the prospect of presenting to an unknown audience a daunting one, but their experience helps them to keep their fears under control.

There are many relaxation techniques, of which one of the most popular is yoga. These are best learned at a class – try your local adult learning centre or college. Further, some presenters find that affirmations and visualisation techniques increase their confidence and others use relaxation tapes. See further reading on page 269.

We recommend that you do 'take a risk' and get into the habit of volunteering to make presentations (sometimes you will be nominated anyway by well-meaning bosses or colleagues). Inevitably you will improve your presentational skills in both formal and informal situations. For instance, you will become more adept at succinctly expressing your point of view in a meeting, even at short notice. You will also increase your profile within the organisation.

We shall now look in more detail at the two stages to making presentations: planning and preparation, and delivery.

*Planning and preparation*

1   The approach. You must establish answers to the following questions:

- Who? – the audience        *A*
- Why? – the purpose         *P*
- When? – the time           *T*
- Where? – the place
- What? – the subject
- How? – the means

In a word, your presentation must be *APT*.

2   The subject matter. There are four stages:

- Do your research.
- Arrange the information logically eg Introduction – Main theme – Summary and Conclusion.
- Prioritise and prune to suit your
  *Audience*
  *Purpose*
  *Time*.
- Prepare concise notes and visual aids. As for notes, cue cards containing bullet points of information are much easier to use and look more professional than scripts on A4 paper. Further, it is very tempting to read out the latter in full and thus break eye contact with your audience. As for visual aids, each type has advantages and disadvantages – but the bottom line is that they should all be aids and not distractions. They should be *big, bold and simple* to be really effective.

3   Plan delivery. This will help you to overcome your nervousness.

- Be thoroughly prepared; carry out at least one full dress rehearsal.
- If possible, get feedback on your rehearsal.
- If you know that you tend to get a dry mouth, arrange to have water available.
- If you know that you get a blotchy neck, wear appropriate clothing.

- If you know that your hands tend to shake, don't hold your papers but place them on a table in front of you.

- Adapt the content of your presentation as necessary to ensure that it will be *APT*.

- Practise deep breathing.

*Delivery*

You will have heard the maxim:

| | |
|---|---|
| Tell them what you are going to say. | *Introduction* |
| Say it. | *Main theme* |
| Then tell them what you have said. | *Conclusion* |

Depending on the length of your talk (and it is important to stick to the time allotted, including time for questions and answers), you will be able successfully to present only a limited number of key points. Pick these points carefully and deliver them effectively by:

- being enthusiastic about your subject

- being yourself, with your own style

- speaking naturally, with only minimal reference to notes (if you are well prepared, your cue cards and visual aids will provide the necessary prompts)

- monitoring reactions ie watch out for body language to gauge interest and understanding

- asking questions to keep the audience on their toes.

So how well do you understand delivery? Try answering the following questions. Should you:

a) start with an apology because you feel that you are not an expert? Or state your credentials for giving this presentation?

b) start with a joke to lighten the atmosphere if you are inexperienced or do not know your audience? Or outline what you are going to tell them?

c) speak quickly in order to get the talk over with? Or speak at a deliberate and measured pace?

d) focus on one friendly-looking person to the exclusion of all others? Or make gentle eye contact with every member of the audience?

e) switch off all the lights and hide behind the overhead projector? Or stand directly in front of your audience with no barrier between you and them?

f) not allow time for questions in case you do not know the answers? Or periodically invite the audience to seek clarification or further details?

g) read straight from comprehensive reference notes to ensure that you do not miss anything out?
Or use brief notes to ensure you cover your key points and not worry if you miss some details?

h) keep your head down because you are worried that if you look up you will see that everyone is bored (or has left the room)?
Or look at your audience so that you can check their body language for comprehension and interest?

i) make extensive use of a whiteboard or flipchart because it provides an opportunity to turn your back on the audience?
Or make occasional use of differing visual aids to provide variety?

j) nail your feet to the floor and not move your hands and arms?
Or trust your own body language?

k) try to copy the style of someone you admire?
Or be yourself?

NB As you'll have realised, the preferred answers to all these questions are the second ones!

---

**Activity 54**

Volunteer to make a presentation to an outside body (eg a local school) on, say, the work of a personnel practitioner or on your organisation as an attractive employer. Follow the guidelines provided in this chapter.

---

## Making a business case

It is likely that, when writing reports or making presentations, you are seeking to influence managers to agree to some sort of change. In the section that follows we look at the need for personnel practitioners to develop the skills of negotiating, influencing and persuading. These skills are obviously critical to success if you do wish to be proactive in seeking improvements or responding to the need for change.

Here we are concentrating on those factors you should consider if you wish to strengthen your business case. There is no exact science in determining which are the most appropriate ones as this will depend on the organisational culture. Your learning sources may be able to help you to select wisely from the suggested list below:

1   Legislation – is the proposed change necessary to comply with existing or forthcoming legislative requirements?

2   Good practice – is there a case for suggesting that the organisation goes beyond minimal legislative compliance and adopts good practices, perhaps in response to competitive pressures?

3    Risk – what are the risks associated with not making the change, eg employment tribunal claims, loss of key individuals, theft of commercial knowledge, industrial disputes, safety issues, etc?

4    Retention and absence – can you demonstrate the benefits that would result from your proposals in terms of increased retention and/or decreased absenteeism?

5    Productivity, profitability and growth – are there strong arguments to suggest that successful implementation of your plans will bring about discernible improvements in company performance?

6    Customer care – can you show that the quality of customer service will improve if your proposals are adopted?

As you are no doubt aware, decision-makers are less interested in views and beliefs and more interested in facts. To convince them you invariably require evidence. You firstly need to make it clear where your arguments are backed up by research evidence, eg workforce profiles or employee attitude survey results. Secondly, managers will not be swayed by vague promises of future benefits so you will need to translate your proposals into credible and realisable financial benefits. Very few business decisions are taken without being backed by a clear financial case. Here are a few hints to help you to identify the relevant cost/benefit information:

- Use plausible estimates – familiarise yourself with some typical costs such as average salaries for different grades of staff.

- Remember opportunity cost – people are employed for more than their salary cost because in addition to direct employment costs there are indirect ones such as office space and the cost of providing employee benefits. When they are not engaged in normal day-to-day activities, employees will not be contributing to organisational performance in the usual way, so there is an opportunity cost to their being on a training course, being absent through sickness etc.

- Distinguish between 'one-off' and ongoing costs and benefits – eg absence management policies and training may cost several thousands of pounds to prepare and implement but this is a 'one-off' cost whereas the resultant benefits of reduced absenteeism should continue year after year. Further major investment is unlikely to be necessary though there will be some annual 'maintenance' costs attached to managing absence.

We hope that you find the above guidelines useful in seeking to improve your communication skills and in making a business case, both verbally and in writing. We shall now consider the associated skills of negotiating, influencing and persuading.

## Negotiating, influencing and persuading

As a personnel practitioner, you are likely to find yourself in situations, formal and informal, that require you to use negotiating skills in order to reach an agreement. Further, you will find it difficult to promote your ideas, affect decisions and 'sell' changes without well-developed influencing skills. Both of these need to be backed up by powerful persuasive techniques and assertive behaviour (the latter subject will be discussed in a separate section later in this chapter).

There are several definitions of negotiation, but we shall use that provided by Alan Fowler (1998):

> *Negotiation occurs whenever there is an issue that cannot be resolved by one person acting alone; it occurs when the two (or more) people who have to be involved begin with different views on how to proceed, or have different aims for the outcome.*

Negotiations do not have to result in win/lose outcomes but may lead to win/win results. For example, if I have an orange that you and I both want, and we negotiate, there are various possible outcomes:

- I keep the orange.  — *I win, you lose*

- You get the orange.  — *You win, I lose*

- We cut the orange in half.  — *I win, you win (compromise)*

- We divide the orange so that I keep the peel for baking a cake and you get the fruit to decorate a drink.  — *I win, you win (collaboration)*

Fowler (1998) also provides us with definitions of influence and persuasion:

> *Influence is a broad concept, involving the effect on each person of the whole context in which the discussion takes place, including the quality of past and present working relationships as well as each participant's unspoken ambitions or fears. Persuasion involves all those skills of argument and discussion that can be used by one person to obtain another's agreement.*

Thus as personnel practitioners you will frequently be in situations, ranging from formal meetings to chance corridor discussions with other parties, when you will need to use influence and persuasion to reach an agreed outcome. For instance, we mentioned in Chapter 8 that sometimes there is no satisfactory resolution to a grievance. In such cases you will need to persuade the employee(s) concerned to accept that there is no point in continuing to pursue the grievance to the next stage,

**Table 24** Assess your powers of persuasion

| | Rate yourself on a scale of 1 to 5 | | | | |
| | Rarely | | | | Always |
| | 1 | 2 | 3 | 4 | 5 |
|---|---|---|---|---|---|
| 1  I adopt a positive and collaborative style. | | | | | |
| 2  I am successful in avoiding confrontation. | | | | | |
| 3  I assess the other person's viewpoint. | | | | | |
| 4  I adapt my position to reflect the other person's viewpoint. | | | | | |
| 5  I encourage a dialogue and do not set out all my case immediately. | | | | | |
| 6  I do not interrupt the other person when they make statements I disagree with. | | | | | |
| 7  I am a very attentive listener. | | | | | |
| 8  I use questions, not statements, to probe or challenge the other person's case. | | | | | |
| 9  If I need time for thought, or for emotions to cool, I seek an adjournment. | | | | | |
| 10  I first introduce proposals for compromise or concession on a no-commitment basis. | | | | | |
| 11  I link my proposed concessions to moves by the other person. | | | | | |
| 12  I emphasise the benefits to the other person of proposed compromise. | | | | | |
| 13  I use summaries to ensure mutual understanding and move the discussion on. | | | | | |
| 14  I take the initiative in bringing the discussion to a constructive close. | | | | | |
| 15  I ensure any agreement includes details of how it will be implemented. | | | | | |
| 16  I ensure any agreement is mutually understood and is not ambiguous. | | | | | |
| 17  I observe body language for clues about attitudes and intentions. | | | | | |

because the answer there will be the same. You would be advised to pre-pare yourself by considering the influencing factors listed below.

Fowler describes the range of influencing factors that are used in such circumstances and points out that:

- you should be aware of them so that you are not unduly influenced by them

- you should use them to your own advantage when they apply in your favour.

You should therefore compare yourself with the other party in a negoti-ating situation by examining the following influencing factors:

- the personal relationship ie past history

- any status differences

- connections with sources of organisational power

- the formality of the location and the negotiating situation (and whose style this suits best)

- the level of information and experience

- gender, race and age differences

- reputations – for success or failure

- expectations about outcomes

- timing – duration and deadlines

- work pressures.

Once you have carried out this analysis, you can use some of these fac-tors to your advantage and resist the temptation to be adversely influ-enced by those that favour the other party – or you may positively take action to counter them. Let's now consider Case Study 22 in order to demonstrate this last point.

Returning to your powers of persuasion. Fowler (1998) provides an excellent self-assessment questionnaire to investigate this. Analyse the range of negotiating situations that you are currently involved in before responding honestly to the statements in Table 24. Think of situations that are formal and informal, and that take place inside and outside the workplace.

Obviously you are aiming to develop your powers of persuasion so that you will eventually be able to award yourself a rating of 5 on each crite-rion; to be realistic, this may never happen, but in the meantime the results will show which areas you should start working on.

We have now looked at the three areas of negotiating, influencing and persuading, and have seen how interlinked they are. Another connected behavioural style is assertion, which is dealt with later in this chapter.

## CASE STUDY 22

Under the earlier section in this chapter on self-development we considered a situation in which you might wish to influence the outcome of a management decision under discussion at a meeting. In this case study the topic for discussion was the reduction of car parking spaces due to the erection of a Portakabin for contract workers. The car park was used by technical and office workers during the day and at night by shopfloor workers and a small number of technical staff who worked nights on a rotational basis.

The administrator for the technical department was due to attend a staff consultative committee meeting, and saw that this item was on the agenda circulated. This topic had been the subject of much discussion within the department and the administrator was concerned at the effect that it would have. There was already pressure for spaces at night-time because the shift for the technical staff commenced after that of the shopfloor workers. He carried out an informal analysis which showed that 90 per cent of the technical staff brought their own cars to work, and all would have concerns for their safety and that of their cars if they had to park further away from the main building at night-time. The administrator decided on two possible solutions: to designate three spaces for the use of the technical staff at night-time (but he was not confident that this would be adhered to) or to relocate the Portakabin.

The administrator knew that the chairperson would normally introduce such a measure as a *fait accompli*, and he realised that there were several influencing factors that acted in the chairperson's favour: he was senior in status and had more influence with important members of senior management. Further, he was known to be fairly dogmatic in outlook but was also under a lot of work pressure at that time

The administrator completed his research, considered alternatives and decided to put forward proposals, backed up by sound reasoning. He also decided to canvass support from one of the engineers present at the meeting (thereby discovering that the engineers' 'on call' system would provide them with similar problems). He successfully gained some 'air time' and, in 'making his business case', the administrator highlighted those factors (listed in the above section) which would help to strengthen his arguments, eg the safety issues, as well as putting forward the cost/benefits of the alternative proposals. The *pièce de résistance*, from the chairperson's point of view, is that he then offered – on the condition that the committee accepted his proposal – to talk to the chief engineer and health and safety officer to decide on an alternative location for the Portakabin.

The chairperson, faced with sound reasoning and someone prepared to take responsibility for the problem, was much less inclined to make the influencing factors work in his favour. The administrator, on the other hand, had not only resisted the urge to be daunted by those factors but had found a way of working around them!

Let us now turn to another important communication skill – counselling.

## Counselling

What do we mean by counselling? We will commence by stating what counselling *is not*:

- giving advice

- giving opinions

- sympathising

- giving practical help, eg taking over the problem and solving it.

Counselling is not better than these helping devices, but it is different from them and more suited to certain situations. In fact, in one meeting you may need to use a range of helping devices. For instance, when discussing early retirement options with an employee, you will need to:

- counsel the employee to help him or her decide whether to retire early or not

- give practical help by providing the pensions calculations

- give advice, if requested, about the advantages and disadvantages of a lump sum payment versus an increased annual pension.

Counselling *is* about – in simple terms – *helping people to help themselves*.

Thus a professional counsellor aims to assist 'clients' in exploring their problems, considering the range of options available to them, and deciding on their chosen course of action. Professional counsellors are generally independent third parties with no vested interest in the outcome of the process. As a personnel practitioner this may not be the case, because it is often the actions of the organisation that you represent that have led to the need for counselling. For instance, a potential applicant for early retirement would perhaps not have considered this option if the organisation had not recently announced a major restructuring exercise that may greatly change his or her job role in the future. Thus the personnel practitioner should aim to counsel the 'client' following the tips described below, though inevitably with one eye on the organisational circumstances, ie the need to equip the organisation with new skills to meet future market needs.

Counselling is a complex subject, as is evident from the number of professionally trained specialists in the field. As a personnel practitioner, you will increasingly find that managers and employees expect you to be the person responsible for dealing with those problems that require counselling as the helping style. We do not wish to suggest that, after a little practice, you would be competent in dealing with every possible situation requiring counselling skills in the workplace. As the saying goes, a little knowledge can be a dangerous thing. You should seek to develop your counselling skills so that you are able to help some employees in some situations, even if it is only in a very limited way. If you have a tendency to try to avoid dealing with employees who you know have particular problems, you will be seen as an unapproachable and uncaring employer. You may even lose good employees because you did not take the appropriate action at the time.

## CASE STUDY 23

One story worth relating is that of a young brother and sister who lost their father. Both went straight back to work on the day after the funeral, but each had rather different experiences. On her return to work, the sister was invited into the office of the personnel officer, who expressed his sympathy (he had previously sent a note signed by the young woman's colleagues together with flowers from the company). He reassured her that if she felt she could not cope with coming back to work so soon, she should just inform him and he would make the appropriate arrangements with her manager. On the other hand, when the woman's brother returned to work, nothing was said by his supervisor at all, though he had known why the young man had been absent. In fact, a couple of days later, when he was feeling very disheartened, his supervisor said to him in the hearing of other workers, 'It's about time you pulled yourself together.' Can you guess which employee remained longer with their employer?

Unfortunately, employees seem to suffer from a vast range of problems, such as addiction to drugs or drink, bereavement, debt, AIDS, physical or mental ill health and troublesome relationships (to name but a few). If you are faced with an approach – usually prefaced by 'Have you got a minute to spare?' – from employees, then, when they are unburdening their souls to you (and taking considerably more than a minute to do so), remember this safeguard: *know your limitations*. In other words, if you feel out of your depth, you should acknowledge this and help the employees by referring them to a specialist for advice.

There are, however, a number of commonly occurring situations that you will be expected to deal with personally. These include redundancy, early retirement, sickness absence, work-related problems and some personal problems. In fact, organisations often have in place formalised counselling procedures to deal with such situations. In such cases the counselling procedure replaces, or runs in parallel with, other procedures. (See the ACAS publications *Discipline at Work* (section 4) and *Redundancy Handling* for further details.)

It is not our intention to provide a comprehensive guide to suit every occasion, but a few simple tips are offered below. These should be read and implemented in the context of each situation that you deal with and in accordance with the appropriate organisational procedures.

### Tips

- Listen actively.
- Show empathy ie non-critical, non-judgemental acceptance.
- Reflect back and paraphrase what has been said.
- Use open questioning.
- Ask questions to ensure that the client focuses on the problem.

- Prompt (but do not direct) exploration of a range of options.

- Provide summaries throughout of what has been said or agreed.

- Encourage the client to find his or her own solution and set his or her own goals.

- Agree an action plan.

- Summarise at the end.

- Monitor and review (if appropriate, ie if you are dealing with work-related issues).

A word of caution here: don't expect too much from a 30- to 60-minute counselling session. Counselling takes time, because clients are often trying to work through complex problems. Don't, though, be tempted simply to allocate a larger chunk of time on the next occasion, because short sessions with 'thinking time' in between are usually more fruitful. If you have practised good counselling skills, your client can leave the meeting better equipped to think through the options before reaching a decision on what to do next. He or she may decide not to *do* anything but, as a result of the counselling, may feel better equipped to deal with the situation than before.

## Time management

Like all busy managers, personnel practitioners are likely to find that there appears to be a serious mismatch between their volume of work and the time they have to do it in. This is especially so when a large part of each day seems to be taken up dealing with queries from employees and other parties. A lot of people attend courses in order to learn about good time management techniques. They often get very enthusiastic about how they will revolutionise their working (and personal) life by employing these techniques at the conclusion of the training course. The problem is that when they get back to the workplace, nothing (and no one) else has changed, so they find that they lack the time to try out any new ideas or to develop the necessary skills. In fact, 'it takes time to save time' initially because good time management involves more planning and preparation; it is often easier to slip back into old habits and react to emergencies and crises rather than thinking ahead to try to avoid them.

It is also difficult to initiate the application of good time management skills at home because if this involves persuading other family members to take more responsibility for, say, certain household chores, they may be inclined to be unco-operative, as the benefits to them are not immediately apparent. Here we can see the link between the previous section on negotiating, influencing and persuading and good time management, as well as a link with the following section on assertiveness. It is necessary to use and develop all these skills if you really want to change your time management habits.

As we have already said, developing skills usually means changing behaviour. With time management in particular you are attempting to change patterns of behaviour that have been ingrained over many years, so don't expect a miracle cure. The good news is that once you begin the process and start to see the benefits, you will be greatly encouraged to carry on. The new patterns of behaviour in the workplace will start to spill over into your personal life as you gain the confidence to try to change others' behaviour along with your own.

First, let's examine some fallacies about time management (see Table 25).

A fundamental stage in time management is to decide on our goals and priorities and then choose to work on tasks that help us to achieve them. Those tasks that do not fall into this category will then either come lower down our list of priorities or will cease to be performed at all. In discussing time management we are referring to the distinction between efficiency and effectiveness: *efficiency is doing things right, effectiveness is doing the right things*.

**Table 25**   Time management

| Fallacies | The truth |
|---|---|
| Time management will mean that I have to work efficiently all the time. | Time management *will* help you to work efficiently, but only when you want to. You may choose to work efficiently for just some of the time – for example, on priority tasks. |
| Time management will mean that I'll be so busy that I'll miss out on things like gossiping with colleagues or taking my time over a favourite job. | Time management helps you to choose the right things to do and to work through them more quickly. You will then free up extra time and you can decide how to spend it. |
| Time management will mean that I can no longer be spontaneous eg agree to help out a colleague or accept an invitation from a friend. | Time management will help you to avoid crisis management but should not remove spontaneity. You can choose which aspects of your life you wish to retain. |
| Time management will mean that I have to work a lot harder overall. | Time management should mean that you do less work overall because you will decide which tasks are the important ones, ie the ones that contribute most to your goals. **You will work smarter, not harder**. |

**Table 26**  How to avoid time-wasters

| Time-wasters | Techniques |
|---|---|
| Interruptions (telephone calls, drop-in visitors) | • Operate a limited 'open door' policy.<br>• Remove yourself to work undisturbed elsewhere.<br>• Stand up when answering the telephone; tell the caller that you will call him or her back at a mutually convenient time.<br>• Get someone to screen your calls and callers – either an assistant or a colleague (in the latter case you could set up a reciprocal and mutually convenient arrangement to cater for periods of intense pressure from work deadlines).<br>• Make deals with your boss about availability and priorities.<br>• Reschedule impromptu meetings for more convenient times. |
| Poorly conducted meetings | • Have a personal agenda covering what you want to achieve during the meeting and work towards it.<br>• Be assertive and suggest time limits for each item.<br>• Gather support to suggest changes to the meeting eg limited duration, less frequent, more informative/participative.<br>• Meet in other people's offices; it is easier to leave!<br>• In your own office have two clocks, one you can see and one your visitors can see. |
| Too much paperwork | • Keep a tidy desk and tackle one task at a time (do not 'grass-hop' between different tasks).<br>• Speed-read; you won't need to remember every detail of the communication – just the gist of it.<br>• Adopt a simple filing system and stick to it.<br>• Thin files out periodically to save time when referring to them.<br>• Handle pieces of paper once only using the RAFT* system.<br>• When possible, reply with short notes/memos/telephone calls rather than long-winded responses. |
| Poor delegation | • Delegate finite or routine tasks.<br>• Ask for regular status reports.<br>• Resist the temptation to get involved in the minute detail of a task. |
| Reverse delegation (when staff offload their tasks on to the boss) | • Listen to the problem but resist the urge to take it over.<br>• Insist that staff present problems *and* some suggestions to solve them.<br>• Support your staff in making *their* decisions. |
| Poor work-scheduling | • Use an 'organiser' to list your 'to do' tasks, and keep this up to date.<br>• Set your own deadlines and priorities and stick to them; whenever feasible, don't allow other people's priorities to override your own.<br>• Always allow for some undisturbed time during the day, and use this for thinking time or work on major projects (preferably when your energy levels are at their optimum). |
| Perfectionism | • Attention to detail has its place but don't allow this to get in the way of achieving the task.<br>• Allow yourself to produce the standard of work that is appropriate to the circumstances (and helps you to achieve your goals). |
| Poor use of technology | • Get up to speed with time-saving technology eg word processing, spreadsheets, database packages.<br>• Use telephone memories/answering facilities/divert systems.<br>• Listen to self-development tapes while driving. |
| Lack of leisure time | • Schedule in leisure time/treats to your day.<br>• Resist the temptation to use your leisure time to meet other needs eg to complete a large project.<br>• Keep fit: a healthy body helps you to perform better mentally. |

*RAFT: Refer it     Act on it     File it     Throw it away

These memorable definitions help us to remember that we should always aim to be effective rather than efficient. Many people pride themselves on being efficient, but that may mean that they are simply working hard to achieve tasks rather than working towards goals. Thus they may be wasting a lot of their time and will probably see other (more effective) people being promoted over them.

Good time management results in

- more productivity
- more control
- more time for leisure
- less stress
- more effective decision-making
- success.

We shall now consider the most common time-wasters for personnel practitioners and suggest some time management techniques for you to try out – see Table 26 opposite. Some of our suggestions assume that you have responsibilities for staff and can therefore delegate some tasks. We have suggested alternative techniques where this is not the case or where delegation is not appropriate (see below for guidance on this latter point).

Remember that you will need to take time out initially to decide on your goals and priorities and to plan how you will achieve them. Don't try to implement everything at once: practise one or two new techniques at a time to see which ones work for you.

### Delegation

The following list shows those activities that you can or should delegate:

- work that you don't have to do yourself
- work that others can do more efficiently or more effectively
- whole jobs
- more demanding tasks that you closely supervise in order to pass on skills or knowledge
- tasks that have been completed incorrectly.

Compare this with the following list which shows those activities that you should not delegate:

- work entrusted to you personally
- your own work that has gone wrong, eg a mistake has been made
- mundane routine work that is not a whole task

- critical tasks where mistakes cannot be tolerated

- work that you do not understand (as you will not be able to judge the outcome)

- staff and team roles and responsibilities

- confidential matters.

We have covered several aspects of this important skill here. Now you need to take *time* to do some further reading around this subject, making use of self-assessment questionnaires to determine your strengths and weaknesses in this area. Plan next to do something specific in order to improve your time management. It can be done: many others have been successful before you.

We shall leave this section with the following five steps to developing good time management habits:

1 *Recognise* the difficulty in changing.

2 *Develop* a better way.

3 *Launch* the new habit strongly.

4 *Practise* the new way often.

5 Allow *no exceptions*.

---

**Activity 55**

Make a log of your activities over a period of a few days. There are numerous formats you could use but a simple record of activities and duration would be a good start. Then analyse your log by designating each activity as

A    Important and urgent

B    Important but not urgent

C    Not important but urgent

D    Neither important nor urgent

and calculate the proportion of time spent on each category.

Ideally, at least two-thirds of your time should come into the B category and only a fifth to a quarter into the A category. All being well, a minimal amount of your time will be spent in category D. But do not be dismayed if these figures do not reflect your distribution of time. Apply some of the time management techniques in this chapter and then repeat this exercise.

---

# Assertiveness

Assertiveness is probably the most useful skill of all. Developing it will have an immediate impact on your working and non-working life. Assertiveness is clear, honest and direct communication that pays heed to our own needs and the needs of others. It is best described by comparing it to the two extremes of submissive and aggressive styles of behaviour; see Tables 27 and 28 below (both adapted from Back K. and K. (1986)).

Once you are familiar with the differences between these three behavioural styles, you should note the following three essential skills of assertive behaviour, summarised by Anne Dickson (1984: 22) as follows:

1  Decide what it is you want or feel, and say so specifically and directly.

2  Stick to your statement, repeating it, if necessary, over and over again. (This is commonly known as the Broken Record Approach.)

3  Assertively deflect any responses from the other person which might undermine your assertive stance, ie acknowledge the response but do not allow yourself to become sidetracked or involved in an argument, eg 'I know that you're tired as well but I still want you to help with the housework'; 'I know that you're disappointed but I still have to say no'.

Successful assertive behaviour is demonstrated in Case Study 24.

**Table 27**  Behaviour styles

| Assertive | Submissive | Aggressive |
|---|---|---|
| Communicates impression of self-respect and respect for others. | Communicates a message of inferiority and results in lowered self-esteem. | Communicates impression of superiority and disrespect. |
| Our wants, needs, and rights are viewed as equal to those of others. | Allows the wants, needs, and rights of others to be more important than own. | Puts own wants, needs, and rights above those of other people. |
| Achieves own objectives by influencing, listening, and negotiating. Others are able to co-operate willingly. | Ignores own rights and needs in an attempt to satisfy the needs of other people. | Achieves own objectives by not allowing others a choice. Violates the rights of others. |
| Behaviour is active, direct and honest. | Anger towards others is directed inwards. | Behaviour is domineering, self-centred, and self-enhancing. |
| *I'm OK...You're OK* | *I'm not OK...You are* | *I'm OK...You're not* |

**Table 28**  What are the differences?

| Assertive | Submissive | Aggressive |
|---|---|---|
| *Verbal*<br>'I' statements that make it clear you are speaking for yourself eg 'I think', 'I would like', 'I feel'. | Few 'I' statements, and those often qualified eg 'It's only my idea but. . .'. | 'I' statements that are boastful or too numerous, and the use of the royal 'we' when it is really 'I' eg 'We don't want to do that.' |
| Distinctions made between fact and opinion eg 'As I see it. . .', 'My opinion is. . .'. | Opinions qualified with such words as 'maybe', 'perhaps', 'I wonder', 'possibly'. | Opinions expressed as facts eg 'The scheme's crazy.' |
| Statements or questions that acknowledge disagreement and seek to resolve it eg 'We have a disagreement on this, so how can we move it forward?' | Statements that downplay a disagreement or pretend that it does not exist eg 'Well, having aired that one, I think it's best if we move on.' | Statements that inflame or keep disagreements going eg 'Anybody with an ounce of common sense can see that won't work!' |
| *Voice*<br>Tone – steady, firm, clear. | Tone – apologetic, wobbly, dull, monotonous. | Tone – harsh, sarcastic, blaming, challenging. |
| Volume – not overloud or quiet; may be raised to get attention. | Volume – quiet, dropping away at the end. | Volume – overloud, rising at the end. |
| *Body language*<br>Gestures – open hand movements used with firm, measured pace to emphasise or demonstrate. Arms open or lightly crossed. | Gestures – covering mouth with hand, tight and nervous hand movements eg fiddling with pen. | Gestures – dismissive hand movements. Pointing with finger/pen, thumping table, 'steepling' (ie finger tops pressed together as sign of superiority), arms crossed high (ie unapproachable). |
| Posture – upright but relaxed, moving slightly forward. | Posture – shoulders hunched, huddled over papers. | Posture – head in air, chin thrust out, leaning far back, hands behind head. |
| Eyes – direct, relaxed gaze. | Eyes – averted. | Eyes – glaring, hostile. |

## CASE STUDY 24

From personal experience, we have found that the approach above can work very effectively and have recommended it to others. Recently a colleague was finding that she had taken on more than she had realised when she agreed to do some tutoring on an open learning programme. She hadn't realised that some students would require additional support from her, either face-to-face or on the telephone or via e-mail correspondence. The tutor was paid by the hour for running workshops and was paid a set amount for marking assignments. There was no provision for student support outside of these provisions.

Initially the tutor was happy to provide the support as she was committed to the programme and wished to give the students as much assistance as possible. Gradually, however, she became more and more resentful and thought about withdraw-

ing from the programme, even though she enjoyed the work. Luckily she took our advice before taking this step and talked to the programme manager. She decided what she wanted and explained the position, having kept a record of her recent contacts with students. The programme manager was sympathetic to her case. They agreed that, in future, the tutor would ensure that she acted assertively in seeking to limit the tendency for some students to become overly dependent on her advice. However, where the additional support was warranted, the tutor could make a claim for any additional hours worked. Several months on the tutor has found that setting ground rules for student contact has reduced the additional demands made on her time and the working relationship between the tutor and programme manager continues to be a happy one.

We can see in Table 28 that assertive behaviour involves lots of 'I' statements. It also involves the use of the word 'no', which can be a very difficult lesson for us to learn. If, for instance, a colleague asks you to help out with some salary calculations so that she can meet a deadline for a report on anticipated labour costs, your first inclination is likely to be to agree. This is acceptable so long as:

- your own work does not suffer

- you know that your colleague will be glad to return the favour at a later date

- you do not feel that your colleague is taking advantage of your better nature (and is only in this predicament through her own fault).

However, if any of these preconditions do not exist, then you should seriously consider saying no. Remember that by saying no *you are refusing the request, not rejecting the person.* You will find that if you say no assertively the person concerned will not consider that you have let him or her down or hurt his or her feelings. It will instead be clear that you simply cannot help him or her to solve this particular problem. So, in appropriate circumstances, practise saying no *clearly and definitely* without excessive apology or excuses and *directly* without lying or letting the other person down.

As a personnel practitioner, you will be dealing with all sorts of people in a variety of emotional states, eg upset, nervous, under pressure, angry, dogmatic, inconsiderate. There will be occasions when you feel that submissive or aggressive behaviour is more appropriate than assertive behaviour. An example of the former situation might be when you are not as interested in the outcome of a discussion as the other party and so allow their views to override your own. An example of the latter might be when you use aggression in a controlled way to indicate that you really have come to the end of the road in a negotiating situation.

The choice of behavioural styles is always open to you. However, by practising assertive behaviour you are ensuring that you do consciously choose a particular style rather than rely on whichever behavioural style is your natural tendency.

## CPD

Two terms are commonly used when discussing personal effectiveness: they are continuous development and, increasingly, continuing professional development (CPD). The first term basically means learning from real experiences at work on a continuous basis, eg not assuming that a two-day skills training programme will provide delegates with all they need to become fully competent in the skill concerned. Thus learning continues throughout our working lives through formal events such as training programmes, but also through our day-to-day experiences, planned and unplanned.

The second and connected term is increasingly being adopted by professional bodies such as the CIPD to reassure outside parties that members of the Institute are fully competent in today's working environment ie that they did not put all their books and journals away on qualifying but take great pains to keep up to date with legislation and other developments in the field of personnel management. Thus CPD is a requirement for Corporate Member status of the CIPD, and evidence will be required at the time of upgrading membership and on a random selection basis at any time. Records should show a mix of learning activities, such as courses, seminars, conferences and self-directed or informal learning including reading, networking, special projects or indeed anything that develops your professional abilities. Ideally it will not all be directly work-focused and will include reference to activities that take place outside work. Most importantly you must include a synopsis of how the learning has been used or will be used in future activities. This, for example, could be the writing of a policy or a specific change in the way in which you will do your job or approach a particular situation in the future.

The CIPD Policy on CPD states five essential principles:

- Development should be continuous in the sense that the professional should always be actively seeking improved performance.

- Development should be owned and managed by the individual learner.

- CPD is a personal matter and the effective learner knows best what he or she needs to learn. Development should begin from the individual's current learning state.

- Learning objectives should be clear and wherever possible should serve organisational or client needs as well as individual goals.

- Regular investment of time in learning should be seen as an essential part of professional life, not as an optional extra.

The main message here is that the acquisition of skills is not a finite exercise. We can never be fully effective in all situations and are constantly thrown into new experiences that promote new learning.

---

**Activity 56**

If you are a member of the CIPD, obtain the CIPD's pack on CPD. Use it to set up a record of your CPD and a development plan. Discuss your development plan with one or more of your learning sources in order to gain their support in putting some of your action plans into effect.

---

## Summary

In this chapter we have looked at a range of topics pertinent to your role as a personnel practitioner. We have not tried to provide a comprehensive coverage, either in range or content, but an introductory guide to a number of skills areas. As your career progresses, you will find that you need to develop these skills in order to perform tasks and activities in as professional a manner as possible.

We chose the skills and techniques of report writing and making presentations as prime examples of communication skills that help you to 'sell' your ideas and proposals. We also considered the connected skills of negotiating, influencing and persuading and their application in both formal and informal situations. Next we examined the counselling skills necessary to deal with the vast range of problems that are likely to face members of your workforce as well as the vexing problem of managing your time. If you cannot manage yourself, it may be difficult to convince others that you are worthy of promotion to a position in which you will also be managing others.

Finally, we proposed that assertive behaviour is appropriate in nearly every role played by the personnel practitioner in the workplace (and in many other situations occurring outside it, too). It is an important skill that backs up the others necessary for you to achieve personal effectiveness. We ended with assertion because, of all the skills areas we have considered in this chapter, this is one you cannot afford to ignore. Assertive behaviour is enormously powerful and, used correctly, helps to build your credibility in the workplace. Try it at work and at home – you'll be amazed by the results.

Completion of a number of appropriate activities, referred to throughout the chapter, will provide you with a useful starting-point before you undertake some further reading into those skill areas that you decide are priorities for you. A number of recommended video titles are also included at the end of this chapter. You will find these particularly useful if visual messages are more appropriate to your learning style.

You should by now be aware of the importance of self-development and the need continually to keep up to date and seek further to improve your skills and knowledge in order to warrant the title of 'P & D professional'. *You should aim continuously to develop yourself throughout your working life.*

We wish you every success!

---

**Activity 57**

Buy a book on one of the topics covered in this chapter, eg negotiating, time management or assertiveness. Apply the techniques that you learn about to any important situation that you are currently facing. Use any self-assessment exercises and questionnaires provided in the book to begin the process of increasing your self-awareness. (Recommended titles are detailed in the further reading listed on page 269.)

---

## APPENDIX I to Chapter 9

### Checklist: the mechanics of report writing

Terms of reference
- Are you clear about the purpose of your report?
- Have you specified its aim and objectives?
- Are you clear about who will read your report and their level of knowledge?

Collecting information
- Have you used a workable recording system?
- Have you collected information from as many sources as possible?

| Organising information | • Is your report presented in clear sections? |
| | • Are they logically sequenced and easy to follow? |
| | • Do you provide signposts (subheadings, for example) for the reader? |
| Grammar and style | • Are your paragraphs short, clearly defined in material and easy to read? |
| | • Have you chosen simple, unambiguous wording? |
| | • Have you checked sentence construction, spelling and punctuation? |
| | • Is the style appropriate to the content of the report, your organisation and the reader(s)? |
| Checking your work | • Have you checked structure and language? |
| | • Have you asked for a third person's comments? |
| | • Have you proofread your final draft? |
| Layout | • Have you presented your report in the accepted organisational format? |
| | • Are the sections numbered and headings highlighted consistently? |
| | • Are quotes/illustrations/appendices/cross-references all referred to correctly? |
| Final presentation | • Have you given the typist clear instructions? |
| | • Have you chosen the most suitable form of presentation and distribution? |
| | • Have you allowed enough time for these final stages? |

## APPENDIX II to Chapter 9

### Checklist: The layout/contents of your report

| Title page | • Does the report have a short, self-explanatory title? |
| | • Does the title page contain other appropriate identification data, eg name of organisation, name of author, date of completion? |
| Summary | • Does it give the reader a framework showing the main features of each section? |
| | • Does it include any conclusions reached? |
| | • Is it self-contained and self-explanatory? |

| | |
|---|---|
| Acknowledgements | • Do they record a debt for help or use of facilities? |
| Contents page | • Are section/page numbers clear and accurate? |
| Introduction | • Does it refer to the terms of reference, limitations or constraints, scope, and the research method(s) you have adopted?<br>• Does it contain appropriate background information (depending on the needs of the reader(s))? |
| Body of the report | • Do you provide an analysis of the perceived problem and include the research findings?<br>• Does the discussion lead naturally on to the conclusions and recommendations of the report? |
| Conclusions | • Do you summarise your main research findings?<br>• Do you state clearly your interpretation of these results?<br>• Do they lead logically to the recommendations you are intending to make? |
| Options | • Have you considered the pros and cons of a number of alternatives before deciding on your final recommendations?<br>• Do they address the issues identified in your conclusions? |
| Recommendations | • Have you written clear recommendations that identify specific actions and assigned responsibility for those actions?<br>• Are they supported by good reasoning that is provided either here or earlier in your report?<br>• Have you costed them and made some assessment of the benefits?<br>• Have you included timescales? |
| Appendices | • Do they contain lenghthy or technical information?<br>• Are they correctly referenced in the report? |
| References | • Has a consistent referencing system been used?<br>• Have you included full details: surname, initials, title of article/book/journal, date of publication, volume/issue/page numbers? |
| Bibliography | • Do you acknowledge other works used and those for useful further reading? |

## References and further reading

The following are available from the Advisory, Conciliation and Arbitration Service (ACAS), ACAS Reader Ltd, PO Box 16, Earl Shilton, Leicester LE9 8ZZ; tel. 01455 852 225:
*Advisory Booklet on Redundancy Handling.* (Revised 1997) Leicester, ACAS.
*Advisory Handbook on Discipline At Work.* (Revised 2000) Leicester, ACAS.

BACK K. *and* K. (1986) 'Assertiveness training for meetings'. *Industrial and Commercial Training.* Vol. 18, No. 2, March/April. pp26–30.

BENNETT R. (1994) *Personal Effectiveness.* London, Kogan Page.

BLANCHARD K. *et al.* (1990) *The One Minute Manager Meets the Monkey.* London, Fontana.

COOK M. (1993) *Slow Down and Get More Done.* Cincinnati, Ohio, Betterway Books.

COVEY S. (1994) *First Things First.* London, Simon & Schuster.

DICKSON A. (1984) *A Woman in Your Own Right: Assertiveness and you.* London, Quartet Books.

DRUCKER P. (1999) *Effective Executive.* Oxford, Butterworth-Heinemann.

ERNST & YOUNG (1994) *The Manager's Handbook.* London, Warner Books.

FISHER R, URY W. *and* PATTON B. (1997) *Getting to Yes.* London, Arrow Business Books

FOWLER A. (1998) *Negotiating, Persuading and Influencing.* London, Institute of Personnel and Development.

FOWLER A. (1999) *Managing Redundancy.* London, Institute of Personnel and Development.

FRITCHIE R. *and* MELLING M. (1991) *The Business of Assertiveness: A practical guide to being more effective in the workplace.* London, BBC Books.

GILLEN T. (1998) *Assertiveness.* London, Institute of Personnel and Development.

GILLEN T. (1999) *Agreed! Improve Your Powers of Influence.* London, Institute of Personnel and Development.

HONEY P. *and* MUMFORD A. (1986) *The Manual of Learning Styles.* Maidenhead, Peter Honey.

INSTITUTE of PERSONNEL and DEVELOPMENT. (1997a) *IPD Guide on Counselling at Work.* London, Institute of Personnel and Development.

INSTITUTE of PERSONNEL and DEVELOPMENT. (1997b) *IPD Key Facts on Redundancy.* London, Institute of Personnel and Development. (No longer available but visit www.cipd.co.uk/Infosource)

INSTITUTE of PERSONNEL and DEVELOPMENT. (1997c) *IPD Careers Information Sheet on CPD and Career Breaks.* London, Institute of Personnel and Development. (No longer available but visit www.cipd.co.uk/Infosource)

INSTITUTE of PERSONNEL and DEVELOPMENT. (1998) *IPD Key Facts on Stress at Work.* London, Institute of Personnel and Development. (No longer available but visit www.cipd.co.uk/Infosource)

INSTITUTE of PERSONNEL and DEVELOPMENT. (Undated) *IPD Code of Professional Conduct and Disciplinary Procedures.* London, Institute of Personnel and Development. (No longer available but visit www.cipd.co.uk/Infosource)

JACKSON T. (2000) *Career Development.* London, CIPD.

JAY A. (1990) *Effective Presentation: The communication of ideas by words and visual aids.* B.I.M.

KOLB D. A. *et al.* (1974) *Organisational Psychology: An experiential approach.* Hemel Hempstead, Prentice Hall.

LEIGH A. (1997) *Persuasive Reports and Proposals.* London, Institute of Personnel and Development.

MACDONALD J. W. (1992) *Report Writing.* London, Croner Publications Ltd.

MAITLAND I. (1999) *Managing Your Time.* London, Institute of Personnel and Development.

PEDLER M., BOURGOYNE J. and BOYDELL T. (2001) *A Manager's Guide to Self Development.* London, McGraw-Hill.

SIDDONS S. (1999) *Presentation Skills.* London, Institute of Personnel and Development.

SUMMERFIELD J. and van OUDTSHOORN L. (1995) *Counselling in the Workplace.* London, Institute of Personnel and Development.

URY W. (1992) *Getting Past No.* Random House Business Books.

## Videos/audio cassettes

*Can You Spare a Moment?* (1987) Video Arts (counselling).

*I Wasn't Prepared for That.* (1996) Video Arts (making presentations).

*Negotiating: Tying the Knot.* (1996) Video Arts.

*The Unorganised Manager.* (1996) Video Arts (time management).

*Report Writing.* (1993) Video Arts.

*Straight Talking.* (1993) Video Arts (assertiveness).

ROSS A. (1999) *Relax for Success.* London, Relaxation Centre Cassettes.

## Websites

BBC Education             www.bbc.co.uk/education/home/

Chartered Institute of Personnel and Development   www.cipd.co.uk

*People Management*            www.peoplemanagement.co.uk

# • Index

THE LEARNING CENTRE
HAMMERSMITH AND WEST
LONDON COLLEGE
GLIDDON ROAD
LONDON W14 9BL